# Music
# for the Movies

*By the same author:*

Ustinov in Focus

The Films of Errol Flynn
(with Rudy Behlmer and
Clifford McCarty)

# Music for the Movies

by

**Tony Thomas**

South Brunswick and New York: A. S. Barnes and Company
London: Tantivy Press

© 1973 by A. S. Barnes and Co., Inc.

A. S. Barnes and Co., Inc.
Cranbury, New Jersey 08512

Tantivy Press
108 New Bond Street
London W1Y OQX, England

Library of Congress Cataloging in Publication Data

Thomas, Tony, 1927–
    Music for the movies.

    "Film music on record": p.
    1. Moving-picture music—History and criticism.
I. Title.
ML2075.T54          782.8          72-37818
ISBN 0-498-01071-6

First printing April, 1973
Second printing March, 1975

SBN 90073063 3 (U.K.)

Printed in the United States of America

*To the memory of
my father
Ernest William Thomas*

# Contents

# Acknowledgments

Let me make no bones about it—I had a lot of help in putting this book together. I am indebted to all the composers here discussed but especially to Ernest Gold, Laurence Rosenthal and Miklos Rozsa for supplying whole chunks of text. I wish to thank Page Cook, the film music critic of *Films in Review*, for allowing me to quote from his excellent columns, and Henry Hart, the editor of that estimable magazine, for permission to do so. My gratitude goes to Gerald Pratley, the CBC film commentator, for access to his considerable library of film music recordings and his own taped interviews with these composers. A particular vote of thanks to Clifford McCarty for putting together, after long and meticulous research, the listing that comprises the last chapter of this book. Finally, a general doff of my cap to those who, over the years, encouraged me in my enthusiasm for film scoring, even though their ears probably suffered under my zeal.

# Introduction: Main Title

Enjoying film music has been one of the staples of my life. I can pinpoint the beginning of my interest—December of 1938, a few days before Christmas. I went to see *The Adventures of Robin Hood* at the Odeon Theatre in Hastings, Sussex, and it was a case of love at first sight. It's still my favourite film. I was then eleven and *Robin Hood* prompted a long lasting adulation of Errol Flynn, but more importantly it touched off an awareness of the value and the stimulation of music in films. I clearly recall walking into that theatre as the credit titles unrolled to the lusty, martial strains of Erich Korngold's music for Robin and his Merry Men of Sherwood. I might explain that I was susceptible to military music, having spent the previous five years living in the Royal Marine barracks in Deal, Kent, where my father was a career musician in that distinguished branch of the British services. It occurs to me now that I had probably reached the age of eleven without realising that there was music in the world other than military. Perhaps that's why Korngold's jaunty "main title" march made such an immediate impression on my young and eager mind. However, this is not a book about military music or my mind, young or middle-aged.

Apart from enjoyment, the most important thing for me about my interest in film scoring is that it whetted my appetite for music in general; it led me to explore all kinds of music. It was the best kind of education because it was self-propelling. Years later, as a Hollywood reporter for the Canadian Broadcasting Corporation, it also led me to an acquaintance with many of the composers whose work had sparked my thousands of hours in hundreds of movie theatres. In producing radio programmes about these composers and their music I was in the happy position of indulging my interest and being paid for it, which is about as fortunate a situation as a man can hope for, and more than he has a right to expect. I was also fortunate in not being disappointed. A dozen years of writing and recording items about Hollywood diminished my fascination for the glamour and the glory of filmdom but not my appreciation for the composers, who are, in my opinion, the sanest and most enlightened group among the convoluted film folk.

My enthusiasm for film music has also brought me twinges of pain, mostly in younger years when I failed to understand that not everyone derived the same enjoyment from the sound of music in the movies. The thing that stung me most was the bleak question, "What music?" This was most often the reply to my innocent inquiry of a friend who had just seen a picture whose score had impressed me. "How did you like the music?" I would ask. A puzzled pause from the friend, and then, "What music?" With time I became more and more cautious about placing that question, especially with girls.

Recently, I couldn't resist asking my nine-year-old son David if he noticed the music in a Western he had seen twice and obviously enjoyed. From the bewildered expression on his face, I knew I was about to hear a chillingly familiar question. I explained, "the background music—the music behind the picture." "I didn't hear any music," said David, "and I was sitting right down in front!" Well, as someone once said about religion: to those who understand, no explanation is necessary. To those who don't, none is possible. This book is for those who understand. As for David, time and exposure will tell. I hope so. I'd hate to think I'd sired a son who doesn't understand me.

TONY THOMAS, 1972

# Music
# for the Movies

# 1
# What's the Score?

During the making of *Lifeboat* at Twentieth Century-Fox in 1944, composer David Raksin was stopped in the studio commissary by a friend and told, perhaps a little too pointedly, that Alfred Hitchcock had decided against using any music in the score of the film. Raksin, inured to snide comments on film music, mused for a moment and asked why and how that unusual decision had been reached. Said the friend, "Well, Hitchcock feels that since the entire action of the film takes place in a lifeboat on the open ocean, where would the music come from?" Replied Raksin, "Ask Mr. Hitchcock to explain where the cameras come from, and I'll tell him where the music comes from."

Amusing though it may be, this anecdote puts its finger on a sore spot—the general lack of understanding about the role of music in films. It is a role that is not even fully understood in the film industry itself, possibly because music is the most abstract of the film arts as well as being the most abused and the most exploited. Famous producers and directors have been heard to say that if pictures were better made they wouldn't need music, to which the composers reply—good pictures are made by the presence of talent, not the lack of music.

Film composers operate on strange terms. A good score can't save a bad film and a bad score can't kill a good picture. There is a certain stigma to film music and it is partly warranted by the large amount of appalling material that has been written over the years. Ironically, the general level of film music is not alone the responsibility of composers. The composer is a hired man—he works for a producer. Unfortunately, far too many producers have tin ears to match their itching palms and in craving only the most obviously commercial music for their films, they are rather like the man who would march into Tiffany's and say, "Show me what you have in chrome."

A chilling example of musical ignorance on a high level occurred during the completion of *The Battle of Britain*. Sir William Walton was hired to score the film, a logical choice, not only in view of his skill but the fact that

15

his soaring music for *Spitfire/First of the Few* in 1942 is a highlight in the annals of film music. After Walton's score for *The Battle of Britain* had been recorded, the tapes were flown to New York. There a high ranking officer of United Artists, who deserves the distinction of being anonymous, listened and said, "The music stinks, get somebody else." A lighter weight composer, Ron Goodwin, who had written an agreeable score for *Those Magnificent Men in Their Flying Machines*, was brought in and wrote a competent, straightforward score. Goodwin is an undeniably tuneful composer, and he was probably somewhat embarrassed over the Walton matter. But a job is a job—particularly the job of scoring a multi-million dollar picture. On hearing about this dumping of his friend Walton's score, Sir Laurence Olivier made it known to the producers that he would have his name removed from the credits unless some part of the Walton score was retained. This would have been an ugly bit of publicity since Olivier's role as Air Marshall Dowding was the most crucial one in the film. The producers decided to keep Sir William's scoring for the five minute segment towards the end of the film in which a montage of aerial dog-fights are presented minus the sounds of the planes and almost like a surrealist ballet. Beautifully photographed, this sequence, dramatically and eerily scored by Walton, is easily the highlight of a generally disappointing film. Olivier's action, which he never allowed to be publicised in order not to embarrass Sir William, was a rare stand for an actor to take but an understandable one. Walton had scored Olivier's *Henry the Fifth, Hamlet* and *Richard the Third* and Olivier had every reason to know what imaginative, inventive scoring by a skilful composer can do for a film.

Film is a kind of discourse among its component parts, each at its best when doing or saying something that none of the others can do or say as well. In this respect, music comes to bear in helping to realise the meaning of the film, in stimulating and guiding the emotional response to the visuals. Directly and pervasively appealing to the subconscious, music may also prepare the emotional climate of the other film components. It is this unique ability of music to influence the audience subconsciously that makes it truly valuable to the cinema. Moreover, music can complete the total picture and produce a kind of dramatic truth, which the visual element is not always capable of doing.

Hopefully, idealistically, the film will one day take its place beside the musical theatre as a free, unrestricted outlet for a composer's imagination. Ralph Vaughan Williams once said, "Film contains potentialities for the combination of the arts such as Wagner never dreamed of." In the meantime, the best film composers continue to wage a kind of guerrilla warfare in the underbrush of contemporary harmony and counterpoint, battling the disdain of the critics, the indifference of the greater public, the commercial pressures of the recording industry and—worst of all—the lack of musical understanding of film producers and directors.

The art of combining moving pictures with musical tones is still a mysterious art. Describing its values and functions is rather like describing a beautiful woman—there's no way of doing it adequately. But no one should be condemned for trying.

At its most general functional level, film music serves as a kind of cohesive, filling in empty spaces in the action or the dialogue—this is neutral, background music and the composer's most ungrateful job since it must enliven and colour scenes without drawing attention to itself.

Film music must also build a sense of continuity, uniting the visual parts—this is most important because a theatrical film is like a jig-saw puzzle. The most obvious example of this is the cinematic montage—a cascade of varying shots that would be chaotic without some unifying musical thought.

Something else that skilful scoring can accomplish is underlining the theatrical build-up of scenes, pinpointing various emotions and actions, and then rounding it off with a sense of finality. In this respect, music is a definite story-telling device. Another aspect of this device is that of utilising "source music," that is, music that can be seen on the screen—coming from a radio or a record player or from a dance band, a circus, a café or an actor playing an instrument.

On a higher level of accomplishment, film music can do two greatly important things (how well depends on the composer). One: create an atmosphere. Two: colour the tone of the picture. Atmosphere music can be quite obviously geographical or historical, placing the story in a certain locale at a certain time with certain kinds of people in certain kinds of situations, but it's a test of the composer's knowledge and imagination how convincingly he does this.

Now, as to colouring the tone and giving the picture a subtle extra dimension: this is the film music that separates the boy composers from the men composers. This is the psychology of scoring, being able to shade emotions, to lighten or darken moods, to heighten sensitivities, to imply, to suggest, to define character and refine personality, to help generate momentum or create tension, to warm the picture or cool it, and—most subtle of all—to allude to thoughts that are unspoken and situations that remain unseen. Such music plays upon the minds of the audience.

In the hands of clever composers, this is true musical dramaturgy. This is Erich Korngold persuading you that Errol Flynn was really Robin Hood in a previous life, Max Steiner telling you what it was like to be a southern aristocrat and lose the War and a way of life, Miklos Rozsa letting you know how Ray Milland felt on a lost weekend when he craved a drink, or

Bernard Herrmann helping you to die of fright as some weirdo butchers Janet Leigh in the shower. If you believed Dana Andrews really loved Laura, thank David Raksin, or if you shared Dana's mind wanderings as he sat in the nose of a wrecked B-36 and mused on the best years of his life, you might tip your hat to Hugo Friedhofer. If your heart went out to Gary Cooper as he waited all alone for those four ex-cons to come and get him at high noon, you might give a thought to Dimitri Tiomkin, and if you think Jennifer Jones really saw the Virgin Mary, then light a little candle to the memory of the late Alfred Newman. One more point: Joan Fontaine was absolutely right when she felt Manderley was haunted, but it wasn't the spirit of Rebecca—it was Franz Waxman's music.

Film music can do a great many things but something it apparently cannot do is to overcome its own rather dubious reputation. Most musical intellectuals regard film scoring as a medium of slick, conventional, *cliché-ridden* composition, and it is easy to understand why they should take that view. This is the kind of music so many film producers *want*, some of them even insist on it, and with the music publishers and the recording companies breathing down their necks, the composers are hard put to bring artistic respectability to a beleaguered medium. A case in point: during the scoring of *Doctor Zhivago*, David Lean, undeniably one of the world's finest film-makers, urged Maurice Jarre to simplify his themes, to scale them down. Finally Jarre hit upon the renowned *Lara* theme, which became one of the most successful melodies ever to emerge from a film. The album of *Doctor Zhivago* is the best-seller of all soundtrack albums. Jarre also won an Oscar for this score, but in the opinion of most other film composers *Doctor Zhivago* is not a well scored film and the *Lara* theme is resoundingly banal. But how does one argue against David Lean, the Oscar, and record sales in the millions? Another example: at the 1970 Academy Awards presentation Burt Bacharach won two Oscars for his music for *Butch Cassidy and the Sundance Kid*, one for the song *Raindrops Keep Falling On My Head*, and one for the score. No one could argue against the Oscar for the song, and Bacharach is the freshest and most inventive song writer in years, but his score for this film is regarded in film music circles as inept and anachronistic. Quite clearly, he was getting two Oscars for the same thing and he was besieged with offers from producers to score their pictures. Said a veteran composer about today's general run of producers and directors, "You might as well just give them a song or a main theme and forget about the rest of the score, they're just not interested."

Composers also complain that producers turn to them too late, and then expect too much. This is mostly in respect to films that have not turned out well, and the composer is then expected to save the bacon. Adolph Deutsch once commented on this: "A film musician is like a mortician—he can't bring the body back to life but he's expected to make it look better." Virgil Thomson has an even more trenchant view of this odd regard in which producers hold composers: "'If the film is good the composer is expected to subdue his talent. If the film is a poor one, the composer is supposed to perform a miracle."

Writing film music is unique in one respect—it is needed, and this is a situation that is found nowhere else in contemporary musical life. Possibly it is the closest situation we have to that of Bach, who similarly functioned as a provider of a steady, workaday flow of music for his church in Leipzig. Purists protest at the thought of Bach or any great master writing for films but it is more than likely that had they lived in the Twentieth century they would have been thus engaged. A little investigation reveals Mozart and Haydn writing music for patrons even less appreciative than film producers.

The most valid criticism that can be laid against film music is that it fails to live up to its own possibilities. The truly interesting thing about composing for the screen is not so much what it *is* as what it *can be*. Erich Korngold put it this way: "It isn't true that the cinema places a restraint on musical expression. Music is music, whether it is for the stage, the rostrum or the cinema. Form may change, the manner of writing may vary but the composer needs to make no concessions whatever to what he conceives to be his own musical ideology. The screen's uniqueness is a spur to the imagination, a challenge to resourcefulness. The cinema is a direct avenue to the ears and hearts of the great public, and all musicians should see the screen as a musical opportunity."

Korngold proved, as did Walton, Copland and Prokofiev, that good composers write good music—movie or otherwise. Yet critics, both professional and amateur, are steadfastly snobbish about this branch of composition. They seem willing to judge opera and the concert hall by its best examples and film scoring by its worst.

In writing the introduction to Clifford McCarty's book *Film Composers in America,* Lawrence Morton, one of the film industry's finest orchestrators, made a valuable point: "Good film scores may indeed be an overwhelmed minority, but they shine like good deeds in a naughty world." As McCarty's book made obvious, a complete list of all the scores written in Hollywood testifies to the power of mediocrity. And this is a sad realisation because good scores are available at no greater cost than bad scores.

As is obvious to anyone with ears and any degree of musical sensitivity, the majority of film scores are barely worth discussion. They perform a function and they are forgotten. Fair enough. But what has to be borne in mind in evaluating film music is that the majority of any kind of creative art—books, plays, poems, pieces of sculpture, music for the concert hall and the opera house—also perform briefly and quickly vanish. What is needed

Canadian film composer Louis Applebaum, Aaron Copland, Sir William Walton and David Raksin during the taping of the television documentary Music for the Movies, at the CBC studios in Toronto, 1962.

is intelligent criticism, but it is something that has hardly ever been applied.

Lawrence Morton puts his finger on the real problem of film music: "It doesn't have to be good in order to perform its functional duties. Except in rare instances, it has nothing to do with art. It could, and one hopes for the day when it will. In the meantime, it has everything to do with commerce. Above all it must be successful—that is, it must "do something" for the picture, please whoever is paying for it and, if possible, win an Oscar. The film producer does not exist who would not sacrifice even the greatest music if he believed that such a sacrifice would ensure the success of his film. This is something of an anomaly in an industry where first-rate achievement is permitted, even encouraged, in other departments—photography, for instance, or costume and set designing . . . certainly it has been proved that although film music does not have to be good in order to fulfil its function, good music actually performs that function far more satisfactorily than bad music. This truth must be constantly hammered at producers who hire hacks when artists are available. Criticism has been laggard in the performance of this job. Producers will rest content so long as movie critics, like the movie-going public itself, continue to exhibit their altogether remarkable insensitivity to all film music except popular songs, folk tunes, ballads, or familiar concert and opera classics; and so long as music critics continue to ignore film music completely."

Lawrence Morton is well qualified to criticise the critics and to be disappointed in both the public and the film producers. He has for some years been the director of the Monday Evening Concerts in Los Angeles and he is well aware of the range and the quality and the quantity of the musical talent available to the film studios. Most of the best Hollywood musicians participate in these concerts and their programmes are among the most intellectual available anywhere. The material ranges from rescued music of the Renaissance Period to the most avant-garde of contemporary composition, and it is not uncommon to find Elmer Bernstein as the pianist in a rare Haydn trio or Andre Previn performing the abstract music of Anton Webern. To anyone who has heard these concerts it is astounding also to hear disparaging comments from elsewhere about the quality of musicianship involved in the making of films. It is amazing to find people who ordinarily shy away from generalisations leaping to embrace the obvious and tiresome canards about film music.

It is, of course, very easy to side with the composers and condemn the producers. But the situation has to be viewed in the widest perspective. Films are made because it is in someone's interest to make them and in order to make a profit there must be a return on the investment; this is guaranteed by the wideness of the appeal of any given picture. David Raksin sees the situation with a clear eye: "Hollywood is a business. It is not run for the edification or the enjoyment of people—it produces these things peripherally because it is to somebody's profit to do so. Those of us who work within this framework of profit-making are often engaged in trying, one way or another, to do something we think is art or artisanry— this place is full of people who are talented and highly skilled—but our films are made for the widest possible public and they are therefore less specialised, less intellectual and less satisfying in terms of everyday life. The popular taste doesn't need to have anything bad said about it by me. It's a fact of life, one of the more unfortunate facts and one of the real ones. This popular level of comprehension, of intelligence, of taste, is the level to which most films, to re-coup their investment, must cater. Pictures are, in their way, a rather accurate reflection of the state of public mores."

It is difficult not to be nostalgic in discussing Hollywood. As a townindustry Hollywood is not, and can never be again, what it once was. The world has changed, the public and its tastes have changed and methods of making films have changed. Many of the changes in filmdom are for the better—it is faintly absurd to imagine all films made thirty years ago to be more enjoyable than those made today. But there was a kind of Golden Age in Hollywood and out of its very vastness came worthy works. The big studios, for all their faults, were able to hire the best available talents and sometimes the talent was tough enough to overcome the tastes of the people for which it laboured. An examination of the history of Hollywood leaves one with the odd thought that many of the finest pictures must have been made in spite of the executives in the front offices rather than because of them. This is especially true of the music departments; those music directors who were men of genuine talent and taste were often left to rule their bailiwicks without interference. Alfred Newman, for example, as head of music for Twentieth Century-Fox had the complete confidence of studio boss Darryl F. Zanuck and made his own decision. Newman hired the best players, arrangers and composers. But with the break-up of the major studios the music situation changed. Composers, like actors, writers and directors, became free-lancers, represented by agents. This independence of talent resulted, in the main, in better and more interesting films but not necessarily better and more interesting music scores.

The decline in the standards of film scoring are obvious to those who have collected film music recordings since the advent of the LP record. The LP was a welcome revolution; it opened up the music world as never before. It also changed the music world as never before. The recording industry grew into a multi-million dollar giant, with the music business becoming a major industry. The mass merchandising methods could hardly be expected not to affect standards. Much of the enormous change was allied to the social cultural convolutions of the post Second World War era—which needn't be discussed here—but in terms of film scoring it soon became apparent to the producers that the LP and the 45 rpm disc were powerful means of publicity for their films and that a good, obviously melodious theme or song were the best and cheapest forms of promotion.

The LP came along too late, in the opinions of devotees of film music. It also came along at the unhappy time when the advent of television had thrown the Hollywood studios in a panic, a panic that spelled the end of the old studio system and gradually an end to the days of studio orchestras and a stable of staff composers.

The film music enthusiasts, ever a minority, welcomed the LP, but enthusiasm waned with time. The recordings issued in the first few years of the LP are vastly more interesting than those of the past decade. Had the LP happened fifteen years previously, all the scores of Erich Korngold would be on discs, as would all the finest work done in the "golden age," the great film musicals as well as the serious scoring. However, the showing of old films on TV and the ownership of a tape recorder permit the enthusiast to indulge himself.

In the age of high fidelity recording the primary characteristic of film scoring has become its ability to advertise the picture. During the Sixties more and more scores emerged with "pop" orientated music, with the worst examples having as much application to the films as Muzak. Musicians whose fame came from other fields, such as arranging dance and vocal music, now assumed importance in film scoring.

Highly skilled and entertaining as they were in their own fields, they could not score subtle, serious pictures. For all that, they pleased the film producers who enjoyed the exposure they received in record sales and from radio broadcasts. The record album thus became a major factor in scoring and composers found they were subject to at least as much, if not more, pressure from record company executives as from film producers.

The truly sad thing about the rise of the record album in respect to film scoring was that the best composers were gradually eased aside. Franz Waxman, for example, scored barely a handful of films in the last ten years of his life. Miklos Rozsa scored nothing for five years. Hugo Friedhofer has scored only one film since 1964. None of these men voluntarily retreated from the work for which they were acclaimed—acclaimed, that is, by the musically knowledgeable, not by film producers in general or the men whose job it is to sell records. The finest composers of film music were not alone in their dilemma. Joining them on the sidelines were the great American song writers—Harold Arlen, Vernon Duke, Cole Porter, Hoagy Carmichael, *et al.*—all of them puzzled by the disparity between the generous royalties that flowed in from their old songs and the fact that no one asked them for anything new.

The most scathing denunciation of the decline in the standards of film scoring came from Page Cook, the film music critic of *Films in Review*. Writing in the March 1969 issue he commented:

All too much of today's film music is an inchoate mass of: (1) the Mersey beat, i.e. Liverpudlian imitations of Negro jazz in which both verbal and sonic echoes of English balladry can be heard. (2) Ganges sound, in which the sitar and other instruments are used to 'release the mind from actuality.' (3) the San Francisco sound, which couples sonic bedlam with illiterate lyrics. (4) folk-rock and rock-folk-pop, which are variations on the combinations of jungle drumbeats with the folk rhythms and verses of the US South and West, and (5) progressive jazz-and-rave, i.e. uninhibited rock.

It's possible nowadays to hear on the soundtrack of *one* picture *all* these variations of the same feebleminded 'thing.' Such jumbling is rationalized by the 'composers' with the assertion that it's necessary to look at *everything* from more than one point of view.

The unfortunate young who think listening to this cacophony will help them emerge from the infantilisms of protracted adolescence, to escape from the lonelinesses and pessimisms of emergent maturity, and to allay the universal hunger for love, are victimized by the shrewdies who promote, and profit from, 'the mod scene.' Hallucinogenic music, like hallucinogenic drugs, may prolong the 'now feeling' for a little while for the immature but reality has to be faced ultimately. How sad it will be when the young discover their youth has been wasted in listening to the debilitating meaninglessness of rock.

When movie producers substitute the primitive juvenilia of rock for relevantly interpretive music they abet the a-cultural rise of non-music, and help to destroy one of the motion picture's most potential components.

The main point of film scoring is a simple one: the music must be intimately related to what is on the screen—it must be appropriate. If what is on the screen shows imagination and substance, then a good composer has the opportunity to create something worthwhile, provided he isn't working for people who are musically musclebound.

Another point, equally simple but apparently not obvious to all filmmakers: scoring allows for the use of any and every kind of musical composition. Any kind of music is *serious* if it has teeth in it, if it expresses honest emotions and is relevant to the visual. Film music does not have to be romantic-symphonic; it needn't flirt with emotions in the way that too many of the old scores used to do, and neither should it ignore emotions as too many of the new scores do. Just as there are many ways to skin a cat, so there are many ways to score films. Whether the musical idiom is derived from jazz or classicism, from contemporary "pop," avant-garde or electronic is not the point. In appraising a film score, the question is: did the composer succeed in complementing the story, and is his contribution meaningful in terms of human experience?

In describing the mechanics and the aesthetics of actually scoring a film, it occurred to me—with nothing that can be interpreted as brilliance, looking for the easy way out would be closer to the truth—to ask a couple of composers to do the job for me. Namely, Ernest Gold and Laurence Rosenthal.

Ernest Gold comes of a musical Viennese family (in fact, his maternal grandfather was a pupil of Anton Bruckner and later the President of The Society of Friends of Music, an organisation that was launched by Brahms). Gold's mother was a singer of *lieder* and his father an amateur violinist who had studied with operetta composer Richard Heuberger. Hence, young Gold had a serious musical influence on one side of his family table and a lighter one on the other side, which is about as equable a background as a film composer could wish. He recalls that his aunts and uncles would ask, "Little boy, what are you going to be when you grow up?", to which he would reply, "I'm going to Hollywood and become a movie composer." They all laughed. As a teenager in Vienna in the Thirties, Gold did in fact become one of those peculiar people who go to the movies to listen to the background music, he grew particularly fond of Max Steiner's scoring and went to see *The Garden of Allah* seven times. Years later, the family having moved to New York in 1938, Gold wrote a piano concerto which was per-

At the recording of George Antheil's score for The Pride and the Passion. In the centre of the picture is Ernest Gold, who both orchestrated and conducted the score. To the left of Gold is composer Antheil and to Gold's right is producer Stanley Kramer.

formed at Carnegie Hall. The critics all said, "It sounds like movie music." With this condemnation Gold in 1945 went to Hollywood and played the concerto for various music department heads, all of whom said, "It sounds like movie music." However, in Hollywood this wasn't a condemnation. He was given a job. What followed was years of hack work, scoring cheapie Westerns and Grade B's, arranging, orchestrating and wondering when and if the chance would ever come to do something worthwhile. The chance came in 1958 when George Antheil, with whom Gold had been studying and for whom he did orchestrations, fell ill and couldn't score Stanley Kramer's *On the Beach*. He recommended Gold, who almost turned the job down when Kramer told him he wanted *Waltzing Matilda* used right through the score. But the need for a good film was too great and Gold brought himself to look upon Matilda as a challenge. Never has the old Aussie song been put through a set of more brilliant variations. Gold's score for *On the Beach* impressed Kramer; it was the start of a long association and it resulted in Gold's excellent scores for *Judgment at Nuremberg, It's a Mad, Mad, Mad, Mad World, Ship of Fools* and *The Secret of Santa Vittoria.* These films allowed Gold to range from scoring Nazi pageantry

**Ernest Gold during the recording of his score for** The Secret of Santa Vittoria.

and horror to a gargantuan comedy romp, from character studies of passengers on an ocean liner to a glowing musical accompaniment for Anthony Quinn as a lovable lout in a little Italian wine town. In 1960 Ernest Gold was hired by Otto Preminger to score *Exodus.* Preminger believes in hiring a composer at the start of a film and letting him see the picture made. Under this entirely reasonable arrangement Gold spent several months in Israel and traipsed around with a musical notebook, sketching ideas as he went. The effort paid off—the resultant score was a classic of scoring and brought an Oscar, not to mention a lifelong annuity on the famous *Exodus* theme.

**Ernest Gold on the Mechanics of Scoring, or The Sheer Hell of Trying to Fit Music to a Picture:**

The first thing the composer usually deals with is the nearly finished film (called a "rough cut") which lacks only the score and some of the sound effects that were not recorded during the actual filming of the movie, such as telephone bells, police sirens and the like. Occasionally the composer has the opportunity to read the script beforehand which gives him a little head start in his frantic efforts to acquaint himself with the contents of the film he is about to elucidate musically. Having seen the picture run in continuity he now runs it once more, reel by reel. Each reel contains nearly 1000 feet of film and lasts about ten minutes. At this second running the producer and director are present as well as the film editor and the music editor. The music editor does not, as the name implies, edit music but he edits film containing music. He assists the composer with the many technical problems that arise in the course of preparing a movie score and at the recording sessions, as well as thereafter. At this second running, called "spotting," decisions are made by general discussion, which parts of the film are to receive music and which ones are to be left "dry." Since it is not always possible to ascertain exactly what sound effects may yet be added to certain scenes or what their precise location is likely to be, it may turn out to be necessary to do a fair amount of guessing about the ultimate destiny of sections of the score to be written. A favourite axiom is "Let's write it, we can always throw it out later."

Nevertheless, spotting is an exacting task and demands great precision. For example it may be decided that, as our star Hilda Lamont slams the door, the music is to start and to continue until, 3 minutes and $25\frac{1}{3}$ seconds later, the ringing of a telephone in a police station "takes it out." The projectors used for spotting runs are equipped to run film in either direction so that it is possible to go back and forth over a scene until the exact spot is found in every case where the music is to start and where it is to stop.

When this is done the music cutter takes the picture to his cutting room and puts it in a machine called a Moviola, which permits the action to be observed through a small viewing screen, about 4 inches wide, while the sound issues from a speaker mounted next to the viewer. One or two counters are connected with the driving mechanism by means of gear. These show the footage of film run through the machine and the time elapsed. Since film travels at a constant speed of a foot and a half per second, the counter would show, for instance, that at a given point fifteen feet of film have passed through the Moviola and that this equals ten seconds of projection time.

The music cutter now starts with the first section that is to receive music (each such section is called a cue and may be as short as a few seconds or as long as ten minutes). He sets both counters at zero and then proceeds to write out a minutely detailed description of everything that can be heard and seen for the entire duration of the cue in question. He attaches precise timings to every bit of description, starting at zero and continuing to the end of the cue, a spot where an 'X' grease pencilled on the film marks the point where the telephone ring sound effect will be placed. His second counter now reads 4:25⅓. Then he "runs down" to the next cue and starts all over again with zero. While all this is being done the composer has a few days to sketch themes, research native music in case the film requires any ethnically unusual material and kiss his wife and children goodbye; he will see little of them during the weeks to come as there just is not time for anything not directly connected with his impending job.

The composer may now wish to run each scene once again, making marginal notes on the cue sheets as he views the film in the moviola or on the screen; or he may prefer to rely on his memory and commence composing immediately, using the cue sheets as his guide. As he makes his musical sketch he puts timings directly in the music, perhaps every other bar or so which will serve as signs when he conducts the orchestra. As the work progresses he must be careful lest a conflict between music and dialogue prove harmful to both. Usually it is safest to write music which is slow, keeps out of the speaking register and is of fairly even dynamics and colouring to avoid confusion on the soundtrack. With increasing experience the composer learns how to use more freedom without inviting disaster when music and other sounds are combined. Owing to the great pressure under which a composer must work it is the usual practice to make more or less comprehensive indications of orchestral intentions on the sketch but to leave the job of actually writing out the full orchestral score to an orchestrator. Some composers prefer to orchestrate their own music but there are perhaps only three or four composers in Hollywood who do so as a matter of course. Since it is often a question of having to rob Peter to pay Paul, i.e. take away from the time available to think about the music itself in order to be in complete control of the orchestral articulation, this question of whether or not to use an orchestrator is by no means easily decided.

When the score is finally completed and the parts have been copied out, the day or days of recording are at last at hand. While the composer had been busily at work, the music editor had not been idle. For the sake of a perfect match between the picture and the music, it is frequently necessary to put certain aids at the disposal of the composer and conductor. Such aids are the click track and "streamers." While the score is being recorded the film is projected on a screen mounted behind the orchestra and the conductor can, if he wishes, follow the dialogue by means of ear phones while conducting the music. He also has a large stop watch which is started simultaneously with the music and which affords him a close check on the timings he had put in the music previously. The click-track, mentioned above, is, in effect, a metronomic beat on film that the conductor and the orchestra follow, again, of course, by using ear phones. This insures absolute accuracy with respect to the intended tempo but, of course, makes for a certain rigidity of performance which is best avoided whenever possible. These click-tracks are made by hand by the music editor. This can be a very time-consuming job as it involves punching holes in the film at equidistant intervals which create an audible click when the hole passes over the sound gate of the reproducing machine. Streamers are another method of insuring perfect "sync" in places. The editor puts a long (three to five feet) diagonal scratch on the picture. When projected this scratch is seen as a wide line moving slowly across the screen. Just as it touches the side opposite that of its origin, a hole is punched in the film. This creates a very bright flash on the screen. As the conductor approaches a point in the music where such a streamer occurs he looks up at the screen as the flash pin-points exactly where a particular musical event, such as an *sfz* chord in the trombones or a weird tremolo in the strings, is to commence. It is then up to the conductor to "catch the cues" whilst continuing to preserve the musical flow of the whole.

When all the music has been recorded (incidentally, most movie music is practically sight-read by the orchestras which have developed an incredible proficiency along those lines), the music editor now has the job of building the "dubbing units." The process known as dubbing involves the combination of all sound elements, up to that point spread over a great number of soundtracks all running concurrently, onto one single track. There may, for example, be one or two tracks for the dialogue; perhaps three tracks for the music, one carrying the orchestra, one a soloist, another a chorus. Again there may be ten or more tracks containing the elements that combine to give a realistic sound picture in terms of sound effects. For instance a scene shows a man saying goodbye to his wife while walking to his car. As he is getting in, a motor cycle passes in the background. The scene is laid in a suburban street with trees and children playing nearby. In terms of separate tracks this means there must be one carrying the dialogue, one for the footsteps, another for general street sounds, another to bring in the passing motorcycle, yet another to indicate an occasional bird call in the trees and one for the sound of children at play. I might point out that this description applies to monophonic recording only. In the case of stereophonic sound the whole thing becomes yet more complicated although the principles involved are the same.

The dubbing is done reel by reel, the picture being projected on a screen while from two to four "dubbing mixers" combine the sounds using a huge control panel that makes one think of space travel rather than motion pictures. On the average it is impossible to dub more than about two reels a day as there are so many variable elements that must be controlled. It is at this point that the composer frequently feels that his fee is not so much in the nature of monies earned for services rendered but rather a reparation paid by the studio in view of the occupational injuries sustained. What fiendish tortures await the composer at those sessions! That tender cello solo, his favourite part of the entire score, lies completely obliterated by a siren which the director decided was necessary at that exact spot in order properly to motivate the reaction on the hero's face! Or that splendid orchestral climax, the ONE place in the entire score which the composer decided to orchestrate himself, held down to a soft $pp$ because of a line of narration that had to be added at the last moment in order to clarify an important story point.

When the picture is finally finished it is previewed in an out-of-the-way cinema to test audience reaction. This has the same function as the pre-Broadway out of town try-out of a new stage production. Depending on the problems uncovered there, minor or major changes must be made in the picture, many of which may necessitate changes in the music as some of the affected scenes may have to be shortened or lengthened or even may be transposed with respect to their sequence. Since it would be too time consuming and expensive to re-write the music, the procedure in most cases is to make such cuts and changes in the score as are required by editing the original magnetic film directly. Then the entire picture or parts of it may have to be dubbed once again and finally the day arrives when the composer is once more a free man, ready to return to the bosom of his family, which has learned meanwhile how to get along pretty well without him.

\* \* \*

**Laurence Rosenthal** owes his apprenticeship in film scoring to the United States Air Force—seldom has a man used his years in the service to better advantage. Rosenthal graduated from the Eastman School of Music in Rochester, New York, and then proceeded to spend two years in Paris studying with the venerable Nadia Boulanger. Returning to America at the outbreak of the Korean War he found himself highly eligible for duty under the colours. With great luck and/or shrewdness, he discovered the Air Force was in the process of setting up a film unit. Rosenthal appealed directly to the Commanding Officer of the unit and put to him the idea that it might be a good thing to have a composer on his staff to score his films. The CO was an empire builder with probable dreams about becoming the Sam Goldwyn of the Air Force. He jumped at the idea of having his own composer and Rosenthal spent the next few years scoring docu-

**Laurence Rosenthal.**

mentary and historical pictures. It was an apprenticeship without a master, Rosenthal's only guidance being what other composers were doing in films. As a student of composition he had found himself increasingly drawn to the use of music in dramatic forms, opera, ballet, incidental music for the theatre, anything that involved a literary or dramatic format, and with his golden opportunities in the Air Force he was able to solidify his ideas and his techniques. By 1960 Rosenthal was getting first class films to score, the first of distinction being *A Raisin in the Sun* and *The Miracle Worker*. In the latter film his score substantially increased the poignancy, the despair, the melancholy and the few moments of joy of an emotionally powerful film. Rosenthal also did interesting scoring for *Becket,* supplying a musical canvas that blended medieval cadences and elements of plainsong with an orchestral texture of a much later period. Absolutely accurate historical music of the period would not have worked for *Becket,* except

**Laurence Rosenthal conducting his score for** A Gunfight. **The image on the screen is Johnny Cash.**

for the scene of the consecration of the Archbishop—here Rosenthal used an authentic Gregorian chant. The job of scoring historical pictures is difficult and the one the critics most like to attack. The composer can really only use period music to colour his score just as the script and the direction can only suggest and approximate what people sounded like and behaved like long ago.

Rosenthal was unlucky with his next two films, *Hotel Paradiso* and *The*

*Comedians*, both heavily cast, expensive failures on which he lavished much careful scoring. In both cases his music helped the pictures play a little better, particularly so with *Hotel Paradiso*, the action of which was very stylised. The Feydeau comedy, whether well made or not, required an almost balletic score to bring the scenes to life. Writing a pseudo turn-of-the-century Parisian score for a small orchestra, Rosenthal was able to inject some of the Gallic charm, whimsy, and naughtiness the actors were labouring to achieve.

### Laurence Rosenthal on the Aesthetics of Scoring Films. Or—Old Composers Never Die, They Simply Fade Away in the Dubbing Room:

Anyone watching a film in its preliminary stages of preparation, even after the rough assembly of sequences has been refined into a more definitively edited version, cannot fail to be amazed by the effect of music, the first time it is introduced into the flow of images. It is difficult to describe it exactly. Something extraordinary has been added, perhaps warmth, perhaps a kind of life-energy, or an "atmosphere" in the sense that the film begins to breathe in a new way. In any case, a new dimension has been opened. And once music exists in a film, its absence must then be reckoned with. Silence itself becomes a kind of music, and the impact when music stops is as great as when it begins.

This is, in fact, one of the first questions the composer discusses with the director, once he is well enough acquainted with the film to be able to consider its musical possibilities. Here, the musical sensitivity of the director can be of enormous help, since solutions to the musical problems are often far from obvious. What kind of music? What style, what attitude, what sort of instrumental or perhaps vocal sound? And then the matter of exactly where in the film music is needed.

At this early stage, it is dangerous to make final decisions and sometimes, in fact, it is only when the actual marriage takes place on the sound stage, in the presence of projected film and orchestra, that the true musical requirements of a scene become clear. Often a minor revision, on the spot, will correct an error in the conception, sometimes a complete re-write is necessary, and, occasionally, no music whatsoever is the answer.

It is curious how in certain situations in a film, music—even very good and interesting music—will lessen rather than increase the impact of a scene. This may be especially true, for example, when good dialogue is being spoken by good actors. I have learned to become very suspicious when the right music for a scene keeps eluding me. When a scene seems to resist music of any kind, it may mean that there should indeed be none. For example, in *The Miracle Worker*, in that long fight scene in the dining room between Annie and the child, music would have spoiled the scene; whereas in the climactic scene where Annie finally breaks through to the child I felt music was needed to increase the sense of ecstasy. Music somehow encased the scene—it was sentimental in a certain way yet still tinged with that melancholy that coloured the whole picture. *The Miracle Worker* was for me a bewitching job. I was deeply touched by it, the communication was so direct that the music flowed effortlessly.

Film, unlike the theatre, is essentially a visual-aural rather than verbal-intellectual medium. Even though the two obviously share certain properties, such as dramatic action, dialogue, and character, the basic nature of the film is quite different.

One of the chief differences is that, in a film, sound becomes a highly expressive sensory element, whether it be music, sound effect, or speech. Total silence is an unnatural vacuum in a film. The ear seems to insist on filling it—whether with a few harp notes, the rustle of clothing, or a human voice. Of course, a great express train could race by on the screen, accompanied by perfect silence or with its natural sound replaced by that of a plaintive woodwind, and that might be enormously effective, but the point is that some sound—or silence—in relation to preceding and subsequent sounds, seems essential. In principle, dialogue plays a lesser role in the aural complex of a film than it does on the stage, where, of course, it enjoys complete supremacy. Hence the correspondingly greater importance of music and sound in motion pictures.

I would wish, however, to avoid giving the impression that music is an absolute essential in any film. It is quite possible, for example, to make a dry, hard, factual, journalistic picture which music would completely destroy by softening or theatricalising. Or there is the austere visual poetry of Ingmar Bergman, who uses very little music in his films. Of course, one might say that a single, resonant, stroke of the guitar after twenty minutes of musical silence is indeed a very special use of music. But there is no question that a film can be conceived in which the complete absence of music is an essential feature of the style.

However, since music and dialogue exist in most films, they must be combined with great care. It is a question of aural clarity. The composer's problem in accompanying dialogue is to find a transparent texture which will allow the words to emerge in clear relief and yet has enough substance to be heard and to achieve its dramatic purpose. This becomes a rather special study. Certain actors' voices can take more music than others, owing to their specific timbre and range. Some instruments—especially woodwinds like flute and oboe—can get seriously in the way of dialogue if they play a busy figuration, while in sustained passages they may not fight the voice at all. The effective transparency of the orchestra's string section is well known. But a composer does not wish always to rely on that particular timbre, especially since it has the curious property of sounding much more sentimental in a film than in the concert hall. So he must experiment with other sonorities. Keeping the orchestra well away from the pitch-range of the speaker—low instruments against high voices, and vice-versa, is sometimes the answer. Many sins in this domain can be covered by a resourceful mixing engineer, but obviously a right initial conception is preferable.

There are, of course, certain special and unorthodox effects of great power, such as the device in *On the Waterfront* of obscuring with Leonard Bernstein's music certain lines of dialogue, emphasising their intended banality. Here the emotional line of the music tells much more than would the obliterated words. In another scene in the same film, sound and music violently drown out the actors to produce an extraordinary feeling of frenzied impotence. The spectator may not be aware of how this has been achieved, but he is nonetheless affected by it. Unfortunately, this very imaginative and unusual psychological use of the soundtrack is all too rare.

Many films have special musical considerations to be dealt with and *The Comedians* was certainly one of them. Against a background of the Caribbean island of Haiti, with its mixed musical heritage of African, Western, and, more recently Latin American and jazz influences, is played a drama of complex, unhappy Europeans, who live in and are related to this environment but are not essentially of it—hence the title. The musical ambiance of Haiti, is, of course, unavoidable, and yet an entire element of non-Haitian character is superimposed on it, neurotic, sophisticated, disoriented. The tone is anti-romantic. The island is certainly no tropical paradise, and the "love story" is one of anguish, irritability and frustration.

How one deals with this musically is a delicate question, since a miscalculation in the general tone of the score could completely distort the point of the film. Even the exact use of Haiti's indigenous music has to be considered. Since the film, though piercingly acute in dealing with a very real situation, is in no exclusive sense a documentation, a mere reproduction of Haitian folk-music would be inadequate.

Problems of this kind lead one to many of the subtler and more elusive questions about film music, and, in fact, brings the composer into confrontation with its very *raison d'être*.

For example, one convention accepted in theatrical media such as opera, ballet, or mime, is the underscoring or emphasising of an action or mood by a corresponding kind of music. Hence battle-music, love-music, storm-music, suspense-music, etc. This is a venerable technique, and though it has been much abused—even to the point of ludicrousness—by the untalented, its effectiveness in the hands of a master cannot be denied.

Anyone who has experienced the opening storm of "Die Walkure," the terrifying scene of the underground vault in "Pelleas," or the brilliant fair in progress when the curtain goes up on "Petrouchka," must recognise the validity of this approach. Of course, in these great masterpieces, the artistic level rises far above anything that could be described as genre-music.

Even today, underscoring still remains a basic means of enhancing musically what the eye sees. But somehow in films, owing perhaps to the objective power of the close-up and the ability of the camera to put the viewer into the very midst of the scene, it often seems redundant and obvious to underline a dramatic moment with descriptively "appropriate" music. Why repeat in the score what the film is already saying visually? So composers have experimented with creating in music what is invisible on the screen. Sometimes it is in the expression of an emotion or mood in "counterpoint." Sometimes a kind of set-piece, often of a popular character—perhaps jazz or rock 'n' roll—which may ignore the specific action on the screen but weaves an overall fabric of sound designed to produce a certain dramatic climate. Occasionally an entire score is composed of such a piece or group of pieces, as in *The Third Man*, where the effect is compounded by the exclusive use of one solo instrument.

Again, a musical atmosphere can be created which actively contradicts what the eye sees. Certain imaginative composers have done this to great effect. An example comes to mind from the recent Russian film *War and Peace* in which a battle scene of grimness and ferocity is accompanied by courtly eighteenth-century dance music, elegant and graceful, carried over from the preceding scene of a palace-hall. The intended irony is clear, perhaps rather too clear and not necessarily the subtlest way of "going against the picture" but, finally, what could have been a completely conventional scene became an extraordinary and unexpectedly poetic moment.

Suddenly the possibilities become fascinating. What other responses could be evoked by film music which has no visual counterpart? And what other musical means can be brought into play? What of the use of electronic music? Or of other new (or even very ancient) theories about the precise effect on the listener of certain musical pitches, timbres, and rhythms? In a way, film music is still in its infancy, and before it lies an endless path of discovery about the relation of sound to image, emotion and idea.

*    *    *

So much for the mechanics and the aesthetics of film scoring, thanks to Mr. Gold and Mr. Rosenthal. A few lines now about the history of film music.

Films have always needed music but they needed it particularly in the early days of the silent screen for two good reasons: one, to overcome the lack of the spoken word, and two, to drown out the sound of the projector, which, prior to the building of cinemas with separate projection booths, sat in company with the customers. Except for the plush city theatres that could afford orchestras, the lot of film accompaniment fell to the lowly pianist, who was almost always left to his own devices to improvise music to cover the gamut of emotions and situations. It's safe to assume that the effect in most cases must have been little better than dreadful.

The man who invented the film music cue sheet was Max Winkler, who was not a composer or even a musician but a clerk in the music publishing house of Carl Fischer in New York. Winkler came into contact with the many conductors and pianists who came into Fischer's and asked for advice on appropriate music to play for pictures. Winkler was the perfect music clerk—his mind was a catalogue of thousands of pieces of music of every kind. He was also a man bright enough to spot a golden opportunity. In his autobiography, *A Penny from Heaven*, published by Appleton-Century-Crofts in 1951, he tells of spending a sleepless night thinking about how to organise the supply of music for films and then hitting upon a brainwave. Winkler got up, went to a table and wrote the following:

**MUSIC CUE SHEET**

for

**THE MAGIC VALLEY**

Selected and compiled by M. Winkler

Cue 1.  Opening—play Minuet No. 2 in G by Beethoven for ninety seconds until title on screen "Follow me, Dear."

Cue 2.  Play—Dramatic Andante by Vely for two minutes and ten seconds. Note: play soft during the scene where mother enters. Play Cue No. 2 until scene of hero leaving room.

Cue 3.  Play—Love Theme by Lorenz—for one minute and twenty seconds. Note: play soft and slow during conversations until title on screen "There they go."

Cue 4.  Play—Stampede by Simon for fifty-five seconds. Note: play fast and decrease or increase speed of gallop in accordance with action on the screen.

The film for which Winkler invented this cue sheet was imaginary but the music selections were drawn from the vast listing in his mind, music he had known from years of contact. His next move was to approach the Universal Film Company in New York and explain to them that he could compile such a cue sheet for every one of their films. In this manner, the films could have their music prepared before they arrived in the theatres. Universal immediately saw the value of the plan. They put Winkler to the test by showing him sixteen film subjects in one screening and challenging him to think of appropriate music—a slapstick comedy, a Western, a love story, a newsreel, a travelogue, etc, etc. They gave him a desk, a stop watch, a pile of paper and some pencils. With each picture, Winkler straightaway came up with a music listing. And a new career was born.

Max Winkler's cue sheets were soon turning up on the music stands of every movie theatre in America. His methods were quickly copied by others but the market was big enough to allow for competition and still succeed handsomely. Winkler formed his own company and supplied music and cue sheets for the films of Douglas Fairbanks, William S. Hart, Mabel Normand and the studios of Fox, Vitagraph, and Goldwyn. Winkler hired composers to write music for films, not the prominent concert and theatrical composers of the day but highly proficient hacks who specialised in supplying music for silent films. It was an age of musical abundance, with the theatre managers and conductors specifying that they didn't want any repetition. Ironically, the music of these now obscure and forgotten composers was heard by more people than the music of all the great masters combined.

Max Winkler's catalogue listed all the compositions under categories—action music, animal music, church music—sinister, chase, sad, mysterious, majestic, furious, etc, etc. Despite his staff of busy composers, he still could not turn out music in sufficient volume to meet the demand. In his book Winkler charmingly admits, "We turned to crime. We began to dismember the great masters. We murdered the works of Beethoven, Mozart, Grieg, J. S. Bach, Verdi, Bizet, Tschaikowsky and Wagner—everything that wasn't protected by copyright from our pilfering. Today I look in shame and awe at the printed copies of these mutilated masterpieces. I hope this belated confession will grant me forgiveness for what I have done."

Throughout the Twenties, Winkler and other music publishers prospered as music publishers had never prospered before or since. But the tower of plenty toppled with the coming of sound in films. It was a sweeping change and a disaster for many thousands of movie theatre musicians. Supplying enormous amounts of music for silent films suddenly became a thing of the past. Winkler sold seventy tons of printed music to a paper mill for fifteen cents a hundred pounds. He reconciled himself to becoming a minor operator in the publishing business but his fortunes picked up again when the film companies realised that they still needed music for film. They turned to him, and other publishers who had specialised in providing music for films, for the rights to his catalogue. But as Winkler said, "I knew it couldn't last long. The film companies were paying millions of dollars to publishers and composers for the use of published music. They soon found it more profitable to hire composers to write original music and to organise their own publishing houses. My catalogue was again heading for the junk pile, this time for good."

And in that admission from Max Winkler lies the kernel of what would be a new musical situation—the gathering in Hollywood of men who would create and develop musical compositions for motion pictures.

# 2
# The Golden Daze

The heyday of Hollywood is long gone, and with it the days of the huge, affluent, hyper-active studio music departments with their staff orchestras and stables of music directors, arrangers, orchestrators, and composers. Despite the excesses and the effusions and the egregiousness of this vast mish-mash of epic title music, sentimental love themes and action agitatos, there was also much that was interesting and admirable. The snobs sneered and the critics enjoyed their cavil but the fact remains that the musical activity of Hollywood was the most powerful educational force music had ever known. Only the insensate and the behalt could fail to be affected by the continual exposure to such a variety of music, no matter how subliminal the effect might be. The purists could decry the authenticity of pictures made about the lives of Frederic Chopin and Franz Liszt but no fair minded person could deny the musical craftsmanship of the pictures. That the musicians worked for men of dubious taste and knowledge is another matter. But what no Hollywood musician has ever been able to overcome is the solid barrier of prejudice that surrounds the community. Andre Previn, who began his incredibly varied career as a sixteen-year-old arranger for M-G-M, says: "No matter where I went to conduct, my reputation seemed tarnished by Hollywood glitter. To have written a Broadway show is O.K., even admirable; having played a lot of jazz is O.K., but less admirable. But somehow, having worked in Hollywood is like being a well-known whore. The maligning comes from people who have never lived there, because if they had they would have found a musical community of the deepest culture and the most remarkable musicians."

A much less appreciative estimate of the Hollywood music departments came from the many composers who tried to break in but couldn't. In truth, the departments were much like closed shops. They were managed by musicians who were largely products of the entertainment business rather than the concert halls and they doubtlessly felt somewhat uncomfortable when faced by composers whose tastes and intents were beyond their own. Musically conservative at heart, the music directors were also responsible to studio chieftains whose own concepts on the use of music in films were severely circumspect. Hence, very few avant-garde composers made the Hollywood grade, in the "gravy days."

In defence of the old line music directors it must be realised that they were operating slick, well organised departments handling a great deal of product on tight schedules. And something that quickly became apparent to those composers of serious contemporary music who did get a chance to score films was that the ability to write music was not enough. The mechanical intricacies of scoring, the acute timing, the mixing of music with sound and dialogue, the dubbing, the syncronisation—were not within every composer's ability or interest.

A classic example of the failure to adapt to the mechanics of scoring concerns Richard Strauss and a German film version of his opera *Der Rosenkavalier*. Strauss insisted on conducting the score himself; he was a master conductor and he saw no reason to delegate the job to a film conductor. The great composer changed his mind after hours of frustrating attempts to conduct the score to the timings of the film. He repeatedly missed cues and couldn't follow the time markings on the screen. Confused and irritated, Strauss handed the baton to the studio conductor and walked out.

Several famous European composers migrated to California because of the political climate of the Nazi era. Lionel Barrymore, who was a gifted amateur composer, tried hard to persuade Richard Strauss to leave Germany and be his guest in Hollywood. After much correspondence and consideration, the old composer decided to retire to his home in Bavaria and "sit things out." Admired by the Nazis, Strauss was later required to conduct some of his famous works for them, which caused his reputation to become somewhat blemished. On the other hand, the Nazis were quite happy to have Arnold Schoenberg leave for America; to them his music was a horrible mystery and an insult to German culture. Schoenberg spent the remainder of his life in Los Angeles, where he was avidly sought after as a teacher by many of the movie composers. Schoenberg showed no interest in film music, although his fame was such that a few producers thought it might be wise to get his name on a picture. One of them was the young, shrewd and greatly successful Irving Thalberg. In 1937 Thalberg asked Schoenberg to come to M-G-M to discuss the possibility of scoring *The Good Earth*. He was told by the producer that this film version of the Pearl Buck book was one of the studio's most artistic efforts and presented a rare opportunity for a composer. Thalberg described one scene: "There's a terrific storm going on—the wheat fields are swaying in the wind, and suddenly the earth begins to tremble. Then, in the earthquake, the girl gives birth to a baby. What an opportunity for music." Schoenberg looked at him incredulously, "With so much going on, what do you need music for?" Thalberg was puzzled by this apparent lack of interest. He then asked Schoenberg, "What would be your terms in working for us?" Replied the composer, "I will write music and then you will make a motion picture to correspond with it." Neither Thalberg nor any other producer approached Schoenberg again.

Among the "longhairs" who wrote an occasional film score in Hollywood were Alexandre Tansman, Ernst Toch, Darius Milhaud and Mario Castelnuovo-Tedesco, although a complete listing of the films on which they worked revealed a surprising fact—none of their assignments were for films of any distinction. Milhaud, who had written several interesting film scores in France, and who spent the years of the Second World War as head of the music department of Mills College in California, scored only one picture, a dull thing called *The Affairs of Bel-Ami,* and Castelnuovo-Tedesco, an Italian master who tutored some of the film composers on the side, wrote scores for a string of abysmal Columbia Grade B's like *The Black Parachute* and *Night Editor.* Whether this was purely bad luck or plotting on the part of the other composers is open to conjecture.

Igor Stravinsky showed some interest in writing film music but no interest or understanding in how the process of scoring was resolved. Columbia hired him to score *Commandos Strike at Dawn* (1942). At the initial discussion of the film, the plot was outlined to Stravinsky—Norway during the war, the underground resistance of the Norwegian patriots, the raids of British commandos, etc. Stravinsky said he found all this fascinating. Some weeks later he called the producer and said the score was ready, which surprised the producer because the film wasn't. However, the studio arranged a hearing of what Stravinsky had written, and then explained that although the music was admirable, it wouldn't fit the film. Stravinsky lost the job but not the music; with a little adaptation it later became known as *The Four Norwegian Moods,* and was soon greatly admired as a concert work.

Whenever a world-renowned composer came to the attention of the Hollywood bosses, it was usually through the machinations of other parties. Ben Hecht, a busy script writer in the late Thirties, and his friend George Antheil tried hard to land Ernst Krenek a position when he arrived in California in 1937. Krenek, unlike many of the musical exiles and expatriates of the film colony, was not Jewish. He simply detested the Nazis and refused to continue living in Germany. His musical esteem had been solidified by the success of his opera *Jonny Spielt Auf,* perhaps the most successful new opera of the Thirties. Hecht and Antheil went to see Sam Goldwyn to persuade him to offer a position to Krenek. Goldwyn said he had never heard of the composer. Antheil explained that *Jonny Speilt Auf* was a "smash hit" all over Europe. Goldwyn still showed no interest.

Hecht now decided to stretch a point, "Of course, you've heard of his *Der Rosenkavalier*?" Goldwyn agreed that the name sounded familiar. Antheil chimed in with, "His *La Bohème* is probably his biggest hit." With this, Goldwyn started to show some concern, but Hecht then casually tossed in, "No, George, I think *Il Trovatore* is his Number One smash." Goldwyn flew into a rage, "*That* son of a bitch. His publishers are suing me—just because we used a few lousy bars from his opera. You tell him to keep a long way from me." Krenek never worked for Goldwyn, in fact, he never worked for any film company, it was a line of composition that held no interest for him.

However, the story of Hollywood music is not the story of occasional famous names but the story of the men who made film music their speciality and developed it into a fascinating musical form—despite the general lack of appreciation of their employers and the public. Many are the hard working, consistent, always reliable composers not mentioned in this book. But the mere mentioning of them *en passant* would be an injustice. A hard working, consistent, reliable man is never an "also ran." Let the reader assume that in reading about Victor Young, John Green and Alfred Newman, he is also reading about the similar experiences and contributions of other composers who were cogs in the rapidly spinning wheels of the film factories.

\* \* \*

**Victor Young**'s twenty years in Hollywood spanned the "golden age" of the American sound film, the years of abundance, the years of fantastic productivity. These were the halcyon days when the major studios collectively put out up to five hundred features a year to feed the weekly moviegoing habits of hundreds of millions. Young arrived in 1936—he died in 1956. In between came an enormous volume of musical productivity: he either wrote or arranged, and conducted or supervised the scoring of something like three hundred and fifty films. That wasn't all. There were two other concurrent levels of his musical life—writing and conducting music for many of the top radio programmes of the period, and working as a recording artist for Decca. Since he was also a man who enjoyed smoking cigars, drinking, gambling, and carousing with his friends, it was little wonder that he passed away at the age of fifty-six.

The remarkable thing about Victor Young was not so much the immensity of his output but his seemingly inexhaustible fund of melody. Music was very easy for him—to the casual observer it seemed that all Young had to do was sit at the piano and the melodies fell out of his sleeves. He was a natural song writer. Many of the songs and themes from his pictures are still part of the pop music repertory: Love Letters, Stella

**Victor Young.**

by Starlight, Sweet Sue, Can't We Talk It Over, A Ghost of a Chance, My Foolish Heart, Golden Earrings, When I Fall in Love, Around the World in Eighty Days, etc., etc. Young was slick and facile as well as being greatly gifted with musical expression, and he might have served himself, and music, better had he worked less copiously and more intently. But apparently he was a man who found it hard to say "no," and at the completion of every film, broadcast or recording there were always more films, broadcasts and recordings to which he had committed himself. Occasionally, when he was thoroughly intrigued by a film, such as *For Whom the Bell Tolls*, he would put extra effort into the composition and prove himself capable of deeper, more serious stuff, but it seemed to him that no matter what the degree of effort, the response was always the same, "Vic, that's terrific." So, on and on he went.

Young was born of a Polish family in a tenement district of Chicago. The parents were musically inclined, and the father was an operatic singer and sang in the chorus of the Sheehan Opera Company. Young began playing the violin at the age of six, having shown a fascination with the instrument while still a toddler. His mother died when he was ten, and he and his sister were then sent to live with their grandparents in Warsaw. His grandfather, a tailor, encouraged the love for music, and Young was later enrolled as a student at the Imperial Conservatory in Warsaw. The most prominent of Young's instructors was Roman Statlovsky, who himself had been a pupil of Tchaikovsky. The teaching of this man was doubtlessly the strongest influence on Young, whose own scoring was characterised by long melodic lines and the foremost use of the stringed instruments. Young graduated from the conservatory with honours and soon afterwards made his *début* as a solo violinist with the Warsaw Philharmonic Orchestra. Within a year of concertising, the teenage violinist was presented with a Guanerius violin by the Philharmonic Society of Warsaw.

The First World War interrupted Young's career. In 1917—he was then seventeen—he was arrested after performing a recital in Russia and interned. He escaped through the aid of a Bolshevist officer who admired his playing, and managed to make his way back to Warsaw, where he was then arrested by the German Military Government. His ability with the violin once more saved him from greater discomfort, and he was put on parole, although ordered to remain in Warsaw until after the armistice had been signed. His single interest now was to return to America, and in February of 1920, he arrived in New York. Following a year of barely being able to make ends meet, Young made his American *début* at Orchestra Hall in Chicago.

The *début* brought Young an offer from a vaudeville circuit, with a contract that would have put him on tour at five hundred dollars a week. He was about to sign when it was mentioned that his performances were not to include any classical music, so he tore up the contract. Young eked out a living with the occasional recital until 1922, when he proceeded to Los Angeles to join his *fiancée*, who had arranged an audition for him with impresario Sid Grauman. The outcome of the trip was twofold: Grauman offered him the position of concertmaster with his Million Dollar Theatre Orchestra, and the *fiancée* soon became Mrs. Young. A year later he accepted a contract as concertmaster of the Central Park Theatre in Chicago, the anchor theatre in the Balaban and Katz chain of movie theatres, all of which had orchestras. This job touched off Young's association with film music, and for the remainder of his life he would be exceedingly busy. By the mid-Twenties he was the assistant musical director of the Balaban and Katz chain, which required him to arrange, and sometimes compose the music to be played before and with the more ambitious of the silent films. In 1929 he began his radio life, and two years later he signed an exclusive contract with Brunswick for broadcasts and recordings. By 1935 Young was one of the best known music directors in radio, and certainly the best known arranger, conductor and accompanist in the record business. Almost every artist who ever recorded for Decca was, at some time or other, backed by Victor Young and his Orchestra. In December of 1935, he was offered a contract by Paramount Pictures, and a few months later he arrived in Hollywood, to reach a new plateau in his career.

Victor Young's contribution to the art of film scoring was of a fairly conventional nature. He knew what was needed musically, and what he gave the pictures enhanced them. But he worked at a time and for a studio where nothing experimental or outlandish was wanted or even tolerated. In retrospect, what distinguishes his music is the warmth of melody—no matter what he did, Young couldn't contain this aspect of his nature. Even in scoring a thriller like *The Uninvited* (1944), a picture with a supernatural story, his love theme was so distinctly beautiful that multitudes of people began asking for a recording. Young refurbished the piece, and as *Stella by Starlight* it remains one of the loveliest themes to arise from a film score.

Young was a lusty man. When, in the last year of his life, he was told by his doctor that he would have to give up smoking and drinking if he wanted to live many years more, his reply was, "The hell with that." He was also a humorous man, given to practical jokes, one of which is legend in Hollywood music circles. Young and Max Steiner were the closest of friends, and similar kinds of men—lovers of poker and horse racing and other things. On one occasion Young drove up from Paramount to have lunch with Steiner at Warners. Arriving at the studio shortly before noon, he wandered over to the music department and found Steiner rehearsing the orchestra in the main title to a new film. Standing and listening to what was a typical but distinct Steiner theme, Young had an idea. He, unseen to Steiner, wrote the theme on a piece of paper, left the recording stage, got into his car and drove back to Paramount. Within a couple of hours, Young had made an orchestral sketch of what he had just heard, and the following morning he recorded the piece with his own orchestra. He then called Steiner and invited him up to his house that evening for a poker session. By the time Steiner and a pair of other card playing musicians arrived, Young had wired his record player to his radio. Some time during the game, he switched on the radio, which triggered the record player—and out came the Steiner music. After about twenty seconds, Steiner's eyes came up from his cards and he started to tremble. "Oh, my God." "What's wrong, Max?" innocently asked Young. Steiner shook his head, "I don't understand. That music. Is that something new?" "Hell, no," said Young, "I listen to this programme all the time—they've been playing it for years." Steiner tried to pick up the game but his attention was destroyed. Soon he said, "Vic, I'm not feeling too well, I'd better go."

Young could never explain why he became a movie composer, it was simply something that happened to him. He said, "Why, indeed, would any trained musician let himself in for a career that calls for the exactitude of an Einstein, the diplomacy of Churchill and the patience of a martyr. Yet I can think of no other medium that offers this challenge and excitement, provided that your interest is the universe in unflagging and your knowledge of musical forms is gargantuan."

His appearance belied his music. Young was slim, short and rather tough looking. He used to delight in recalling an occasion when a director who wanted him to score a certain picture took him into an office to discuss the matter with the producer, and the producer turned to the director and asked, "This man can compose music? He looks like a prizefighter to me." Young was often mistaken for a retired bantamweight, which impression was not entirely wrong, because he employed the nimble footwork of a light boxer in sparring with producers, studio executives, and recording engineers. In an industry noted for its "yes-men," Young was a "no-man." He also learned to be devious. He was once told by a producer that "this picture should be scored in the style of Hindemith." Said Young, "I assumed he had only recently heard his first Hindemith recording. I nodded in solemn agreement, and went home to work on a score which he later marvelled at and heralded as being exactly what he had in mind. There was nothing Hindemithian about it—the style was completely my own."

One of Victor Young's last scores was, perhaps, his ultimate achievement—*Around the World in Eighty Days*. The Mike Todd picture was itself a *tour de force* of entertainment, and its gaiety and visual interests were supported all the way by Young's tuneful music. The main theme, later backed by a lyric, became a hit song, and the album remains in the catalogue, as it deserves. Young wrote a series of musical pictures for this film that immediately lift the scenes—scenes of comedy and adventure in various parts of the globe. Sadly, he never lived to receive his prize for the score. He died of a heart attack in Palm Springs on November 10, 1956. Nineteen of his film scores had been nominated for Academy Awards. The following March he received his only, and posthumous, Oscar—for *Around the World in Eighty Days*. He had died during the scoring of *China Gate,* and the music credit frame of that film reads: Music by Victor Young, extended by his old friend, Max Steiner.

Victor Young was always encouraging to young composers who came to him for advice, and one of them was Henry Mancini: "Vic loved life in all forms. He was a man's man. There was no sham, he said it 'like it was' all the time. He gave the impression of being a man you might not readily walk up to, but once you got over your own hang-ups, you'd find he was a gracious man. But he worked too hard, and I think he drove himself to an early grave."

*       *       *

**John Green** has the peculiar affliction of possibly being over-talented. Green has written a number of songs that are among the hardiest perennials—*Body and Soul, I Cover the Waterfront, Out of Nowhere,* etc.—he has music-directed some of Hollywood's best musicals, four of which (*Easter Parade, An American in Paris, West Side Story,* and *Oliver*) have brought him Academy Awards; he has composed dramatic scores; and he continues his career as a conductor of symphony orchestras. Unlike many another successful musician, Green did not have to fight an impoverished background. His output and his varied successes attest not only to talent but to a certain ambitiousness and a powerful ego.

Green began his association with films soon after talkies came in. In 1930—he was then twenty-one—he landed a job with Paramount's East Coast Studio on Long Island, just outside New York City. After two years there, he left the film business and became active in broadcasting and the theatre and it was not until 1944 that he resumed his film life, and then, so to speak, with a vengeance. Green's father was an affluent New York banker and builder, although musically and theatrically orientated. The Green home was ever open to the leading artists of the day. By the age of three, Green was showing an unusual interest in music and "I sustained my first physical injury at the age of four when I fell off a chair on which I was standing conducting the *Poet and Peasant* overture, in front of our Victrola. I sprained my little conducting arm, but not enough to impair later efforts or not enough for anyone to notice. My real impairment came in being a rich man's son and that was the hurdle I had to jump. My father was very opinionated but fortunately also humorous. He did not encourage my musical ambition. He believed there was room in the arts only for the great, and I clearly recall him telling me, 'Son, there's no bum like a pretty good artist, and you're pretty good.' However, I was not about to be discouraged. I was wise enough to go along with his theory that I should have a good liberal arts education and acquire some business skill. I attended Harvard and graduated from their school of Economics, which landed me a job as a purchase and sales clerk in a Wall Street bond house. But I had no intention of following a career in business and after six months I quit to team up with lyricist Eddie Heyman."

Green had actually turned semi-professional while still at Harvard. He participated in all the school musical activities and shows as an arranger and performer, and in his last year he played with the highly esteemed Harvard Gold Coast Orchestra. It was also during that year he wrote his first successful song, *Coquette*. One of his jobs after quitting Wall Street was as a rehearsal pianist for Gertrude Lawrence, during which period he and Eddie Heyman wrote *Body and Soul* for her. "But film had always been a major interest of mine—cinematography is still a hobby—and when I got wind of an opening for a rehearsal pianist at Paramount's Astoria studio I grabbed it—at fifty dollars a week. My first assignment was *The Big Pond* with Maurice Chevalier and songs by Sammy Fain, including *You Brought a New Kind of Love to Me*. Robert Russell Bennett had been engaged to orchestrate the songs but he fell ill. Frank Tours was the music director at studio—a remarkable Englishman whose father had been the original conductor for Gilbert and Sullivan at the Savoy Theatre—I asked him if I could have a crack at the job and he took a chance, in fact, the very first song I orchestrated was *You Brought a New Kind of Love to Me*. This was in the days when the orchestra was right on the shooting stage with the performers as they were being filmed—the singing and the playing was simultaneous—a clumsy, costly process."

Green arranged the music for twelve films during his two years at Astoria, and between assignments conducted the orchestra at Paramount's Brooklyn Theatre, which he describes as invaluable experience for a young musician, not to mention a magnificent sop for the ego—almost enough to atone for falling while conducting at the age of four. His conducting was striking enough to bring an offer from Victor Young, who was then the music director for the Atwater-Kent radio series. "Victor—God love his memory—hired me as an orchestrator and gave me wonderful opportunities, which in turn led to other things. It got me jobs with some of the best bands playing in New York at that time, the chance for my music to be heard on radio, and it brought me to the attention of Broadway-producers. I later wrote scores for some miserable flop musicals, with an occasional hit song, and I went to England to write and conduct a musical for Jack Buchanan—the first original musical broadcast by the BBC, '*Big Business.*' "

The Thirties were busy years for young Johnny Green. By 1942 he had been hired by Richard Rodgers as the music director of the last Rodgers and Hart show, *By Jupiter*. This would lead him back to the movies. "Louis B. Mayer, Arthur Freed and Judy Garland came to the show one evening, and as I came up from the orchestra pit I was met by Freed, who told me he and Mayer wanted to discuss something with me. They insisted I come to Hollywood. I wasn't that interested, I really wanted to stay in New York and do something about my poor batting average in the theatre, in fact, one of my turkeys was playing at the time, and kept from total disaster only by one number—*The Steam Is on the Beam*. However, M-G-M had a way of twisting one's arm by adding ciphers to the offer, and I just couldn't turn it down."

November, 1942, marked Green's arrival at M-G-M and the beginning of a long and profitable association with the studio. His *forte* quickly became the arranging and conducting of musicals, at which M-G-M was the leader in the field. Green had always been an excellent conductor, and no mere sound-stage time beater, and he injected great vitality into the scoring of the lavish, colourful, musical entertainments that delighted the world, not to mention the M-G-M stockholders. Occasionally, Green was able to accept a job from another studio—he wrote the songs for Deanna Durbin in *Something in the Wind* at Universal, and the score of Danny Kaye's *The Inspector General* at Warners. The score of the Kaye comedy was of a high order and clearly pointed to the fact that if Green hadn't been so busy with musicals he would have been one of the industry's foremost composers.

In 1950 John Green's career entered another phase. Louis B. Mayer called him in to discuss the job of heading up the whole music department. Says Green, "Despite the great activity and the abundance of talent, it was a badly structured and badly managed department. Mayer knew this and he told me, 'We want the greatest music department that there has ever been in this entire business—the greatest orchestra and the greatest staff, and we want it managed with the utmost order and system.' I blanched and said, 'Mr. Mayer, it's going to cost a lot of money to have that kind of a department.' To which he looked me in the eye and replied, 'Well, we've got a lot of money.' That was that. It was the beginning of ten years in which I was virtually autonomous—I made the deals as well as the aesthetics. I was paid an awful lot of money. I like to think I was lured not so much by the power but the challenge to build the kind of department they wanted. However, looking back on it, I sometimes regret accepting the offer, it was ten years I could have spent composing, but there were also creature comforts I was shallow enough to be lured by."

**John Green and the MGM Concert Orchestra.**

The M-G-M Music Department under John Green was, indeed, an impressive force. Miklos Rozsa, Bronislau Kaper, Adolph Deutsch, and Andre Previn were the prestige composers, and for the musicals Green had a group of men who, in combination, are never likely to be equalled: George Stoll, Lennie Hayton, George Bassmann, Roger Edens, Conrad Salinger, and others. Green was also very much a working boss—he produced a series of short subjects under the general title, *The M-G-M Concert Hall*, with himself conducting the M-G-M Symphony Orchestra and for which he won the third of his five Oscars. He also assigned himself to scoring the expensive but disappointing epic, *Raintree County*, which nonetheless contains a monumental score. During his reign he also was responsible for commissioning the first twelve-tone film score, Leonard Rosenman's *The Cobweb*, which he also conducted, and the first electronic score, for the cartoon *Robby the Robot*. Green decided that *Executive Suite* should have no score at all, "It's also the function of a music director to know where to be silent, and there's nothing music could have done for that picture except hurt it."

Green's biggest single job as a music director was his work for *Oliver*, and it is entirely due to Green that the music in that film is so vital and lively, in fact, so soaringly effective. Green worked on the picture for two years and recorded the score in London, where he culled top instrumentalists from the five leading symphony orchestras. "I'm the world's worst snob about who plays under my stick, and I can tell you that leaving that particular orchestra was like leaving one's favourite child." Green won a well justified Oscar for his efforts on this film, something that seems to puzzle those who wonder why it didn't go to Lionel Bart, who wrote the stage original. Bart is not a composer; he has the enviable ability to think of melodies—other people write them down for him. And the difference between a simple melodic line on a piece of paper and what was heard on the soundtrack of *Oliver* is John Green, the rich and vigorous creativity of his orchestrations and his conducting. Asked to comment on the success of the film, Green says, "It's enormously complicated and very simple—all of its elements belong to each other."

It was John Green who was largely responsible for Andre Previn's being hired by M-G-M. Previn, born in Berlin in 1929 and musically educated both there and in Paris, came to Los Angeles in 1939. His talent was abundant even as a schoolboy and as Green recalls, "When we hired Andre he wasn't quite sixteen and he could only come to work after three o'clock. He was incredible. After about three years as an arranger we

MGM music chieftain John Green and then 18-year-old Andre Previn (1947).

gave him his first score, *The Sun Comes Up,* and from then on it was: Andre Previn, composer-conductor. I hardly know what to say about Andre, his technique and his facility seem limitless. In scoring, he was so fast and accurate you wanted to kick him in envy. And it wasn't enough to compose brilliant scores like *Elmer Gantry* and *The Four Horsemen of the Apocalypse,* he was also moonlighting as a pianist, both jazz and classical. Now, of course, he's developed into a first class conductor, and I don't imagine he will return to the film world. He and I became good friends. I remember calling him on his thirtieth birthday at 7:30 in the morning, which is something you don't do to him because he's not an early riser. I called and said, 'Andre, today you're thirty, and it's no longer a miracle you can play a C Major chord,' and hung up. He was still laughing when I saw him for lunch. I was with Andre once when he was asked by an interviewer whether having to write music to a deadline, such as we must do in this business, was a good thing for a composer. I remember his answer because it was exactly what I or any of the other composers might have replied had such a clear accounting come to mind. He said, 'I think we need the deadlines because we don't have the luxury of waiting for that elusive muse. Very often we're not too terribly interested in the project at hand—you can get tired of even a good film after you've seen it several times—and if some of us were left to our own devices the score would never be recorded, or we would procrastinate to the point where they would get someone else.' So you might bear that Previn reply in mind whenever you are tempted to think how wonderful it is to be a film composer."

There is nothing particularly new in the concept of marrying music to film, in the opinion of John Green. "It's the continuation of a theatrical tradition—Shakespeare's plays at the Globe Theatre had musical accompaniment. As for the particular value of music on film, I think if you were to see a major film whose score you liked, and then saw the picture without the score, you would find one of the major elements—and by major I mean almost as important as the photography—missing."

*   *   *

If the Golden Age of Hollywood Music can be epitomised in the experience of just one man, he would have to be **Alfred Newman.** When Newman arrived in Hollywood in 1930, sound in film was going through the fledgling period and the use of music, other than for visual performance, was an uncharted road fogged with ignorance and uncertainty. Newman paved that road, not only as a composer but as a superlative conductor and music director, and later as the head of a major studio music department. He worked ferociously and prodigiously all through that Golden Age, and when he died in 1970 he knew that its deflation and demise had preceded him. He had outlived it.

David Raksin, who worked as a composer under Newman at Twentieth Century-Fox from 1944 to 1950, says this about him: "He was a totally remarkable musician with an amazing sense of theatre and timing. He was also a taskmaster, he always wanted your best and no one who ever worked for him for long ever gave him anything else. Al was a self-regenerating man—just when everyone thought he had said all he had to say about film music, he would surprise everyone and come up with a great score. He could also be self-deprecating and he would occasionally refer to himself as a 'hack musician.' It's a strange thing, but if you have any kind of a gift, there seems to be—in some cases—an inner bargain with yourself not to use it. It's tough to write music on demand, it doesn't always come when you want it, and Newman was a rather reluctant composer. I think he was more instinctive than profound musically, but what he did have was an unfailing sensitivity to the dramatic meaning of a film scene and the ability to translate that meaning into the language of music."

Alfred Newman was the eldest of ten children born to a working class family in New Haven, Connecticut. His father was a produce dealer with no interest in music but his mother liked music and realised her first-born was gifted with unusual talent. The boy responded to the sound of music and craved to play the piano. A piano would have been a major luxury for this family, but they prevailed upon a friend who had one to let the boy use it. Since they couldn't even afford bus fare, Newman walked ten miles to and from his daily practice session. His first teacher was a house painter who had once taken a few lessons, and charged twenty-five cents for his own tutoring. By the time he was eight, Newman was playing in public and earning money from clubs and organizations in New Haven. The money was saved and used a year later to send him to New York to study with Sigismond Stojowski, one of the finest teachers of that time and fortunately a warm-hearted man who was generous enough to take the boy on at little expense. Stojowski was also the teacher of Oscar Levant, who recalls him as not only a brilliant pedagogue but a sympathetic and humorous man. It was Stojowski who said of Saint Saens's Second Piano Concerto, "It begins with Bach and ends with Offenbach."

Newman continued to earn money as a child pianist during his years with Stojowski, and at the age of twelve he was sponsored by Paderewski for a recital in New York. There seems little doubt that Newman would have developed into a major concert pianist but the financial circumstances of his family ruled out any further study. He literally went to work in order to send money home. He accepted an offer from Gus Edwards, the impresario who specialised in young talent, to perform five shows a day at the Harlem Opera House. At thirteen, he undertook a vaudeville tour in which he performed while dressed as Little Lord Fauntleroy. His success was continual, and while touring with musical comedy road companies he asked, and was allowed, to occasionally conduct the orchestra. It is a matter of record that Alfred Newman, age seventeen, was hired as the conductor of *The George White Scandals,* and for the next twelve years he went from job to job as the conductor of many of the famous Broadway musicals of the Twenties. In 1930, when Irving Berlin contracted to make a film of his *Reaching for the Moon,* he insisted that Newman go to Hollywood as the music director, and what was originally set up as a three-months' visit opened up into a career that would keep him in Hollywood for the remainder of his life.

When Newman arrived in Hollywood in early 1930 he found that the Berlin film was not ready to be scored, and the head of the studio, Joseph M. Schenck, then lent him to Sam Goldwyn. Newman worked on five other films before he got around to scoring *Reaching for the Moon.* He found his musical comedy experience invaluable in this new profession of arranging music for film tracks. He also found a friend in Goldwyn, who not only used him steadily over the next decade but cheerfully recommended him to other producers. Newman was the only composer Goldwyn ever really knew or liked, and whenever he wanted advice on who to hire, he called Newman—even when Newman was head of music at Twentieth Century-Fox Goldwyn would call and ask who he should get to score his films. In this way, Newman was of help to many composers.

The first Newman score to win wide attention was *Street Scene,* a 1931 filming of the Elmer Rice story of life on New York's East Side. The main theme of that score, later adapted by Newman into an orchestral piece called *Sentimental Rhapsody,* became not only popular but a hardy perennial of the film music world and turned up in half a dozen other films over the years—films scored by composers working under Newman. Other Newman themes became popular: one melody from *The Hurricane* took on a life of its own as *The Moon of Manakoora,* and any musically inclined person who enjoyed *Wuthering Heights* could hardly have failed to leave the theatre humming the haunting *Cathy* theme. The score of this film helps it to maintain its life as a masterpiece of romantic film making.

The quality of Newman's composition varied from time to time, most probably because he took on too much and because composing was not a job he enjoyed, but the quality of his conducting never strayed from excellence. His ability to lead an orchestra was perhaps his outstanding talent. His timing and his nuances and his precision were near perfection.

He once told me, "I'd much rather conduct than compose. Composing is a lonely business, really lonely. Conducting is gregarious, you work with anywhere from five to a hundred men, the lights are always on and there's an excitement to being with talented musicians and making music. I studied composition as part of my musical training but I never wanted to compose. I studied music because I wanted to be a good conductor."

Newman was the most decorated of the Hollywood musicians—nine Oscars came his way, although only one was for composition, for *The Song of Bernadette.* The others were for musicals and he never made any secret of the fact that the awards were for group efforts, representing a team of arrangers and orchestrators of whom he happened to be the boss. The first was *Alexander's Ragtime Band,* in 1938, followed by *Tin Pan Alley* (1940), *Mother Wore Tights* (1947), *With a Song in My Heart* (1952), *Call Me Madam* (1953), *Love is a Many Splendored Thing* (1955), *The King and I* (1956) and *Camelot* (1968). On his final trip to the Academy Awards stage, Newman showed all the excitement of a father wearily walking into a maternity ward to look at his ninth child.

Newman had written many distinctive scores before he picked up his Oscar for *Bernadette*—outstanding were *The Prisoner of Zenda* (re-used in its entirety in the 1952 re-make), *Wuthering Heights, How Green was My Valley,* and *This Above All*—but *Bernadette* enabled those who were sufficiently interested to study the score closely because it was the first to be released as a commercial recording—an eight side 78 rpm Decca album, later transferred to LP. It was also the first of several scores of a strongly religious nature, the scoring of which revealed Newman himself to be a man of quite some faith, something his manner tended to belie. He wrote especially well for the strings, and the strings in these religious pictures had a strikingly spiritual quality. In *The Song of Bernadette,* the musical highlight is the revelation scene, one which gave Newman considerable problems. "My first reaction to the scene was to 'hear' it in terms of the great religious experiences that had previously been interpreted by Wagner in his Grail music and Schubert in his Ave Maria, which is a terrifying standard to have to approach. I first wrote for the scene in this vein but I wasn't happy with anything I did. It then occurred to me that I was wrong in thinking of the scene as a revelation of the Virgin Mary. I read back over Werfel's book and found that Bernadette had never claimed to have seen anything other than a 'beautiful lady.' I now wrote music I thought would describe this extraordinary experience of a young girl who was neither sophisticated enough nor knowledgeable enough to evaluate it as anything more than a lovely vision. With this in mind, I thought the music should not be pious or austere or even mystical, or suggest that the girl was on the first step to sainthood. She was at that point simply an innocent, pure-minded peasant girl, and I took my musical cues from the little gusts of wind and the rustling bushes that accompanied the vision, letting it all grow into a swelling harmony that would express the girl's emotional reaction. And it was important that it express *her* reaction, not *ours.*"

**Alfred Newman in his studio at Twentieth Century-Fox in 1941.**

Newman's style of composition was essentially operatic—lyrical, dramatic and expressive, and his method of scoring was predominantly one of mood settings rather than leitmotifs and music counterpointing the action of the film, which was basically the style invented and employed by Max Steiner. Between the two of them, Newman and Steiner were the two major influences on film scoring in Hollywood in the years between the mid-Thirties and mid-Fifties. Any newcomer who could successfully study, understand and utilise both styles had found the magic formula.

Quite a few of the best Hollywood composers were men who drifted into the business with no particular ambition to remain, but because of the suitability of their talent, the copious opportunities and the high pay, they stayed, never to return to their previous musical environment. This was a situation peculiar to the American film industry, which required that a composer devote himself full time to writing for the screen. The studios wanted their composers under exclusive contracts. In England and France, because of the centralisation of the various arts in the capital cities, a composer might go from the film stages to the theatre stages to the concert halls to the ballet—all within a year. The British and French composers were also far less likely to be tied to long running contracts at enormous salaries. In Hollywood, with film factories working at full tilt, the gentlemen in the Front Office were not interested in their men moonlighting, no matter how artistic or admirable the cause.

Newman was a victim of this kind of fate, that is, if a man who ends up earning two thousand dollars a week plus royalties can be regarded as a victim. He had arrived in Hollywood with the right degrees: a classical education and a rich background of experience in the theatre. There were no areas of music mysterious to him and he could thus tackle anything. He also deemed it wise to continue his study of music; all through the busy years on Broadway, he had studied with George Wedge, and when Schoenberg arrived in Los Angeles, Newman was one of his first pupils. Although composing was not a passion with him, any study of Newman's scores shows a deepening of his composition, although it cannot be denied he was a most eclectic composer. By the same yardstick, much of what Newman invented for the screen was widely copied.

Examples of the best of Newman: the ghostly choral music in the main title of *Twelve O'Clock High;* the darkly dramatic and driving title music to Henry King's highly artistic Western *The Gunfighter;* the entire, rich score of the same director's *Captain from Castile,* especially the final spectacular scene of the Conquistadores marching in victory (Newman's exciting march was a deft tribute to Erich Korngold, whom he greatly admired); the asylum scenes in *The Snake Pit,* particularly the horrifying electronic therapy sequence; the gentility of his theme for *Anne Frank;* the anguish of the music that accompanies Christ's carriage of the Cross in *The Robe;* the sombre tone poem in *David and Bathsheba,* that approximates to the cadences of the Twenty Third Psalm; the Easter Service and the Grand Ball sequence in *Anastasia,* and the moody uneasiness of the music for the title character; the exuberance and optimism of the main title of *How the West Was Won;* and the glorious Hallelujahs which were deleted from the score of *The Greatest Story Ever Told* by its producer.

Newman became the General Music Director of Twentieth Century-Fox in 1940, and held the post for twenty years. Darryl F. Zanuck was his boss, and Newman was lucky in working for a man who trusted him completely. He was well paid, although nothing could replace the time and effort the job demanded, and he was given a huge annual budget, which he spent lavishly. Despite his obvious success, he frequently expressed less than contentment with his work. He spoke for the whole colony of composers when he said, "I often wonder what could be achieved if we were given enough time to work on a film score." In the case of *The Egyptian,* there simply was not enough time. Bernard Herrmann was assigned and given eight weeks to write two hours of symphonic music for this sumptuous and dull epic. The management then moved the release date up by two and a half weeks. Herrmann appealed to Newman for help, and the two men resolved the problem by dividing the scoring between them. It was the only time two major composers have collaborated to produce one homogeneous score. And it was no ordinary score. Dealing with ancient Egypt, the music had to reflect an almost unknown culture, and support the rich, exotic visuals. After an initial discussion of modes and scales, and the assigning of the sequences, the two composers retired to their quarters and wrote for five weeks, sending their sketches back and forth but seeing each other only twice during the operation. The scoring was also unique in that both composers conducted their own portions.

Most of the Hollywood composers would write concert works on their own time, perhaps hoping that it might be performed but most probably doing it to "keep in shape." Alfred Newman never wrote anything other than his film scores, and even in doing that he let it be known that they were not the frustrations of a serious symphonist. "If I want to write great music, I've no right to be working in a film studio. Good film music must always be inspired by the picture of which it is a part, not by the desire of a composer to express himself. The effect of music in films is largely one of association, the important thing being to evoke the proper mood and spirit. If you can't accept these terms—stay away from films."

Despite his realistic attitude toward his work, quite a lot of Newman music lived beyond the films and became popular on recordings. Rare is the film music buff who doesn't rhapsodise over his *Captain from Castile* score, or point to the quality of various passages in *The Robe,* which is a scholarly usage of ancient Jewish music. The sincerity of feeling that Newman put into his religious subjects is beyond reproach, and it revealed an aspect of his nature he otherwise never referred to.

*The Diary of Anne Frank* was yet another Newman score with a spiritual character. Despite the severe setting of the story and its horrific *dénouement,* the music avoids atonality or jagged modernisms and focuses on a certain wistfulness and on old European charm. The Frank family, driven from Hamburg and sheltered in the attic of a friendly house in Amsterdam, lived through an unnatural, suspended period, in which their only pleasures were reminiscences and listening to the radio, from which they might hear and enjoy a Strauss waltz. For the sensitive, imaginative young girl, it was a period of fancy, fortunately the fancy of a happy soul who could write in her diary, "In spite of everything, I still believe people are good at heart." Newman visited the house in Amsterdam where the Frank family stayed. He wanted to feel the atmosphere before writing his music, and he said, "It was a strange experience—standing in that room where Anne lived and from where she was eventually led away to die, I had a feeling mixed of exaltation and repugnance. George Stevens had decided that the film shouldn't be one of gloom, but that we should concentrate on the love and humour of these people. During my visit, I had lunch with Anne Frank's father, a charming man, and he wanted to know what my music would be like. I could only tell him in the abstract that what touched me most about the book was its spirituality, and that was what I wanted to say in the music. This seemed to please him. When it came to the actual scoring—I didn't try to illustrate, except in a few places, what was happening on the screen, so much as invoke in the music the remembrance of happier times, and the longings for the future—the longings of an oppressed people."

Alfred Newman was a compassionate man and it was a quality that shone through much of his music. In person he masked his gentle nature with a certain gruffness, as if somewhat embarrassed to be known as a man concerned about humanity in general and his associates in particular. Ken Darby was the choral director on several films scored by Newman— *David and Bathsheba, The Robe, How the West Was Won, The Greatest Story Ever Told,* and most of the Rodgers and Hammerstein musicals that were filmed—and he cites as an example of Newman's sense of values the fact that while they were doing *Carousel* the composer persuaded Darryl F. Zanuck to give Darby billing in the credit titles as his associate—on the same credit card as himself. "That kind of generous recognition was unique in the film industry, but when I said so in front of the crew Newman mumbled gruffly: 'To hell with *that*. Nobody gets credit they haven't earned.' He concealed his kindness just as he concealed the mechanics of music. I remember during the scoring of *How the West Was Won* Alfred shaking his head and musing, 'How in hell am I going to do anything original for *another* Indian chase?' and then going home and doing one. It was a series of brass punctuations in a complex scherzo, with the horses' hooves and Indian yells supplying the counterpoint. His whole score for this film is a beautiful fabric of original material woven with traditional melodies."

Ken Darby recalls *How the West Was Won* as the most pleasant assignment on which he and Newman collaborated and *The Greatest Story Ever Told* as the most miserable. Produced and directed by the brilliant but painfully meticulous film-maker George Stevens at incredible cost, the film was a major disappointment at the box-office. Newman had been particularly successful writing music for biblical pictures and Stevens insisted that he was the one man for the job. Flattering as it was, Newman would have been wise to reject the offer. He was a painstaking, extremely conscientious musician and at this time in his life his prior concern should have been his health.

Darby revealed some of the machinations in the making of this film to *Films in Review:*

Our contract called for twenty weeks of work but we were on it for more than a year. My first contact with the project was after Alfred had met with director George Stevens and been asked to develop a couple of thematic ideas and a melodic line for "Oh, give thanks unto the Lord, for He is good, and His mercy endureth forever." This last involved a male chorus and Alfred and I put our heads together. He completed his other themes and we recorded them on quarter-inch tape. I then took a plane to Stevens' location at Glen Canyon in northern Arizona, intending to stay a few days. My job was to play Newman's themes for Stevens and rehearse the disciples—those who could sing—in the psalm. It was also my job to interview and explore the repertoire of the Inbal Dancers, who had been imported from Yemen.

Whenever I tried to corner Stevens long enough to play him the tape I'd be told: "Tomorrow." So I auditioned the players who were cast as disciples. Six had good voices, one was exceptionally gifted, and the rest were hopeless. The Inbal group proved to be difficult. At first they refused to perform their holy music on the ground of sacrilege, but ultimately I won their confidence and listened to some of the most interesting sounds I've ever heard.

We made all kinds of experiments—group lamentations, women keening in pairs, solos, sextettes. At long last all this was displayed to Stevens who, although he'd been on the set all day and was very tired, came alive and grabbed his script to find places in which to use the Inbals. He told me to stay on and record everything they could do. But little of their music got into that final print.

Months later, after Stevens had gone over every scene of his "final" cut version with us—it ran almost four and a half hours—we started recording. Voices were used in some places as audible scrims, i.e. were interlaced with orchestral color to add a mystic quality (the Nativity sequences, the sorrowing of Jerusalem, the antiphonal Hosanna, the return to Capernaum). The most exciting musical sequences were those of the raising of Lazarus and of the Easter morning and the Resurrection. While we were working on these Stevens began recutting the portions that had already been scored. Which meant the shortened scenes had to be re-scored and re-recorded. Time was running out and Alfred got Hugo Friedhofer and Fred Steiner to help on this.

The Hallelujah that Alfred wrote was intended for the end of Act I (the raising of Lazarus) and the end of Act II (the Resurrection of Christ). We used sixty voices for it and an orchestra of about the same number. Out of the blue Stevens told me it would be replaced with Handel's *Messiah*. I was stunned and I told Alfred. "That isn't the worst of it," he replied. "George has been playing the recording of the score of *The Robe* and wants to use the Crucifixion music from it for the raising of Lazarus."

Twentieth Century-Fox and the publishers of *The Robe's* music were paid a fee, and we recorded it. By this time Alfred and I had lost heart and Alfred took sick. Which is why Stevens asked me to cut bars from Alfred's themes for the scenes he, Stevens, shortened after United Artists insisted the film ran too long. I also conducted the Handel and Verdi *Requiem*. Alfred put it succinctly: "It's my name but it isn't my score. I'd be pleased if my name were removed from the credits." Newman's music for *The Greatest Story Ever Told*, including his Hallelujahs, is some of the finest music ever written for films.

*The Greatest Story Ever Told*, despite all Stevens's hard work and his undoubted sincerity, was poorly received by the critics and the public. As always with historical and biblical films made on grandiose scales, the music score was trounced. The more snide among the critics sneered at Newman's "attempting to glorify his own music by incorporating Verdi and Handel" but once again it was a case of the blame being laid at the wrong door. Stevens had defeated his own purpose by insisting on the *Hallelujah Chorus;* all it did was accentuate an already overly-theatrical film. Sprinkled as it was with dozens of cameo performances by famous faces the film emerged as a rather monstrous vaudeville act.

Alfred Newman remained with film music to the end of his life, but as he passed the age of sixty the strain of his exacting profession began to tell on him. The years of working long hours and the strain of responsibility made a heavy mark, and he was never easy on himself. A heavy smoker, he wracked his lungs with coughing in his last years, and although he was in no way an alcoholic, Newman did love expensive Irish whiskey, which he drank straight. His principal pleasure was his home and his family, his wife and six children. Uncompromising in his business dealings; severe and impatient with those he didn't like, Newman could appear a rough man. To those fortunate enough to be his friends, he was remarkably soft hearted and kind. Speaking for myself, I looked forward to my visits to his home to interview him because he was more interested in being a host than an interviewee. There were a thousand things he would rather talk about than his music, and at the end of the visit there was always that Irish whiskey, which I accepted because I hadn't the courage to tell him it gave me severe indigestion. Later, when I would play back my tapes and look over my notes I would find little actual material about his work. What I did have was the recollection of being with a remarkable man.

When Newman died on February 17, 1970, it was—for many of us—the official parting knell of Hollywood's Golden Age.

Alfred Newman at his last recording session, conducting his score for Airport, at Universal in 1969. With him is his associate, choral arranger Ken Darby. The Newman score was nominated for an Academy Award, but he died before the nomination was announced.

# 3
# The Mittel-Europa Strain

History is full of irony. It is, for example, ironic that the fury and the horror of the Russian revolution and the Nazi regime in Germany actually benefited the culture of the United States. Legions of artists of every calibre and kind left the Soviet Union and all parts of Europe in the wave of historical cataclysms, and many of them found their way to America. Quite a few of them discovered profitable outlets for their ability in Hollywood.

In their prime, the major studios drew their talent from all over the world; wealth and power enabled them to hire the best. But it might also be said that Messrs. Warner, Mayer, Zanuck, Goldwyn, *et al*, were ably assisted by Stalin and Hitler. Four Europeans of deep musical roots, all of whom would have a profound bearing on the development of film composition were Dimitri Tiomkin (Russian), Bronislau Kaper (Polish), Franz Waxman (German) and Miklos Rozsa (Hungarian). Perhaps none would have become a Hollywood figure without a shove from history.

**Dimitri Tiomkin** was born in the Ukraine but grew up in St. Petersburg, which he left in 1919. He was then twenty. Seven years previously he had entered the sanctum sanctorum of Russian music, The St. Petersburg Conservatory of Music. This was at a time when nothing in Russia was more highly esteemed than music, and the director of the Conservatory, Alexander Glazounov, then also at the height of his fame as a composer, was regarded as a minor God. Tiomkin's mother had taught him the piano from infancy, and the father, a doctor who would become distinguished in Berlin as an assistant to Dr. Ehrlich (the discoverer of the salvarsan cure for syphilis), agreed to the boy's becoming a musician even in spite of his own distaste for music.

Tiomkin recalls Glazounov as a kindly professor who pretended to be stern. His taste was classically traditional but romantic in spirit. He frowned on modernism and didn't care much for the impressionistic style of Claude Debussy, who was currently in vogue. "His teaching was not severe, and I think his influence on me was that of a radiant personality. He did have

64

one particular musical influence—he loved fugues and he drilled us in them all the time, and that's probably why I have sneaked so many fugues into my film scores."

Tiomkin studied composition at the Conservatory as part of the overall course, but his major concern was the piano. His teacher was Felix Blumenthal, who also taught Vladimir Horowitz and Simon Barere. Both Barere and Tiomkin earned their first money as pianists in movie theatres in St. Petersburg. Tiomkin remembers pounding away on a piano at the side of the screen and trying to come up with music that was more or less suited to what was on the screen. The knack for scoring showed itself even then. "There was one film in which a woman was being choked, and as her head rocked back and forth, mine did too, and I made the kinds of grunts and groans she might have made in a sound picture. The audience thought that was funny, so the manager told me to 'keep it in,' and I did it every night."

After the Russian revolution, with life grim and opportunities for concert pianists nil, Tiomkin proceeded to Berlin, sponsored by his father, who had left the mother some years previously and re-married, and whose pro-German sentiments and respected medical knowledge had ensconced him in the German capital. Never having had much rapport with his father and feeling upset about his mother, to whom he was strongly attached, Tiomkin decided to strike out on his own. It was an emotional decision, and an impractical one in view of his lack of funds. The parting between father and son was bitter, and the two never saw each other again.

By chance, Tiomkin came into contact with another Russian pianist in Berlin, a man named Michael Kariton, the kind of man who could survive under any circumstances. Kariton offered to share his accommodation with Tiomkin. He also encouraged the young man to continue his studies, and with his help Tiomkin was able to take lessons from Ferruccio Busoni. Busoni, an Olympian pianist-composer, was philosophical in his teaching of music, he dealt with the architecture of harmony rather than pure technique. Looking back on his musical education Tiomkin feels he was fortunate to have studied with two distinct but different men: by Glazounov he had been imbued with the romantic spirit of music and from Busoni he had learned the discipline of form.

Berlin in the Twenties was the centre of symphonic music. Tiomkin lived there for three years and during that time made his *début* as a concert pianist with the Berlin Philharmonic Orchestra. His pragmatic friend Kariton, whose nose was ever keen to the smell of opportunity, persuaded Tiomkin to form a duo-piano team with him, since duo-pianists were then in fashion. The place to go, cried Kariton, was Paris. Actually, Paris at that time could have done with fewer Russians rather than more. The city was swamped with Russian exiles, many of them aristocrats, some of them opportunists, and a few were people of great talent. Stravinsky, Diaghilev and the Ballet Russe were all contributing to the highly active cultural life of Paris. Tiomkin and Kariton made their mark, a sufficiently big enough one to get an American offer. In 1925 they arrived in New York and found themselves booked on a vaudeville circuit. This perturbed the Russians, until they learned of the salary—a thousand dollars a week for six months. The tour taught Tiomkin about showmanship, and it whetted his appetite for American music. Now he could add jazz and musical comedy to his previous knowledge of Russian romanticism and German classicism. The future Hollywood composer was in embryo.

Shortly after his arrival in New York Tiomkin had met Albertina Rasch, the Austrian born ballet dancer and choreographer. After his first American tour, she and Tiomkin were married, a marriage that lasted until her death in 1968. Said by those who knew her to have been a spirited woman, she had some bearing upon Tiomkin's career. With her persuasion he returned to solo concertising, and in 1928 he went to Paris to give the European *première* of George Gershwin's Piano Concerto in F. Back in America, his esteem increased, Tiomkin played Carnegie Hall and embarked on another tour. He specialised in contemporary composers; occasionally he would play Gershwin but his program consisted mostly of Ravel, Poulenc, Auric and Prokofiev.

As Tiomkin concertised, his wife continued her career as a ballet impresario. The 1929 stock market crash hit the Tiomkins hard, theirs were luxury trades and luxuries were suddenly out. But Albertina was an enterprising woman: the concert halls and the opera houses may have turned dark but the movie houses hadn't. Films were an inexpensive form of entertainment and the last the public would have to give up. Sound had brought a new era to Hollywood and the industry was booming. The producers were looking for musical ideas and Mrs. Tiomkin had one for them—short ballet sequences. The idea was accepted and the Tiomkins left for California. While his wife worked at M-G-M, Tiomkin gave recitals in Los Angeles. Albertina quickly brought it to the attention of her employers that her famous pianist husband also wrote music. Tiomkin had, in fact, been composing for years, playing some of his pieces at his recitals and for his wife's ballet company. Publishers had shown no interest in the compositions so Tiomkin would put the pieces away in a trunk. The trunk was raided repeatedly in years to come when he needed material for his films. One of the compositions was a ballet piece called *Mars*. Tiomkin played it for M-G-M and they paid three thousand dollars for it. Flushed with success in a new endeavour, Tiomkin turned out more ballet music for M-G-M but after working on his third picture, *The Rogue Song*, the torrent of movie musicals that gushed from the screen in the first two years of sound quickly dried up as the public tired of the silly sameness of it all.

Dimitri Tiomkin's first original film score was written in 1931, for a filming of the Tolstoy story *Resurrection*. It seemed plausible to the producers to hire a Russian composer to write music for the rumblings of the Russian soul, but Tiomkin feels he must have laid it on too thickly, because they didn't ask for more. He returned to concertising but he was now intrigued with film scoring and kept his ear open for the sound of opportunities. In 1933 he heard that Paramount were making an extravagant version of *Alice in Wonderland* and hadn't yet decided on a composer. Tiomkin arranged a meeting and gave a successful salespitch on his particular abilities to score a film of this nature. In truth, he was completely baffled by the film, the story and the dialogue. English is a hurdle Tiomkin has never cleared. He had studied English music at the St. Petersburg Conservatory and he had a liking for Purcell, which knowledge he knew he could utilise in the scoring, but the Jabberwocky nonsense verses floored him and he would reduce everyone to laughter whenever he asked about them. In garbled English he would say something like, "How give line correct saying Twinkle, twinkle, little star?"

*Alice in Wonderland* was a flop, despite all the stars it used, possibly because they wore masks and couldn't be identified except by voice. The impact of his score was enough to establish his ability but not enough to bring a deluge of offers. Tiomkin scored a handful of minor films over the next few years but his first real opportunity only came in 1937 when Frank Capra filmed *Lost Horizon*, a beautifully made picture. Tiomkin's music was suitably romantic and mystical for the adventures of Ronald Colman in Shangri-La. The success of the film brought Tiomkin not only offers to score more films but a request to return to the concert platform. Fate would allow just one more appearance. He played the Rachmaninov Second Concerto with the Los Angeles Philharmonic and the reception was strong enough to lead him to think of resuming his concert career. Not long after this, he was involved in an accident and injured his right arm. A broken bone never healed properly. The right hand was later strong enough for normal piano playing but never for the arduous pyrotechnics of the concert hall performance. The accident decided Tiomkin's future; he now became a full-time movie composer, with occasional tinges of nostalgia for the lure of the virtuoso and the captivation of an audience.

Tiomkin does not feel much nostalgia for his early years of scoring films in Hollywood. The pay was none too good and the conditions were worse. He claims that the composer in that era was almost a prisoner in a cell, along with a projection booth, a small screen and a piano of dubious quality. "Sometimes the producer, billowing clouds of cigar smoke, would

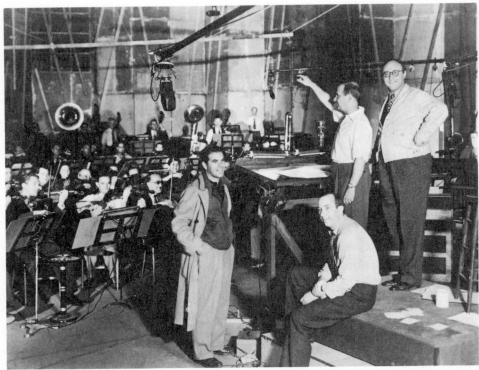

**Dimitri Tiomkin looking pleased with himself during the scoring of** Lost Horizon **in 1937. Tiomkin had reason to be pleased: this was his first major score. Standing in front of him is conductor Max Steiner and standing in front of the podium is director Frank Capra.**

drop in and the poor composer, feeling more suffocated than ever, would give a nervous run-through of all his themes. No wonder the producer didn't like what he heard." With his great success in later years, Tiomkin would refuse to play his score on a piano. If the producer wanted to hear it, he had to supply a studio session and an orchestra.

Tiomkin is the kind of composer who always says 'yes' to a producer and then goes ahead and does what he feels best. In public he speaks well of the producers with whom he has worked but in private his views are likely to be less than flattering. The conditions under which composers worked in the heyday of Hollywood were "terrifying, fantastically stupid. On *Alice In Wonderland* I worked twenty hours a day for ten days, conducting and recording." Tiomkin's most eloquent complaint is against the policy of calling in a composer after the film has been completed, and then handing him a short recording schedule. The speed with which many famous scores have been composed and conducted is incredible.

The film practice that most infuriates Tiomkin is that of denying the composer a say in the dubbing of the picture, the mixing of the voice, sound and music tracks. Often the music is lost in low dubbing, although this is not so embarrassing as over-dubbing. "We seem to live in the strange belief that noise and loudness is a kick for the audience. Some producers want the music played loud, especially the brasses. The audience gets a pain in the ear and curses the composer. I always fight against too much music. The producer says, 'Here we must have music,' and I always ask 'Why?'"

One of Tiomkin's most felicitous associations was with Frank Capra. Capra had been pleased with the music for *Lost Horizon* and wanted to use the composer again, although he felt that since his own forte was Americana, Tiomkin needed to learn more about American music. Capra gave him books containing New England hymns, Negro spirituals, work songs, cowboy ballads, etc, etc. Tiomkin delved into the material, and furthered his own research into long forgotten lyrics and melodies from the cotton fields, the lumber camps, the river boats and the merchant marines. This knowledge of musical Americana proved of immense benefit to Tiomkin, for it enabled him to provide sympathetic music for Capra pictures like *You Can't Take It with You*, and *Mr. Smith Goes to Washington*, and a large number of Westerns.

The Tiomkin Westerns include such spacious epics as *Duel in the Sun, Red River, High Noon, The Big Sky, Gunfight at the OK Corral, Rio Bravo, The Alamo*, and *The War Wagon*. Frequently chided about being Russian and yet able to write music descriptive of the American West, Tiomkin, whose geniality hides a mind like a steel trap, upturns his hands and quips, "A steppe is a steppe is a steppe." Pressed for more of an explanation, he says, "The problems of the cowboy and the cossack are very similar. They share a love of nature and a love of animals. Their courage and their philosophical attitudes are similar, and the steppes of Russia are much like the prairies of America."

*Duel in the Sun* was a gargantuan Western made by David O. Selznick; his idea was apparently to make it the *Gone with the Wind* of cowboy pictures. Everything about the film was overdone, but viewed in the right spirit it remains an entertaining opus, excessive though it undoubtedly is. Selznick was a producer unusually concerned about his music scores, even to the extent of telling a composer what instruments to use and where. For *Duel in the Sun* Selznick wanted a particularly sumptuous score, and he had the unhappy idea of approaching four of Hollywood's best composers and making this proposition: each composer would be put on salary for two weeks and would score one specific scene. At the end of the period, Selznick would review the pieces and make his choice. The selected composer would, however, have the two weeks included in the price of the job. None of the four composers he had in mind would accept the proposition. One of them was Miklos Rozsa, who had provided the greatly admired score for Selznick's *Spellbound*. Rozsa told his agent, "I want you to say to Mr. Selznick, in precisely these words, that if he had never heard a note of my music, I would find his offer insulting. Inasmuch as he has heard it, I regard his manner as criminal, and I never want to hear his name again." Selznick also made the mistake of putting the contest idea to Erich Korngold, who looked at him with mock fear in his eyes as he shook his head, "No. What if I win?"

**Dimitri Tiomkin conducting his score for** Duel in the Sun.

*Duel in the Sun* was scored by Tiomkin, once Selznick cleared from his mind any idea of a composers' contest. The music was rich, lavish and thunderous, sweeping across the plains with hundreds of horsemen, and rising in agonies of passion as Gregory Peck and Jennifer Jones loved and slaughtered each other. Selznick outlined the kind of score he had in mind and gave Tiomkin a card on which he had listed four particular emotions he wanted in the music—a kind of musical medical prescription. The four emotions were: jealousy, flirtation, sentiment, and orgiastic. As soon as Tiomkin had written his themes for these, Selznick wanted to hear them. Tiomkin had already planned on fully covering these obvious aspects of an obvious story but sly diplomat that he is, he graciously agreed to comply. The Tiomkin themes for jealousy, flirtation and sentiment all measured up to Selznick's satisfaction but he didn't like "orgiastic." He felt the Tiomkin theme was too pretty and needed to be more violent. Tiomkin accepted the criticism and went away to write something else. Selznick's reaction to the second try was no more enthusiastic, "No, it still needs more rhythm. I want it to be throbbing and unbridled. This is a rough cowboy and a tempestuous girl." Tiomkin bristled, but it has always been his policy to go three rounds with a producer before taking a stand. Again he retreated to invent another musical solution. This time he scored with plenty of orchestral palpitations. When he played this feverish rhapsody for Selznick, the producer was still unsatisfied. "Dimi, what we must have here is love-making music, and this isn't the way I make love." Tiomkin was outraged. He picked up his score and shook it at Selznick, and yelled, "Look, Selznick, I don't know how *you* make love, but this is how *I* make love." The humour of the situation got to Selznick, he began to laugh and agreed to drop the pursuit. Tiomkin's third try at "orgiastic" is the one on the soundtrack of *Duel in the Sun,* in the scene by the old swimming hole as Greg takes Jennifer against her will.

It often happens with composers that the pieces that become famous are not necessarily those they like best. Tiomkin's own preferences among his scores are *Lost Horizon, The Moon and Sixpence,* and *I Confess.* The interesting point about this choice is the common denominator: the gentility of the music. The tone is quiet, and sometimes tender. Tiomkin has often been criticised for orchestral bombast but these seem to be the scores that have become popular.

Another untypical Tiomkin score of considerable interest is *Cyrano de Bergerac,* with Jose Ferrer as the top heavy hero. The score was never recorded, except by those who siphon the sound from a TV set into a tape recorder. The score is suggestive of Rameau, and perfect for the period. Since the story is one of comedic and romantic exaggeration, the music follows suit. The overture is in the early-eighteenth-century *concerto grosso* style, and appropriate because the opening scene is a theatre stage. A blustering horn figure characterises the nose that marches on before the owner by a quarter of an hour, and this figure is used fugally for the street fight in which Cyrano battles a hundred men. Tiomkin used a ninety-piece orchestra for this score, with a thirty-piece brass choir. The brass is heard to advantage in the military sections, especially as the Cadets of Gascoyne march into the tavern. A particularly good piece of scoring is the tavern scene, in which Cyrano relates his victories, punctuated by taunts from Christian about his nose. A dissonant chord chimes with each mention of the word "nose," as part of an orchestration that points up Cyrano's rising anger.

Although Dimitri Tiomkin is respectfully regarded as one of the handful of men who pioneered film scoring, he sometimes regrets he didn't arrive later in the game, at a time when composers had more freedom, "To achieve anything in those early days was a problem. I think it was Alfred Newman who said, 'Everybody around the studio has two jobs—his own, and music.' To do anything different was almost impossible, for instance, the end of the film always had to be a rising crescendo. I sometimes would try for a quiet musical conclusion, a poetic ending, but no, it had to be loud and definite. The opening title music had to be full of joy and gladness. It was actually forbidden at some studios to use minor keys in the opening music for a picture, their reasoning being that 'minor' meant sad and 'major' denoted happiness. The conviction with which they said these things was incredible, and sometimes funny. Victor Young once told me, when he was working on some picture or another, that the producer called him in and ordered him, 'I want you to have music in the major for the heroine, and music in the minor for the hero. Then, when the two are on the screen together I want the music to be both major and minor.'"

The quality of the music in Tiomkin's more than one hundred film scores has varied noticeably, possibly more so than most of the other major Hollywood composers. Tiomkin is known as a shrewd businessman and he was for some years the highest paid man in the profession. His effort on a score often seemed geared to what he estimates the effort is worth. For example, he scored two large scaled films in 1964 for Samuel Bronston, *The Fall of the Roman Empire,* and *Circus World.* The first is obviously a score on which he worked with enormous patience and interest, and the second is just as obviously a hastily put together pastiche of self-plagiarism. Tiomkin, also unlike most film composers, has enjoyed being a celebrity and living in the grand manner. He was bitterly disappointed at not winning an Oscar for his *Roman Empire* score; it would have been his fifth. His music for *High Noon* had brought him two, for the song and one for the score, and the scores of *The High and the Mighty* and *The Old Man and the Sea* each won him the famed gold statuette. With each nomination, Tiomkin stepped up his usual publicity in order to increase his chances.

John Green describes Tiomkin as a fully effective human being, "Composing expresses his talent; the achievement of international fame fulfils his ego; successful negotiating gratifies his gamesmanship; the use of his epic dialect satisfies his comedic need; his gift for gracious hospitality gives him happiness. You have never been a guest until Tiomkin has been your host."

Tiomkin has often been accused of being commercial. If this is true, it is a sense of commercialism that has served the films as much as himself. *The High and the Mighty* and *Friendly Persuasion* would probably not have done as well at the box-office minus their famous Tiomkin themes. *The Old Man and the Sea* was a failure that might have been a bore without Tiomkin's full blooded music, the closest thing yet to a symphonic poem from the screen. In the case of *High Noon,* the film was literally saved by Tiomkin's invention of a song that was a part of the narrative and a score that generated tension. The film had been written off as a flop by the studio, based on their try-outs, but the addition of the song helped turn the film into a classic of its kind. Unfortunately, the great success of that song started a trend in film-making, the use of songs in film titles, whether they needed it or not. The trend was a godsend for song writers, film publicists and recording artists, but a plague to composers who were forced to include the song as a theme in the score. Very often the song, almost always written by someone else, denied the composer the use of the credit titles for his own statement.

Tiomkin has often endeared himself to the press and the public by making humorous quips about his profession, such as saying he only does it for the money. He denies this when interviewed seriously, "It isn't true that I do it only for money. Writing film music lets me compose in as fine a style as I am capable of. I'm a classicist by nature and if you examine my scores you will find fugues, rondos and passacaglias. I'm no Beethoven but I think if I had devoted myself to concert composition I might have been a Rachmaninov. I'm not in sympathy with the harsh, atonal music of today, it's enough to lacerate your ears. Perhaps that is why I have done well in films—it was music for the masses."

The biggest laugh ever recorded at the Academy Awards presentations was brought about by Dimitri Tiomkin. In accepting his Oscar in 1955 for *The High and the Mighty,* he stepped to the microphone and said, "I would like to thank Beethoven, Brahms, Wagner, Strauss, Rimsky-Korsakov . . ." and that was as far as he got, the auditorium rocked with laughter. Many people had made snide remarks about movie composers filching from the classics, and here was one of the most famous of them apparently admitting it. Tiomkin, whose Gregory Ratoff accent makes anything he says sound funny, claims his intention was to be serious and salute the masters who had developed the art of music. He had to leave the stage before he could finish his speech because the laughter was so great and he was too confused to continue. Many people later congratulated him on his sense of humour—few of them were composers. Several

Hollywood musicians attacked him for casting ridicule on the profession. But Tiomkin admits that he gained more fame in that moment of unconscious humour than in forty years as a musician. Was the humour truly unconscious? With Dimitri Tiomkin it is very, very difficult to know.

One of the composers who was most horrified by Tiomkin's Oscar speech was the late **Franz Waxman**. Waxman was a serious composer and

Franz Waxman.

a serious man. His bearing was rather like that of the traditional stage concept of the German professor, and his humour would not have embraced gibes about music. Shortly after the celebrated incident, Waxman singled out Tiomkin and excoriated him. Tiomkin listened patiently and then said, "I don't know why you're so annoyed, Franz, I don't hear any influences of these great composers in your music." This so confounded Waxman, all he could do was walk away.

About Franz Waxman, a very simple statement can be made: he was among the handful of the best composers who have invented truly superior music for the screen. His craftsmanship and his taste and his understanding of the medium were almost beyond criticism. The subtlety of his scoring was often beyond the comprehension of many of the people for whom he worked, and he suffered because of it. And it's possible that even Waxman himself didn't appreciate his own ability as a film composer. His primary interest was the concert hall and he tended to regard his life in films as secondary.

Franz Waxman was a musician for whom music was an all consuming way of life. The study of his Los Angeles home was a kind of musical mineshaft—books, scores and records were all over the room in huge quantities, not only on the shelves that covered every wall but on the piano, on the desk and on the chairs. Even the fireplace had been converted into a filing cabinet. The forty-seven volumes of the complete works of Bach stood out only because of the brilliance of their red bindings. It was quite clearly the den of a man with an insatiable curiosity about music, and it was a room into which his young son, John, would occasionally wander, look around, and say, "Dad, some day we're going to have to straighten out all this junk."

Waxman was very much a composer of the late romantic German school. His style was texturally rich and strongly expressive in melodic lines. He could bend the style to suit the subjects of his films, he could use dissonances when needed but his private musical nature was never truly influenced by the neo-romanticism of composers like Hindemith and Schoenberg. Waxman was aware of all that had been done by these and other composers but he was adamant in his own convictions about structure and the emotional content of music. Luckily, his convictions were backed by a profound gift for melody. Unluckily, Waxman sometimes took himself and his work too seriously and put enormous efforts into the scoring of films that deserved no such effort.

Waxman believed very definitely in positive melodic lines in film scoring. "Concert music is full of secrets. Brahms, for example, reveals himself slowly and the meanings of his music come only with study. Film music must make its point immediately because it is heard only once by an audience that is unprepared and didn't come to the theatre to hear music anyway. I believe in strong themes which are easily recognisable, and which can be repeated and variated according to the film's needs. But the variations must be expressive and not complicated."

Franz Waxman truly believed in film composition as an art form and any examination of his scores backs up the belief. The examination also shows an increase in his abilities in scoring over the years. This is not true of all film composers, many of whom reached a certain level in expressiveness and stayed there, sometimes profitably. Waxman's scoring in the last ten years of his life showed a clear progress. His death from cancer in February of 1968, age sixty-two, eliminated a man at the height of his creativity.

Waxman was one of seven children born to a Jewish family in Upper Silesia, now a part of Poland. The family was fairly well-to-do, the father being an executive in steel manufacturing. Neither the parents nor any of the other children were musical. Tragedy would strike the family terribly in years to come: one of Waxman's brothers died in infancy, another was lost in action in the First World War and another died in a concentration camp in the Second War. The family name was Wachsmann, which the composer changed when he arrived in America.

Waxman's early fascination with the piano and with wanting to make a career in music was discouraged by his father, who insisted on placing the boy in a bank as a teller after he left school. Waxman studied music on the side, which gradually convinced him of his mission in life. At the age of seventeen he enrolled in the Dresden Music Academy, where his progress was so fast he was transferred to the Berlin Conservatory. He supported himself by playing the piano in night clubs in the evenings, which led to him being offered a job with a then popular jazz orchestra, the Weintraub Syncopaters. Some of the music for the band was written by Friedrich Hollaender, who was soon to win fame writing songs for Marlene Dietrich and who would also turn up in Hollywood a few years later as a movie composer. Hollaender was impressed with young Waxman's talent and introduced him to the daughter of Bruno Walter, who in turn introduced him to her father. Walter was also impressed, and he contributed to Waxman's musical education.

In 1930 Franz Waxman's life took a distinct turn in the direction of his future fame when Friedrich Hollaender introduced him to German movie producer Erich Pommer. Hollaender's own career had moved into a higher gear with his success writing the songs for German films. He suggested to Pommer that Waxman would make an excellent film orchestrator and the suggestion was taken up. One of Waxman's first assignments was arranging and conducting Hollaender's score for *The Blue Angel*, the film that made an international star of Dietrich. Waxman made a good living as a film musician but his ambition was to compose. The opportunity came three years later when he scored *Liliom*, Fritz Lang's version of the Ferenc Molnar story. The value of the Waxman score was quickly appreciated and it would have been the beginning of a career as a German film composer had it not also coincided with the advent of the Nazis. Early in 1934 Waxman was beaten on a Berlin street, which produced an immediate resolve to remove himself and his new bride to Paris.

The rise of Nazism had a profound effect on the German film industry, as well as on the theatre and the musical arts. It decimated the talent. Multitudes of the finest German musicians, actors, writers, directors and producers were Jewish, and with their departure, the German film—then highly regarded for its artistry—suffered a blow from which it never recovered. Among the talents who would now contribute to the development of film in the studios of Paris, London and Hollywood was Erich Pommer. Pommer accepted a contract from Twentieth Century-Fox and his first assignment was to produce a film version of the Jerome Kern-Oscar Hammerstein II stage musical, *Music in the Air*. This seemed logical to the studio—Pommer was German and the story was set in Bavaria. The logic was taken a step further: since the story was about a young composer, why not bring over young Franz Waxman to adapt the score? While Pommer was at it, he also decided to bring over a young German writer to adapt the screenplay—Waxman's friend, Billy Wilder. The film opened at Radio City Music Hall in December 1934, its success heralding a bright and promising new year for Herren Pommer, Waxman and Wilder.

Among the Hollywood directors who had heard Waxman's score for *Liliom* was James Whale. He was then nearing production on *The Bride of Frankenstein* and looking for a composer who could give the film something better than the average "squeal and groan" horror score. He offered the job to Waxman, who accepted even though he had never before thought in terms of musical fear and mystery. What Waxman wrote set a new standard in scoring such films, so much so that the themes for the film became stock items for the Universal Studios music library and were later used in many Universal pictures, notably the *Flash Gordon* serial.

*The Bride of Frankenstein* score also brought Waxman an offer to head the music department at Universal. Over the next two years he supervised the scoring of some fifty Universal films and wrote the music for a dozen of them. Next came a lucrative offer from M-G-M—a seven year contract as a composer, which Waxman lost no time in accepting. Composing was more to his liking than directing a music department, especially for a studio like M-G-M. The studio got its money's worth out of Waxman with an average of eight scores a year.

The first Waxman score to win wide attention was *Rebecca* in 1940, produced by David O. Selznick. Selznick had used Waxman two years previously to score *The Young at Heart,* which had brought the composer his first Oscar nomination. The score for *Rebecca* was a perfect complement to the du Maurier story; it conveyed the innocence of the young girl played by Joan Fontaine, the sophistication of Olivier's Maxim, the icey Mrs. Danvers of Judith Anderson, the mystery of the dark mansion of Manderley and the malevolent spirit of the dead ex-wife, Rebecca. Despite the excellence of the music, Selznick was not satisfied that the score was sufficiently romantic, and called in Max Steiner to spruce up a few scenes. The Steiner style was at variance with the Waxman but Selznick so liked one of the Steiner themes that he made the composer use it again in *Since You Went Away.*

Of the nine films of 1941 scored by Waxman two were outstanding— *Dr. Jekyll and Mr. Hyde,* and *Suspicion.* The Spencer Tracy version of the Robert Louis Stevenson story didn't win critical acclaim but it had great style; the sets and the lighting were on a typically high M-G-M level. The film impressed Waxman deeply; he was struck by a certain religious significance in the story and believed the author had meant it as a moral lesson—the triumph of goodness over evil. Ingrid Bergman appeared as the floosie Hyde takes to and torments, and Waxman skilfully and chillingly used her song *You Should See Me Dance the Polka* in variations that underline her growing fear. Waxman was so taken with the Stevenson story that he worked for years after on an operatic version, but it never came to completion.

Alfred Hitchcock's *Suspicion* was another love story with mysterious overtones. Joan Fontaine played a woman puzzled by the man with whom she was in love. Thus the love theme had to have qualities that would imply a certain strangeness, and to do this Waxman used an electric violin to give the sense of unreality. Combining the instrument with a clarinet and a vibraphone, he was able to suggest a weird atmosphere. Waxman by this time had become fascinated by the possibilities of new sounds in orchestration and it is interesting to listen to what he does in the scene where Fontaine believes her lover has tried to murder her and she cries out for help. For the final scene, an automobile chase, Waxman bases his music on the sound of high speed whirling wheels.

With his M-G-M contract completed, Waxman accepted an offer from Warner Brothers in 1943, joining them at a time when their music department was considered the industry's foremost place for a musician. Among the more interesting scores he composed during his five years at the studio were two Errol Flynn war pictures, neither of them typical of war films of the period. Both films were rather sombre and restrained in their heroics. Lewis Milestone's *Edge of Darkness* allowed Waxman the use of a few Norwegian melodies but what gave his score real strength were his variations, often darkly orchestrated, on *A Mighty Fortress Is Our God.* *Objective Burma,* which caused Flynn to be unfairly lampooned as a man who won the war in Burma by himself but which actually contains one of the actor's most intelligent performances, is a masterpiece of scoring. Waxman conveys the strain of paratroopers dropped behind the lines, their stealthy trail through the jungle, the foreign, exotic terrain they move through, and the single-minded purpose of their mission. The closing sequence of the weary troops laboriously climbing a hill is scored by Waxman in a fugal passage that abruptly stops when they reach the top, leaving the soundtrack silent except for the howling of a wind over the desolate hill.

Waxman's first Academy Award Oscar came in 1950 for writing the score of Billy Wilder's *Sunset Boulevard,* which brought Gloria Swanson back to the screen, rather ironically in the role of a famous movie star. Many assumed the role might be close to her own story. It wasn't at all. Swanson is a notably realistic woman, and in no way given to dwelling in the delusions that afflicted the nutty "Norma Desmond." Waxman said at the time, "To convey the state of her madness I used a shrill, insistent orchestration of the music around her, and let an emphasized violin voice her explanation of her pathetic behaviour." The music underlines the pathos of the woman, and it does so with irony and sympathy, especially in the final scene where she descends the grand staircase of her mansion, believing she is playing Salome in a film.

\* \* \*

Waxman won another Oscar the following year—the only composer so far to have won two in succession—with his score for George Stevens's filming of Theodore Dreiser's *An American Tragedy,* re-titled *A Place in the Sun.* Stevens urged a delicate performance from the young and stunningly beautiful Elizabeth Taylor, and from Montgomery Clift as the young man from the other side of the tracks who murders, his drab, impregnated girl friend (Shelley Winters) in order to pursue rich girl Taylor. The Taylor theme is played by a saxophone and Waxman apparently auditioned a hundred players in order to find one who could give the right inflection to the melody. He felt this was essential in order to make the audience aware of the nature of the girl. At one point the scoring becomes painful: as Clift sits in jail awaiting his execution, Waxman plays a theme that gradually lifts in key changes, as if denoting the stretching nerves of the man. The general appreciation of the score by those who heard it during the recording was not fully shared by director Stevens. He felt Waxman's music was too Teutonic and he asked Victor Young, the head composer at Paramount, where the film was made, to re-score certain scenes in the picture. Young refused, and another Paramount composer was assigned the ignominious task. Two years later, Stevens asked Waxman to go over Young's score for *Shane,* to which Waxman summarily replied, "Definitely not." Waxman showed even more integrity when he resigned from the Academy of Motion Picture Arts and Sciences in 1954 because Alfred Newman's score for *The Robe* was not nominated for an award. Moral stands such as this have been precious few in the history of Hollywood.

Franz Waxman composed scores of depth and quality for two religious films, neither of which deserved his painstaking care—*The Silver Chalice,* and *The Story of Ruth.* No musically sensitive person could fail to appreciate the erudition and eloquence of these scores, or puzzled by why he should have put so much work into such tedious pictures. Waxman also worked hard on a film that was also largely a failure but which deserved a better reception from the public—*The Spirit of St. Louis.* James Stewart, far too old for the part of young Charles Lindbergh, nonetheless performed with sincerity and obvious respect for Lindbergh, whose interest in aviation he well understood. Billy Wilder, who made the film, realised it needed the hand of an uncommon composer and called upon his old friend. The film needed a score that would support the bare dramatics of a man flying the Atlantic alone—the loneliness and the apprehension he must have felt on that pioneering flight. Waxman's music carries the burden; it literally accompanies the lonely aviator and speaks his mind as he looks down at the ocean and the various lands over which he flies. The music also alludes to the danger of drowsiness, his fear of not being able to land the plane, and his prayers. Truly a landmark in film scoring.

The major motif in Waxman's score for *The Spirit of St. Louis* appears in his oratorio *Joshua,* which he conducted at the Los Angeles Musical Festival in 1961. Waxman made more of a contribution to Californian musical culture than any other composer who lived and worked in the film capital. In 1947 he inaugurated the Los Angeles Music Festival, conducting its concerts and bringing great artists to perform in it, as well as introducing compositions never before heard in performance in the city. Walter Arlen wrote after Waxman's death: "His courage in creating and sustaining the Festival despite obstacles and odds is a matter of indisputable record. Over the years he gave equal billing to Schoenberg and Shostakovich, Berg and Britten, Mahler and Milhaud, Hindemith and Harris and

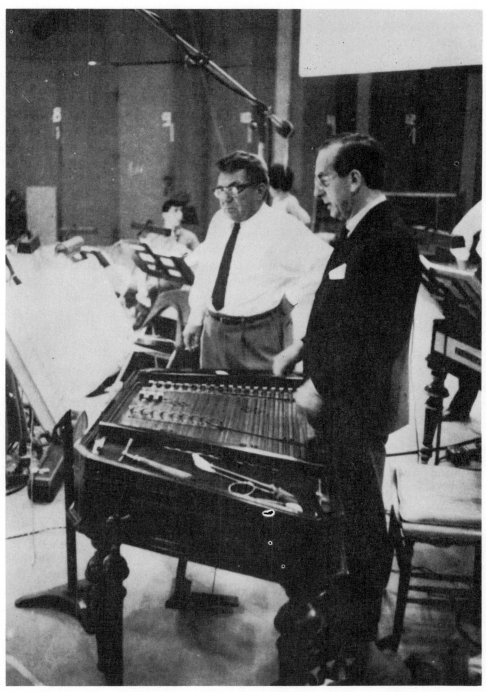

**Franz Waxman, right, with orchestrator Leonid Raab during the scoring of** Taras Bulba.

Honegger, Webern and Walton, Strauss and Stravinsky, even in the face of apathy and malice. Without him, our city would have been musically poorer."

*     *     *

During the Fifties Waxman began to spend periods in Europe visiting various musical festivals and occasionally guest conducting orchestras. These trips, and the directing of his Los Angeles Music Festival each year probably interested him more than film scoring. Yet there was no evidence in the scores of any decline, in fact, the quality seemed to rise. Two scores in particular in the last decade of his prodigious musical productivity are proof that an artist works best when busy: *Peyton Place,* and *The Nun's Story,* two vastly differing subjects. The film *Peyton Place* was that rare commodity—a film that was immensely better than the book on which it was based. Filmed in colour on location in New England, the picture gives a generous viewing of the distinctly beautiful landscapes of that American region, plus the setting of a small town. It's doubtful if any native American composer has described the scenes with more feeling than Waxman. Interviewed about the score, he said, "Music in this film had to be simple in its harmonies, it had to tell of the problems and feelings of young people—I felt the drama could take care of itself. It took between six and seven weeks to write and it was fairly easy going, because I was impressed with the picture. Fortunately I was not pressured to write or use a title song, a ridiculous restriction, and except for an initial discussion with producer Jerry Wald and director Mark Robson as to concept, I was left alone—the ideal situation. I was enchanted by the New England landscapes and in order to get an authentic feeling I studied music of the area and let it color my themes."

*The Nun's Story* is precisely what it should be—a truly spiritual picture, and made the more so by the quality of Waxman's score. Originally, director Fred Zinnemann felt that the film needed no music but Warner Brothers, who didn't care much for the project and doubted that it would make any money, insisted that the film's austere subject be made more appealing by one of the better composers. The choice fell on Waxman, who then spent half a year preparing and writing the score in Rome, where it was also recorded. "It was a most enjoyable assignment—a fascinating depiction of religious life, quiet in character and archaic in feeling. My thematic material is derived mostly from Gregorian chants, which I found while doing research in the library of the Papal Institute of Religious Music in Rome. Oddly enough, I have used the twelve-tone scale only once in my film career and it was in this picture, for the sequence in the insane asylum."

Waxman was nominated for an Academy Award for *The Nun's Story*, but lost to another religious subject—*Ben-Hur* by Miklos Rozsa. Waxman was in no way a commercially minded man and he set little store by the awards that seemingly mean so much to movie folk. On the subject of *Ben-Hur*, he said it deserved to win and, "Rozsa is the best film composer anyway."

**Bronislau Kaper.**

Waxman's last concert composition was his choral and orchestral work *The Song of Terezin,* commissioned by the May Festival of Cincinnati and performed there in May of 1965. The work is based on a collection of poems called *I Never Saw Another Butterfly,* illustrated by some of the children who passed through the Terezin concentration camp near Prague. The work consists of eight songs sung by a soloist, a children's choir and a mixed chorus with orchestral backing. Most of the songs express the wonderment of children concerning the beauty of nature and of animals but the last is titled *Fear,* in which the chorus sings of the will to live. The final line sings, "We must not die." Tragically, the composer himself would die a few short years after this *première,* and it would be a bitter loss to the world of music.

Clever composers can, if they so wish, use their music to shield themselves. Depending upon the extent of their talent, they can produce a style that may not be a true reflection of the inner man. In the case of **Bronislau Kaper**, the warmth of his music is so genuine that it is, indeed, a true statement of the man. Kaper is, as any of his colleagues will testify, a man of sentiment and wit, and his best work in films has been for pictures that he openly admits he loves—*Lili, The Swan, Green Dolphin Street, The Glass Slipper,* and *The Brothers Karamazov.*

Kaper is a composer who loves music. This may seem an odd statement to those who assume all composers to be music lovers. This is a matter of degree—composers obviously like music, most of them enjoy it and take pleasure from their ability to create it but rare are those who love it with a passion. To visit Kaper in his home is to share his delight in listening to anything from a Polish song to Berg's *Wozzeck,* or better still, to hear him play the piano. What the listener is most likely to hear is a stream of beautiful melodies from a Middle European of the Old School who readily admits to an occasional tear while watching heart-rending scenes in some of his films.

Kaper's ability to convey human feeling in musical terms has helped many an actor. Edward G. Robinson came up to him after a screening of *The Stranger* and said, "Bronny," "I owe you something. My acting became so much better after they added the music." George Peppard admits this: "There's a long scene in *Home from the Hill* where the camera stays on me as I walk to a cemetery. People are always saying what a fine piece of acting it was. Actually, I didn't do anything but walk and stare ahead. All the acting was done by Kaper."

John Green worked closely with Kaper during the years when Green was in charge of M-G-M's music department, and he conducted many of Kaper's scores. Kaper, unlike most of the film composers, is not a conductor. Says Green, " I think he's an unequalled master of music that

Bronislau Kaper rehearsing his music for Lili with star Leslie Caron.

occurs simultaneously with dialogue. He has an uncanny gift for it—he has a built-in computer that somehow records the actual pitch and rhythm and variations of projection and impact of spoken voices. I would study his scores prior to conducting them, and there might be a scene with peppery dialogue—fast, loud, high pitched, rhythmically complicated dialogue. I would see the score he had written for the scene and it would be black with notes—there would be high multi-noted woodwind passages, and I would wonder how we could run all this under dialogue. Then Bronny and I would play the score on the piano—four hands—and it worked. I was amazed at how he did it, the timing cue sheets couldn't possibly give him every little syllable. But he had it all in his head—the music would fit in and out, and flow among this dialogue miraculously. I've never known another composer who could do that."

Kaper was the child of a non-musical family in Warsaw. To please his father, a businessman, Kaper completed a course in law, although he had no intention of following it as a profession. His interest in music began at the age of seven when a piano was brought into the family home. It was discovered that the boy could play it, even though he had received no instruction. Within a year, he was showing off to his relatives by stopping in the middle of a piece, getting up and running around the piano, and then picking up immediately on the right note. His early improvising revealed a characteristic that has stuck with him through the years—that of instinctively playing in the key of G Major.

Along with his study of law, Kaper had also taken a course in piano and composition, and with both courses completed he headed for Berlin. There, in the mid-Twenties, he found a richly productive musical atmosphere. New and creative strides were being made in the theatrical and cinematic arts in Berlin; Kurt Weill was only one of many young artists making an impression in a city wide open to experimental artistry. Kaper quickly got a job writing songs for cabaret, and used the money to further his musical education. His introduction to the film world came through a young German producer with a complicated name, a name so difficult to non-German ears that when he went to Hollywood a few years later he decided to call himself Sam Spiegel. The film was called *Honeymoon for Three*, and from then on, Kaper was a film music man. He spent six years working on German films in Berlin, and then, with the rise of the Nazis in 1933, he and his wife moved to Paris. The move had been a hasty one, and the Kapers arrived with little more than their clothes. "But luck was on our side. Luck, what a wonderful thing. One evening we decided to live it up, despite our lack of funds, and we went to an expensive café on the Champs-Elysées. As we sat, a man came up and greeted us. He was a film cutter I had worked with in Berlin. 'We've been looking for you—we're doing a French version of one of our films and we need your music.' So right away I got a job."

Kaper spent two years writing music for French films and had several hit songs. One of them was *Ninon*, which sounds similar to Johnny Mercer's *Dream*, written years later, and in the summer of 1935 the Jan Kiepura recording of it was played on every European radio station. Louis B. Mayer happened to vacation in Europe that summer and seemingly heard the song everywhere he went. He found out who had written it and invited the composer to meet him. "I went to his suite at the Ritz Hotel in Paris and played a lot of music for him. He didn't say much but he nodded his head a lot. Then I noticed him hitting his left hand with the edge of his right, as if cutting something in two. I asked him what he was doing. 'This means half your salary is against your royalties.' With this understanding, I was hired."

Kaper arrived in Hollywood in 1936 and immediately began writing songs for M-G-M. His contracts with that studio were renewed time and again, until they stretched over a thirty year period. Within months of his arrival at M-G-M Kaper had written a smash hit—the title song of *San Francisco,* which remains an American anthem. A year later, something equally American: *All God's Chillun Got Rhythm,* with Harpo Marx acting as a pied piper to an enthusiastic black chorus in *A Day at the Races.* More typically Kaper was the beautiful ballad *While My Lady Sleeps,* sung by Nelson Eddy in *The Chocolate Soldier.*

Kaper was not allowed to score a film at M-G-M until four years after his arrival. "In Europe, we had done everything—songs, score, arrangements, directing—but in Hollywood you weren't allowed more than one job. With my first M-G-M picture I also supplied the connective passages. They were horrified. They had so much money to spend, they couldn't think of a man doing more than one job." Later, when he began scoring, he ran into the problem in reverse—they wanted to bring in song writers to add to his score.

Kaper scored a half dozen films a year at M-G-M, most of them run-of-the-mill products, the glossy film entertainments for which the studio became famous and wealthy. Occasionally he would get a picture that provoked an emotional response in him, such as *Gaslight* in 1944, "because Ingrid Bergman has such a marvellous face—I looked at it and couldn't help but write music for it—every time she spoke, I was moved." It has not escaped the attention of the Hollywood community that beautiful women seem to affect Kaper in this manner.

*Green Dolphin Street* was another film Kaper enjoyed scoring; its romantic nature again brought forth beautiful themes. The main theme, picked up some time later by Miles Davis, has become a staple of the jazz world, although its original inspiration was far removed from jazz. Another peculiarity of the score: "There was an earthquake in the picture, and I decided to score the scene with music leading up to the eruption, stopping, and then starting the music after the subsiding. Amazingly, people are always telling me how much they liked my music for the earthquake. Also, with the earthquake in *San Francisco*, they say the same thing, although there wasn't a note of music in the sequence. I've had some of my biggest successes with the lack of music in earthquakes."

The Kaper scores range from intimate drawing room comedies to epics. But what he obviously likes best are those vehicles that coincide with his own tastes, such as *Lili*, and *The Swan*. The score of *Lili* brought the composer an Academy Award Oscar, although he feels sure he wouldn't have got it had the score not contained the song *Hi Lili, Hi Lo*. "I like pictures like *Lili*, and another one with Leslie Caron, *The Glass Slipper*, because they contain songs and dances that are part of the story line and they have to shoot to your music. This way, you are not carrying the burden of somebody else's mistakes. Usually, you come to a picture that is finished, and it's like inheriting cancer. The worst thing that can happen to a film composer is being asked to score a film that someone else has already scored. Sol Siegel asked me to score a miserable picture about the Spanish Civil War called *The Angel Wore Red*, with Ava Gardner and Dirk Bogarde. It had an Italian score, and with a few notable exceptions, the worst scoring is done in Italy—stupid, arrogant, monotonous, tasteless. It's a terrible experience to follow a bad example but in this case they wouldn't have released the film otherwise."

*The Swan* was right down Kaper's alley. "I love this period. Right at the start of the film you see the legend, '1910—somewhere in middle Europe.' I get terribly attached to some films and this was one. There were tears in my eyes at the end, and I knew I was going to write good music. The story was delicate and stylish and elegant, with Grace Kelly as the princess, beautiful but cool, Alec Guinness as the prince to whom she is betrothed, and Louis Jourdan as the tutor who falls in love with her. I had to treat the first part as a subtle pantomime, and not give away much of the romantic feeling. Then, Jourdan tells her he loves her, and the music takes over, so to speak. The end scene is one of the most delightful I've ever scored: Guinness is talking to Kelly and telling her why she is like a swan, as Jourdan, still in love with her and knowing she feels something for him, leaves the palace forever. There was a beautiful sadness to it. The Molnar story had a 'once upon a time' quality—almost a swan song for a bygone era."

Two expensive disappointments were scored by Bronislau Kaper: *Mutiny on the Bounty*, and *Lord Jim*. In both cases, the music represents a high level of effort and interest but not enough to save the films. Kaper philosophises that both films allowed for travel—to Tahiti and Cambodia— and for some fascinating musical research. Other films on which he has laboured hard but largely in vain are *The Red Badge of Courage* (1951) and *A Flea in Her Ear* (1969). *The Red Badge of Courage* is an anomaly in the listing of Hollywood films. Produced by Gottfried Reinhardt and directed by John Huston, the film was a beautiful but unwanted child of M-G-M. Lillian Ross wrote an entertaining and perceptive book, *Picture,* (Rinehart & Co. Inc. 1952) about the internecine affairs in the making of what was obviously, except to the M-G-M Top Brass, an exceptional piece of cinematic art. Butchered by the studio in cutting it from almost two hours to a mere sixty-five minutes, the film still is the finest screen version of a Civil War story. Kaper was deeply touched by Stephen Crane's account of a young boy's reaction to warfare. "The music had to tell his story, how he felt about the death of his friends, why he ran from battle and how he overcame his cowardice. These soldiers were simplistic men, they were of the earth, and they were put in the ironic, ridiculous position of having to kill their own countrymen. When the boy's regiment win their first battle and they are happy about it, I felt I had to underscore the tragedy of it all. And when the boy later runs away, I had to communicate his fears—with spasmodic music, like a heartbeat. When the boy writes a letter home, I scored it with a banjo to get a funny sound to a sad situation—to point up the absurdity of men at war."

*A Flea in Her Ear* was a flop at the box-office, and a great pity because Kaper's score is utter delight. His music for this Feydeau farce is a non-stop tuneful romp, and it gives substance to what is essentially *frou-frou.* The score tinkles with Gallic wit, flirtations and breeziness: bistro music, bedroom music, promenade music, a few graceful waltzes and a sprightly march for the cavalry rescue of a young lady. "The point with this film was its farcical quality. Almost vaudeville. There was no depth to the story or the characters and there wasn't meant to be. It was a surface exercise and it seemed to me that the Offenbachian route was the way to go."

A film for which Kaper had an affinity was Richard Brooks's version of *The Brothers Karamazov.* "The story was one of the closest things to me. I wanted to score the version that was made when I was working in Berlin but other commitments kept me from it. This time I was determined it wouldn't get away from me. As a child I read the book and for weeks afterwards I couldn't talk to anyone. Doing *Karamazov* I had to tell the audience how I felt about the story, and yet I had to do it in a language they would understand. The gypsy music of that Russian period was a useful coloration but I wrote in a rather Prokofievien style because of the violence in the story. I feel the music must always be an emotional reaction. Many people commented on the rather startling dramatic music I used with the credit titles. Well, I didn't want them to think this was just another family picture."

Kaper has also proved adept at scoring comedies, of which *Auntie Mame* is a prime example. "Comedy is difficult because of the emphasis on dialogue. You cannot waste time in a comedy, and that's a bit of a strain on the composer. You don't have long stretches of music to express yourself—with dramatic subjects you have time to build but with a comedy every note must count. With *Mame* the first temptation is to comment musically on her gay, vivacious manner, but you see that on the screen, you don't have to say it again. What I did was to try and show that beneath this frivolity was a woman of deep sentiment, with problems, and that she was genuinely concerned about her nephew. To have scored her comically would have cheapened the film. When something is very effective on the screen, you add little to the music."

The bromide about film music not being heard seems to irritate Kaper less than most of his colleagues. "Let's put it this way: if you don't hear the music on any level of consciousness, then it has served no purpose. At certain moments in films, nobody knows the difference between what is visual and what is acoustical. It all comes together. It's like seeing and hearing lightning—it's one effect."

There are no rules about film scoring. Kaper has often pointed out to producers that the film they want him to score actually needs so little music they had best hire an arranger to provide a few transitions. Other films call for almost constant scoring, "But music can do bad things, it can punctuate wrong lines, and it can turn a warm scene into a cold one and vice versa. With dialogue, the most effective technique is the use of silence, to lull the audience with neutral music into a sense of half security and then stop when something really important is said—nothing is as loud in films as silence."

The real test of a composer is being given a long sequence that has no dialogue or sound, and being required to tell the story with music. Kaper did this brilliantly in the opening sequence of *Butterfield 8*. The first few minutes of the film begin with Elizabeth Taylor alone in bed, then getting up, brushing her teeth and choosing what clothes to wear. The scene is simple but the implications are not, "I had to tell the audience that this is an unhappy, neurotic girl. To suggest her character and her intentions. This wasn't easy—Elizabeth Taylor in bed looks so gorgeous, why should she be unhappy? This is where music comes in, this is the value of the composer in film-making: to add something that isn't otherwise apparent. And if you can't add something, don't bother to write it. Music without a statement is no music."

Bronislau Kaper is a man whose interest still lies in living a full life. His vitality has yet to ebb and his charm continues to captivate those who are fortunate enough to come into contact with him. He contrives to look some twenty years younger than his age and maintains his interest in an athletic life. Kaper still fences with foils and sabres, and, at this writing, was taking lessons in Japanese wrestling.

After forty years of writing music for films, Kaper does not feel that everything has been said and done, "No, if you're excited by something, you'll come up with new ideas. How many women have you known in your life? Then along comes another and you love her. You've seen eyes before, legs before, but wait—there's something different about this one, something in the eyes, in the voice, a smile, an expression, something in the way she walks. It's the same with films—all you need are a few little things and off you go again. If I were bothered by the *clichés* of the past, I couldn't live. Not just music. Life is also full of *clichés*. Don't fall for them."

\* \* \*

It's very likely that when the roster of twentieth-century composers is finally completed, the name of **Miklos Rozsa** will be listed near the top. Rozsa has managed what few composers have been able to accomplish—a distinguished and highly profitable career writing film scores while also writing music for the concert hall and having it frequently performed and recorded. His *Violin Concerto,* and his *Theme, Variations and Finale,* are among the most popular of contemporary compositions. Together with his doctorate in music, his penchant for musicology, an enviable gift for melody and a distinctly individualistic 'sound,' Rozsa has long established a niche for himself as a cultured, affluent man of the world. His mansion atop one of the Hollywood hills bespeaks a degree of success that is rare in the world of music—marble statues of ancient Rome, bronze artifacts, oriental rugs, Rembrandt etchings, and paintings from various periods of Dutch, Flemish and Hungarian artists. It is not the home of the average musician.

Rozsa did not set out with the idea of becoming a film composer. It was the persuasion of a friend that brought him into the business, at a time when, as he candidly says, "I knew nothing about film music, nor did I care." Rozsa was born in Budapest in April of 1907 to a mother who loved the piano but to an industrialist father who not only cared little for music but doubted that a decent living could be made from it. He tried to advise his son against making it his career but the boy's talent for music was obviously too large and his enthusiasm too passionate to be contained. Rozsa could read music before he could read words, and he began violin lessons at the age of five. Two years later he played a movement from a Mozart violin concerto. He was elected president of the Franz Liszt Society at his school and won the society's composition contest at the age of

Miklos Rozsa.

eighteen with a trio for flute, oboe and cello. Rozsa left Budapest to attend the University of Leipzig but within the first year he decided to devote himself entirely to music, and enrolled in that city's famed Conservatory of Music.

Rozsa's father wrote to his son's teacher, Hermann Grabner, and asked for an opinion of the boy's musical worth. Grabner replied that the boy seemed to be showing rather amazing promise as a composer, an opinion that was strengthened shortly afterwards when the esteemed music publishing firm of Breitkopf and Haertel put student Rozsa under contract. He was then twenty-one, and they are still his publishers. After his graduation in 1929, Rosza stayed in Leipzig and acted as an assistant to Grabner, in addition to composing a steady stream of music. Two years later, after several of his chamber works had been performed in Paris, Rozsa decided to make the French capital his home. The success of his *Theme, Variations and Finale, Opus 13* in 1934 established him as one of the outstanding young composers of the day. His ballet *Hungaria,* performed by Anton Dolin and Alicia Markova, took him to London in 1936, and it was the reaction of French film director, Jacques Feyder to this ballet that lead Rozsa into films. Rozsa had known Feyder in Paris and one evening in London he received a call from the director inviting him to join him for dinner at his hotel. He then took Feyder to the theatre to see the ballet, "Jacques seemed very impressed and insisted we go out afterwards and celebrate my success. Champagne was ordered at his behest—I knew he enjoyed drinking it, but I had never touched the stuff. As the champagne went down, my value as a composer went up. By the end of the second bottle I was better, according to him, than Beethoven had ever been. He told me I was the greatest composer alive, and why wasn't I writing for films? I said I'd never thought about it, mostly because I didn't write fox-trots. He replied, 'You're out of your mind. I don't want foxtrots, I want serious music.' Said I: 'In films?' Feyder then let it be known he had made up his mind I was to do the music for his new picture and that we were to meet for lunch the following day at the Green Park Hotel."

Rozsa's blithe ignorance of the film world continued to manifest itself at the luncheon. "I met Jacques and his actress wife, Françoise Rosay, at one o'clock and he said he was expecting another couple. We had a few cocktails and the time slipped by. My main interest was eating—I was hungry, and more interested in the arrival of food than his guests. Around three o'clock they came in, an attractive German couple who were intro-duced as Mr. and Mrs. Sieber. She sat on my right, and Feyder was on my left. I noticed people looking at us but I couldn't understand why. Suddenly she turned to me and asked, 'Is my song ready?' I must have looked blank, and I felt Feyder nudging me. I came out with something like, 'No, but I'm working on it.' She then said, 'Mr. Feyder tells me you're going to write the music for our picture.' I smiled idiotically. A little later I leaned over toward Feyder and whispered, 'Who is she?' and he snarled back under his breath, 'Marlene Dietrich, you damn fool.'"

The film in question was *Knight without Armour*, starring Dietrich and Robert Donat, and produced by Alexander Korda. Feyder told Korda he wanted Rozsa to do the score, to which Korda replied, "Who's Rozsa?" Feyder looked astonished, "He's the greatest friend of your brother Vin-cent. They practically live together." Korda was finally talked into using Rozsa, although it might not have been possible had the great producer realised that until the previous day, the composer had neither heard of him or his brother. Capricious though the entry may have been, it launched a firm association between Rozsa and Korda, and one of the most produc-tive careers in film composition. Rozsa confesses that at the outset he knew so little about film scoring he bought a book to find out how to do it. "I also went to see many films and found the scores mostly appalling, especially in American films. Some of the better French pictures had scores by Honneger, Ibert and Milhaud, and they served to inspire. But I had a lot to learn about film scoring and I learned the hard way, by making mistakes."

Rozsa scored half a dozen pictures for Korda and in 1939 was assigned to write the music for an extravagant fantasy, *The Thief of Bagdad*. The war broke out after the picture was in production just a few weeks and Korda was unable to get enough money together to finish the picture. United Artists offered to supply the finishing funds but only if the film was completed in Hollywood. Arrangements were agreed upon, and Rozsa proceeded to Hollywood in the spring of 1940, where he turned out a richly melodic score, well suited to the romantic and exotic needs of the Arabian Nights story. The score would have landed Rozsa a job in any studio but Korda retained his services for three more pictures he had planned to make in England but which he would now do in Hollywood, even though they were largely British topics. The first was *Lady Hamilton*, with Laurence Olivier as Lord Nelson, and Olivier's new wife, Vivien Leigh, as Nelson's inamorata. Next, *Lydia* with Korda's famous wife, Merle Oberon, in the title role, and *The Jungle Book*, starring Korda's Indian discovery, Sabu.

*The Jungle Book* is a film which leans heavily on its music score. Fortunately, the score was a brilliant one, and packed with imaginative descriptions of jungle animals. Rozsa later adapted it into a concert suite with narration, and twice recorded it—first with Sabu and some years later with Leo Genn. Neither the accompanying text or the quality of the narration in the two recordings serves the music well. With a strong but simple text, Rozsa's concert version of *The Jungle Book* might well take its place alongside Prokofiev's *Peter and the Wolf* in the far from overcrowded field of musical stories for children. The film itself was a condensed version of Kipling's two Jungle Books, focusing on Mowgli, the boy who wanders off into the jungle and is reared by a family of wolves. Rozsa's score is fully descriptive of the images and the mysterious depths of the jungle. The scoring of the various animals is particularly deft and tuneful: the elephants are characterised by roaring trombones and tubas, wolves by glissando horns, Baloo the Bear by a chuckling contra-bassoon, Bagheera the Black Panther by slithering strings, the hyenas by gurgling alto saxophones, the monkeys by high, perky piccolos, and Shere Khan the Tiger by muted, low brass. The score is a delightful lesson for young people in instrumentation.

Miklos Rozsa's first contract with a Hollywood studio was at Paramount in 1943. Two of the scores he wrote for that studio are of particular interest: *Double Indemnity*, and *The Lost Weekend*. The first is lean and slightly dissonant, with few themes. Rozsa relates that the score was condemned by Paramount's musical director. "I was asked to appear in his office, where he there explained that the music was very bad. He told me it belonged in Carnegie Hall. I thanked him but he said he hadn't meant it as a compliment. He then asked why I hadn't written something attractive, to which I replied that Billy Wilder's film was about ugly people doing vicious things to each other. Anyway, he and I had to go to the *première* together. The film went over quite well but I still had the feeling I was in the doghouse. My music director and I started to walk away when Buddy de Sylva, the head of the music department, yelled after us to come back. I felt like Marie Antoinette on her way to the guillotine and I'm sure the music director felt even worse. De Sylva then let it be known that he thought it was a wonderful score. He turned to the music director and said, 'And you're to be congratulated for hiring him.' With this, our music director beamed and said, 'Buddy, I always get you the right man, don't I?'

*The Lost Weekend,* which won Ray Milland an Oscar for his portrayal of a dipsomaniac, was another film that needed something more than a conventional score. The film fascinated Rozsa because he himself drinks but little and it was an exercise in imagination to musically underline dementia praecox and the craving for alcohol. Of particular help in this score, and the one for *Spellbound,* was an electronic instrument called the theremin, manipulated by a hand held over it and moved back and forth and up and down to produce sound oscillations. Some wag described the theremin as the wail of a thousand women, but Rozsa's choice of the instrument seemed perfect as the voice of a disturbed psyche. In *The Lost Weekend* it helped Milland to get across his unspoken yen for a drink, without the actor having to mug the feeling. One scene is made horrific by the music: Milland in his dementia sees a mouse running across the floor, and a whining little violin characterises the animal. Then a bat materialises and swoops to kill the mouse viciously with nerve wracking musical jolts. How terrified and unnerved Milland is by this imagined incident is clearly pointed up by the scoring.

*Spellbound* won Rozsa his first Academy Award Oscar. Quickly heralded as a landmark in film music, the score contains a theme that remains one of the most popular ever to emerge from a soundtrack. Rozsa adapted it into the *Spellbound Concerto,* many times recorded. The theremin played its most vital role in this story of an amnesia victim and his fear that he might be a murderer. Its eerie sound blended perfectly with Rozsa's haunting music and contributed mightily to the aural atmosphere of implied madness and mystery. Rozsa used the theremin again in *The Red House,* and then abandoned it, fearing it might otherwise become a trademark. "I didn't want it to be the equivalent of Dorothy Lamour's sarong."

Rozsa began another distinct stylistic phase in 1946 when he scored

*The Killers.* Mark Hellinger's production of this and two other pictures—
*Brute Force,* and *The Naked City,* his last work before his untimely death—
brought a new kind of crime film to the screen: realistically brutal, unsentimental and harsh. Rozsa's thickly textured scores for these pictures, full of sharp accents and terse rhythms and tension chords is unlike either what he had written for the screen previously or what he would write later. The films came during the three years Rozsa spent at Universal and included similar subjects in *Criss Cross* and *Kiss the Blood Off My Hands.* One of the films from this period brought Rozsa his second Oscar: *A Double Life,* with Ronald Colman's brilliant performance as a demented Shakespearean actor. Not content with what he had learned previously about psychosis in scoring *Spellbound,* Rozsa asked psychiatrists for information about the sounds the mentally sick are predisposed toward, and then used the knowledge in scoring Colman's scenes of paranoia. The scoring for these scenes contrasted sharply with the concerto grosso style for the theatre sequences of Colman playing *Othello.*

In 1949 Miklos Rozsa accepted a long term contract from M-G-M, whose music department had been put in fine functioning order by John Green. The orchestra was first rate and the recently introduced LP recording process, with M-G-M having its own label, promised a new era in Rozsa's career. It turned out to be exactly that; his assignments were consistently interesting and it soon led to his becoming a specialist in the scoring of historical subjects.

Rozsa's composing style has often been described as polyphonic—full, chromatic and intricately textured. It's the music of an educated composer, and the tastes are definitely those of early-twentieth-century Europe. His music is quite clearly his own, there is a Rozsa "sound" and it is easily recognisable both in his film scoring and his concert works. Being Hungarian also works in his favour, for there is an inbuilt exotic quality to native Hungarian music. "We stand alone in a Slavic sea. Hungarian peasant music is unique, it has no connection with other musical cultures just as the Hungarian language is unconnected with other languages. Our gypsy music is especially valuable, as Brahms discovered long ago and as Bartok and Kodaly made apparent with their marvellous treatments. There is a certain oriental color in the gypsy scale, and it is a very useful palette to have in one's heritage."

One of Rozsa's most famous concert works is the *Violin Concerto* commissioned, performed and recorded (RCA Victor LSC 2767) by Jascha Heifetz, and in 1970 it was put to use as film music through the interest of Billy Wilder. "Wilder approached me at a party and said he loved my violin concerto, and that he had worn out his copy of the record and wondered if I had another one. I was as intrigued as much as flattered

**Miklos Rozsa with director Billy Wilder during the scoring of** The Private Life of Sherlock Holmes.

but all he would say was, 'I've got an idea.' Some months later he called me into his office and revealed the idea: he had written a screenplay called *The Private Life of Sherlock Holmes* and he had written it around my concerto, inspired by the fact that Holmes liked playing the fiddle. The theme of the first movement is somewhat nervous and this apparently suggested to Wilder Holme's addiction to cocaine. (I've scored music for dipsomaniacs, amnesiacs and paranoids—now I have a drug addict to add to my list of dubious characters). The theme of the second movement of the concerto brought a lady spy to Wilder's mind, and the turbulent third movement conjured up, for him, the Loch Ness monster. He said, 'This is perfect monster music.' I wasn't flattered but he was right, it did work out quite well. I agreed to score the film for him, using the concerto. He seemed to think this would be easy because I wouldn't have to think up any new themes. Actually, it was very difficult. The concerto was not written with any images in mind and the timings had to be altered to fit the film sequences. It would have been much easier to invent something fresh."

Rozsa's contribution to the art of film scoring has been enormous, and the decline in the number of his assignments during the Sixties was a sad comment on the decline in the general artistic integrity of film-making during the decade. He laments this decline but philosophises that the changing times find him somewhat reactionary, and out of step with newer concepts in cinema. It remains for others to point out that Rozsa has scored the widest possible variety of subjects with never failing effectiveness, and with a subtlety and sensitivity that perhaps misses the ears of many of the newer film producers.

Film music, ideally, is an extension of what Wagner began, his idea of the all encompassing work of art comprising acting, drama and music. Within his particular framework—opera—music was the most important ingredient. In film, it isn't. But to understand just how powerful the contribution of music is to film, one has only to think of Rozsa's historical film subjects and imagine what their impact might have been minus the score. However, the following pages by the composer are here presented not so much to prove any point but rather to illustrate the interesting ways in which the musical decisions were made.

### Miklos Rozsa on Musical Archaeology in the Movies, or, The Pilgrim Fathers Meet the Knights of the Round Table along the Appian Way

Films with historical backgrounds always present interesting problems to the composer. There had been innumerable other historical pictures before *Quo Vadis,* and they were all alike in their negligent attitude toward the stylistic accuracy of their music. It is interesting to note what painstaking research is usually made to ascertain the year of publication of, let us say, 'Yes, We Have No Bananas,' if it is to be used in a film about the Twenties, but no one seems to care much if the Christians in the First century sing 'Onward Christian Soldiers' by Sir Arthur Sullivan, composed a mere eighteen hundred years later. It is hard to believe, but I was asked to use 'Adeste Fideles' for the Nativity scene in *Ben-Hur.* My argument that it is a medieval Latin hymn fell on deaf ears. Only when I threatened to leave the picture was I allowed to disregard this notion.

No one expects to hear sixteenth-century Minnesänger music in *Meistersinger,* ancient greek music in *Electra,* or ancient Hebrew music in *Salome.* The orientalism in *Aïda, Samson and Delilah,* or *Queen of Sheba* is only used as colour, and they are full-blooded, romantic operas mirroring the style of the period of their creation with no attempt whatsoever to represent the true style of the period of their action. But motion picture art is different. It is realistic and factual. It not only tries to capture the spirit of bygone eras but also tries to make believe that it projects before the eyes of the spectator the real thing. There are no painted backdrops, fake props, cardboard shields and wooden swords as in an opera, but everything is realistic to the fullest limit and if the public doesn't believe that the Christians were actually eaten by the lions, the film has failed in its object.

When *Quo Vadis* was assigned to me I decided to be stylistically, absolutely correct. First, thorough research had to be done. Though my old studies of the music of antiquity came in handy, I was greatly aided by George Schneider, the M-G-M librarian, who produced every reference to the period that could be found in libraries throughout the world.

Our first job was to prepare the blueprints for the antique instruments which had to be made. We reconstructed these from Roman statues (in the Vatican and Naples museums), antique vases and bas-reliefs on columns and tombstones, giving exact measurements for all details. The actual instruments were then produced by Italian instrument makers, so a great array of lyras and cytharas (the chief instruments of the Romans), double pipes (aulos), curved horns (buccina), straight trumpets (salpynx or tuba), tambourines, drums, sistrums, clappers and other percussion instruments were made with amazing likeness to the real ones.

Then the music which was to be performed on scene had to be prepared. To select music for an historical picture of the middle ages, for instance, would have been an easy task, as there is a wealth of material available. But this is not the case with Roman music from the year 64 A.D. In spite of the fact that a great amount of Roman literature, painting, architecture and sculpture has survived, there is no actual record of any music of the classical times of Roman history. There is a lot of reference to music in literary works of the time, so we know what an important part music played in the life of the Romans. Seneca complains that orchestras and choruses grew to gigantic proportions and often there were more singers and players in the theatre than spectators. There were numerous schools of music, and daughters of the rich bourgeoisie had to learn to play the lyre just as they had to play the piano centuries later. The slaves of the aristocrats entertained constantly and Seneca also complains that "at table, no one can talk for the music." All this proves that music was widely practised and belonged to everyday life.

In *Quo Vadis* there were three distinguishable styles in which music had to be created. Firstly, the music of the Romans, such as the songs of Nero and the slave girl Eunice, the sacrificial hymn of the Vestals, and the marches and fanfares. Secondly, the hymns of the Christians, and thirdly, the music performed by the slaves, which could be called the Roman Empire music. As nothing remains of Roman music, this had to be created by deduction. We know that the culture of the Romans was entirely borrowed from the Greeks. Greek civilisation and religion dominated Roman life and Nero himself preferred to speak Greek rather than Latin, and in sculpture, painting, poetry and pottery they copied Greek models. As Greek musicians and instruments were imported and Greek musical theory adopted, the music of the Romans cannot be separated from its Greek models and ideas. It was, therefore, not incorrect to reconstruct this music from Greek examples. About the music of the Greeks we know considerably more. We know their thorough and involved musical systems, we can read their musical notations and we also have about a dozen relics of actual music, preserved mostly on tombstones and old papyri. These were of the greatest value in this attempt at reconstruction.

As the music for *Quo Vadis* was intended for dramatic use and as entertainment for the lay public, one had to avoid the pitfall of producing only musicological oddities instead of music with a universal, emotional appeal. For the modern ear, instrumental music in unison has very little emotional appeal; therefore I had to find a way for an archaic sounding harmonisation which would give warmth, colour and emotional value to these melodies. The hymns of the early Christians also had to be reconstructed by deduction. Saint Ambrose's collection of liturgical music for the Catholic Church appeared about four hundred years after our period and I wanted to go back to the very source from which the Ambrosian plain chant and later the Gregorian hymnology blossomed. As the early Christians were partly Jews and partly Greeks, their liturgical music naturally originates from these sources. These two influences have been prevalent in the Gregorian hymns which are the basis of the Roman Catholic Church music.

The third category of the music was that of the slaves, mostly Babylonians, Syrians, Egyptians, Persians and other conquered nations of oriental origin. There were fragments of the oldest melodies found in Sicily with Arabian influence, and others found in Cairo, which I utilised. The orchestration of the music performed on scene was another problem. None of the old instruments were available and, therefore, an archaic sound had to be created with our modern instruments. I used a small Scottish harp, the Clarsach, and this delicate instrument gave a remarkably true likeness to the sound of the lyre and antique harp. For military music: cornets mixed with trumpets and trombones gave the roughness of the early brass instruments. Bass flute and English horn replaced the sound of the aulos. Our modern percussion instruments come close to the antique ones and therefore it was safe to use tambourines, jingles, drums of different shapes and sizes, and cymbals. Bowed stringed instruments, however, could not be used. These came into usage nearly a thousand years later. For music that was supposed to be performed by a large group of players, I took the liberty of using the string group of the orchestra playing pizzicato to reinforce the main body of the orchestra. Harps and guitars were also added to achieve the percussive quality. Melodic lines, however, were only given to the woodwinds and brass instruments to perform. A romantic, chromatic harmonisation would have been out of place and a simple modal harmonisation seemed to me the closest to the character of this music.

I didn't realise it at the time but *Quo Vadis* turned out to be the first of a dozen historical films, all of them set in different periods and all calling for various degrees of research. I had been type-cast three times before: as a composer specialising in oriental fantasies, next as one dealing in dark psychological subjects, and then a composer of hard hitting crime pictures. Now I became the man the producers cried for whenever vast historical epics took shape on the drawing boards, and with my next assignment I advanced a full eleven centuries.

With *Ivanhoe* I became my own first disciple (I suppose also the only one) and followed the example which I set up in *Quo Vadis*. Having tried to re-create the music of the first century by using, after thorough research, musical fragments from the period, I did the same in *Ivanhoe* by going back to sources of the twelfth century. I found a somewhat similar situation in musical matters between the two films. As Roman music was largely influenced by the Greek, so the music of the Saxons came under the influence of the invading Normans. It is a well known fact that people on a lower level of civilisation readily absorb the culture of the invaders or neighbouring countries which have a higher civilisation, as a subconscious expression of their longing for the higher level of life. The sources of Saxon music are extremely few and far between but there is a large amount of music available of the French troubadours and *trouvères* who brought their music to England with the invaders. The various themes in *Ivanhoe* are partly based on these sources and partly my own. Under the opening narration I introduced a theme from a Ballade by Richard the Lionhearted; the Norman theme I developed from a latin hymn (Reis Glorios) by the troubadour Guiraut de Bornth. The love theme of Ivanhoe and Lady Rowena is a free adaptation of an old popular song from the north of France—the manuscript was found in a collection in the Royal Library of Brussels. For Rebecca I needed a Jewish theme, mirroring not only the tragedy of this lovely character of Sir Walter Scott's but also that of her persecuted people. Fragments of medieval Jewish musical motives suggested a theme to me; in short, my scoring of the film was coloured and inspired by the material discovered in research.

The next film was also English, but one taking place five centuries after the era of the Norman conquest and one dealing with a completely different musical fabric. *Plymouth Adventure* is the story of the Mayflower's journey from Plymouth Harbour to Plymouth Rock in 1620. I now looked for a musical theme which the Pilgrim Fathers might have known, and which also expressed their indomitable spirit of religious, personal and political freedom. The pilgrims had one book with music on board: Henry Ainsworth's Psalter, which was printed in Amsterdam in 1612. This book contained the melodies the pilgrims brought to America and sang in their new country. I decided to use as the theme of the Mayflower, the 136th Psalm, a melody which is imbued with vigour and fervent faith. It has a very interesting history. One can trace it back to French Psalters of the early sixteenth century and fragments of it (according to Waldo Seldon Pratt's book *Music of the Pilgrims*) can be found in early German chorales. It has been called the Huguenot Marseillaise as it has the pulsation of a battle song. It has an unusual rhythm and I found its text most appropriate. I therefore used it vocally with an orchestral accompaniment for the opening of the film: "Confess Jehovah thankfully, for He is good, for His mercy continueth forever." The theme attains its culmination in a sequence of the departure of the Mayflower, when the sails of the ship fill with wind to start a voyage into the unknown. To give an atmosphere of authenticity, I tried to build the other themes in the manner of the seventeenth-century Lutenist composers whose music the Pilgrim Fathers knew and must have brought with them. I didn't use any contemporary material, as these themes had to fit closely the situations and characters of the narrative. Again, it was a matter of coloration and style.

M-G-M's filming of Shakespeare's *Julius Caesar* in 1953 gave me a problem of a different kind. If it had been merely an historical film about Caesar, I would have undoubtedly tried a reconstruction of first-century music. However, it was more than that. It is a Shakespearean tragedy and, with all its language, a true mirror of Elizabethan times—and it is principally this language which dictates its style. In Shakespeare's time, as they had few scruples about stylistic correctness, the music was undoubtedly their own—Elizabethan. Should I have composed in a Roman manner, it would have been wrong for Shakespeare—should I have tried to treat it as stage music for an Elizabethan drama in Elizabethan style, it would have been anachronistic from the historical point of view. I decided, therefore, to regard it as a universal drama, about the eternal problems of men and the timely problems about the fate of dictators. I wrote the same music I would have written for a modern stage presentation: interpretive incidental music, expressing my own musical language, for a modern audience, what Shakespeare expressed with his own language for his own audience. The example set by Mendelssohn with his music for *A Midsummer Night's Dream* was obvious, as he wrote his own, highly romantic nineteenth-century music, which now everybody accepts as authentic to this romantic play of Shakespeare.

Dramatic music for historical films cannot help but be stylised, as the very nature of dramatic music excludes the exact usage of period music, which in almost all cases is quite undramatic. By studying the melodic, rhythmic and harmonic elements of the past, the composer can create a language that is appropriate to the subject while still being his own musical expression. Berlioz once said he had to change his style for each dramatic subject he overtook. This was true also in my own case with my next three historical films: *Young Bess* was the story of Elizabeth the First as a child, and the musical problems were fairly straightforward. *Knights of the Round Table* was an action pageant set in fifth-century England, and here I had to fall back on imagination since hardly anything exists from that period. Far more interesting was *Diane,* the story of Diane de Poitiers and her love for King Henry the Second of France. Unfortunately the film was a dismal flop but I still like it from the musical point of view because it allowed an exploration of the Renaissance period. Sixteenth-century French music was very interesting, composers like Josquin Des Prez and Orlandus Lassus were prolific, and I enjoyed studying their scores and composing music in that style, using viola di gambas, recorders, harpsichords and various medieval instruments. I must confess I like some of my music for this sadly neglected picture. The love theme was later published for String Orchestra under the highly unsuitable title: *Beauty and Grace.* The title is *not* mine.

Hollywood has not exactly achieved world fame for the historical accuracy of its film biographies but *Lust for Life* was a gratifying exception. It not only captured the dramatic highlights of Vincent Van Gogh's tragic life but also with painstaking research remained absolutely factual. Based on Irving Stone's book and written for the screen by Norman Corwin, the film was directed by a man who is an artist in his own right, Vincente Minnelli, and produced by the impeccably tasteful John Houseman. Kirk Douglas not only managed to look like Van Gogh but was entirely believable as the ecstatic and exalted Dutch painter. My problem, as always with historical subjects, was to find a suitable style, one which would form an homogeneous unity with the pictorial happenings of the photoplay. The music that Van Gogh knew and liked was the high romanticism of the Wagner-Liszt-Berlioz school and its numerous satellites in France and Germany. His early impressionistic and pointillistic style, however, corresponds musically with the impressionism of Debussy, although Van Gogh himself could not have known his music. There is a twenty-five year time-lag between pictorial and musical impressionism. The first important impressionistic orchestral work is Debussy's *L'Après-Midi d'un Faune,* which had its first performance in 1894, four years after Van Gogh's death. However, the emotionalism of the musical *fin de siècle,* the daring harmonic and orchestral palette of Debussy corresponds—to my mind, at least—with the early style of Van Gogh, and gives a point of departure for further development as his own style started to develop, too. Nothing was further from my mind than to imitate Debussy's style for *Lust for Life*, but the timbre of this score is that of France at the beginning of the century.

**Miklos Rozsa conferring with the venerable Spanish historian Don Ramon Menendez Pidal in Madrid in 1961 during the preparations for** El Cid.

I thought my career scoring historical subjects had completed itself, but I was quite wrong—the mightiest assignment of them all now came my way, *Ben-Hur*, to be followed, one after the other, by *King of Kings, El Cid*, and *Sodom and Gomorrah*. Happily, Rome is my favourite city, my second home. I love Roman culture, and that was where we made *Ben-Hur*. It involved a year and a half of my life and the conditions were those under which all composers should work—in short, to be with the film from the very beginning and to be regarded as one of the team of storytellers. The film called for a vast musical canvas, surely one of the biggest in film history, with many themes and much interweaving. The drama, the personal conflicts and the pageantry required music which grew out naturally from its atmosphere. Fortunately, I had extensively researched approximately the same historical era for *Quo Vadis*, and discovered fragments of Greek, Hebrew and Oriental music, and being aware that almost no purely Roman music had survived, I decided to stick with my own Roman inventions. The script demanded about half a dozen marches, and it was with these I tried to get as close as possible to the sound of what my research had led me to believe Roman military music might have been.

But *Ben-Hur* was largely a religious story and the biggest problem was deciding on the music for Christ. Everyone wanted me to use the theremin, to get that spellbinding, supernatural and eerie sound. But you can't use electronics for the first century, so I opted for the pipe organ. Every time you see Christ in the film or hear about Him or feel His presence you hear the pipe organ combined with divided high strings, usually playing harmonics. The most interesting challenge with this theme was the scene where Christ appears before the multitude to deliver the Sermon on the Mount. The script specified that at no time was Christ's voice to be heard, so it became the job of the music in this sequence to intimate the revered words of the Sermon. Later I published eleven choruses based on themes of *Ben-Hur* and *King of Kings*, and they are now widely performed in churches of all denominations.

No assignment in my life was tougher than the next one—*King of Kings*. It was made right after *Ben-Hur* and I moved from the one film to the other. Not only was the period and subject material similar but several of the scenes were the same, although treated a little differently. I thought at the time, "this is too much." I couldn't write the same music, or at least I wasn't expected to. What helped was the change of geographical location—*King of Kings* was made in Spain and I worked in Madrid. This helped me to think a little differently. That, and the very great difference in the treatment of Christ, who was here the central figure. In previous films about Christ, He had not been heard, now He was both clearly heard and seen. Thus, the central theme of the score is that of Christ the Redeemer. It usually appears accompanied by female voices sustaining soft harmonies. The Hebrew themes are fashioned after examples of ancient Babylonian and Yemenite melodies, and the Roman music is, again, my own interpretation. From the musicological point of view, it might not be perfectly authentic, but by using Greco-Roman modes and a spare and primitive harmonisation, it tries to evoke in the listener the feeling and impression of antiquity.

Spain was also the setting of *El Cid*, and a thoroughly Spanish subject. Rodrigo Dias de Bivar, the noble Lord (Cid) whose story the picture tells, was an idealisation of a Castilian knight of the eleventh century. Numerous stories and ballads tell of his chivalry and gallantry and his conquests, although one wonders if he was quite as magnificent as the legends would have it. I was fortunate enough to write the score in Spain, to absorb the atmosphere, and to be advised by the greatest authority on the Cid and the Spanish Middle Ages: Don Ramon Menendez Pidal. The Cantigas, a collection of nearly 250 melodies dating from the time of Alphonso the Wise, but undoubtedly containing material from earlier times, proved to be an inexhaustible source. The rich libraries of the monasteries of Montserrat and the Escorial also enlarged my insight into the music of medieval Spain. Stylistically, the score for *El Cid* was influenced by three sources: the medieval, the Moorish-oriental, and the combination of these two elements which resulted in the music of the Iberian Peninsula, and what today we call Spanish.

*Sodom and Gomorrah* was an intriguing subject that developed into a very bad picture. It is the kind of experience composers dread—a huge effort that sinks with the ship. But from the musicological point of view, it was too fascinating to deny. Again, the opportunity to delve into the ancient past and possibly discover something different, something to help the composer describe the evil and perversion of the Cities of the Plain, the Helamite tribes, the love of Lot and Ildith, the sorrow of Lot as he turns away from the Pillar of Salt, and the exodus of his people from the Cities. Could I turn my back on such a challenge?

Idlsohn's Music of the Yemenite and Babylonian Jews provided me again with themes as points of departure and the choruses of the Jews are all based on authentic material, which goes back to Biblical times. However, the picture was a huge flop and the RCA Victor album of the score disappeared from the market as fast as the picture. Love's labour lost again.

I am often asked if I would accept a commission for another large scale Biblical picture. I'm not sure but my first reaction would be to decline. I wonder how Wagner would have fared had he been required to write four operas on the story of *Parsifal* instead of one. But once a musicologist, always a musicologist. The re-creation of "far-gone" areas of music will always interest me and now, after a pause of some years in historical pictures, if a good one comes along, I might be tempted.

# 4
# Themes from the Vienna Woods

And then, of course, there were Max Steiner and Erich Wolfgang Korngold, two Viennese whose influence on film music concepts and standards were commensurate with Thomas Edison's contribution to electric illumination. Hyperbolic as this claim may sound, it's indicative of the enthusiasm these men received, and continue to receive, from their admirers, who would seem to outnumber the admirers of any other composers in film history. Steiner is the primary object among film theme collectors—people who tape records or write down or just memorise his innumerable movie melodies and then play them on the piano for other admirers, who can barely wait to get the piano themselves—"Do you remember this one?" The enthusiast will then bang out (Steiner themes seem to appeal especially to the pianistically frustrated) something that sounds like—DUM DEE DUM, DE DUM DEE DUM, DE DUM DEE DUM DEE DUM DEE DA. The other party will usually pipe up with the instant response, "The Oklahoma Kid, of course." The Korngold enthusiast tends to be a somewhat better pianist, and needs to be, which might be the key to the difference between the two composers. While both were richly melodic and obviously Viennese, Steiner was the product of an operetta background and Korngold came from somewhat further up the street—from the opera house and the concert hall.

It was entirely logical that two of Hollywood's most prominent composers during the peak period should have been Viennese. Vienna, like Hollywood, was an artistic mecca, a gathering ground of the arts, a magnetic milieu full of talented, expressive, ambitious people. And anyone who had successfully functioned in Vienna might well survive in Hollywood because the atmosphere was much the same—an atmosphere of stimulation, redolent with creativity but pock marked with conceit and deceit, conniving and manipulating, jealousies and rivalries.

A Viennese musician of a generation ago, assuming him to be intelligent and well versed, received an exposure to music such as no other city could offer. Vienna, as the capital of the Austro-Hungarian Empire, drew its talents from a fantastic musical hinterland. Not only could a Viennese musician draw upon an epic classical tradition and a flourishing musical theatre but he could cull his ideas from the folk songs and dances of Austria, Bohemia, Hungary, the Tyrol and many other regions of Franz Josef's domain. A musical child growing up in Vienna in the years between the turn of the century and the outbreak of the First World War, as did Steiner and Korngold, would hear the groundswell of modernism pioneered by Schoenberg and his disciples. The world had never before offered, and would never again offer, such opportunities for musical education.

By a similar but much less magnificent token, the Hollywood in which Steiner and Korngold worked also presented a situation of abundant opportunity that is never likely to be repeated. The two composers were the "stars" of the Warner Brothers Music Department, which department deserves more than a mere mention in any book about the history of music in Hollywood.

*    *    *

The four Warner brothers had championed the use of sound in films; others had considered it and dismissed it as too much of a risk—by the late Twenties the best of the silent films had reached a level of artistry and sophistication that was readily acceptable to the public and profitable to the producers. It was argued that the films, accompanied by large orchestras, small orchestras, organists and pianists—as per the magnitude of the house, didn't really need dialogue and sound effects. The brothers Warner were enterprising enough not to believe this line. Their first "talkie," *The Jazz Singer*, met with audience enthusiasm when it was premiered on the evening of October 6, 1927 in New York, but it took a year for the industry to accept the fact that the silent era had ended. Some of the strongest resistance came from the music publishers who had worked up a profitable business supplying sheet music to something like twenty thousand movie theatres in the United States and Canada. In addition to the impending dismissal of hordes of musicians, the film tycoons resented the prospect of spending enormous sums of money for equipment to record film tracks, convert theatres and install sound systems.

But *The Jazz Singer* had opened the way and there was no ignoring the new direction. The Wall Street financiers sniffed a good smell, and loaned several hundred million dollars to the Hollywood moguls to re-tool their plants. 1929 was a sort of second California gold rush. Hundreds of musical people bought themselves tickets to Los Angeles: it seemed to them that the kind of movie most likely to flourish in this new era would be the musical. The Warner Brothers had won their gamble, and in a further shrewd move they aligned themselves with three big music publishing houses—Witmark, Harms and Remick. Other studios followed suit with other houses, and American music moved one gigantic step closer to becoming Big Business.

Jack L. Warner, the youngest of the brothers and the survivor, made a decision early in the game, "Films are fantasy—and fantasy needs music." For all his hard-nosed commercialism and his often dubious taste, it is to his credit that he allowed the setting up of a music department that was, for many years, the foremost of its kind in the film world. Eventually it would be equalled and perhaps surpassed, but for a dozen years or more, from the mid-Thirties to the end of the Forties, no studio paid more attention to the sound of music in its films than Warners.

Warners had actually pioneered film music before the arrival of the "talkie." The first film with a fully synchronised musical score was Warners' *Don Juan*, starring John Barrymore, in 1926. The music was composed by William Axt and David Mendoza, and recorded by the New York Philharmonic under Henry Hadley. Axt had, the year before, written music for *The Big Parade*, and *Ben-Hur*, both scores being played by orchestras in the theatres. The success of his *Don Juan* brought Axt the first studio contract given a composer, not from Warners but from M-G-M, for whom he wrote dozens more scores until his retirement in 1939. Warners then quickly looked around for a musician to set up a music department for them. They decided upon Leo F. Forbstein, who was at that time (late 1928) conducting the orchestra at Grauman's Metropolitan Theatre in Hollywood.

Forbstein was one of the best known of movie theatre conductors during the Twenties; born in St. Louis, Missouri, he had led his own orchestra at the age of sixteen, while still a student, and he had built a reputation as a musician with a talent for organisation. This is what the Warners wanted, and Forbstein began 1929 as head of their music department, entirely responsible for all their musical activities. He held this position for the remaining twenty years of his life. By the mid-Thirties Warners were the producers of Hollywood's best musicals, starting with *42nd Street* and followed by a string of mammoth glittering vehicles, most of which were choreographed by the fantastic mind of Busby Berkeley. Forbstein conducted the orchestras in these early Warner musicals but by 1935 he was able to lay aside his baton and do what pleased him most—manage his growing musical bailiwick. It was Forbstein who persuaded Max Steiner to join Warners, and it was Forbstein who signed Erich Korngold to a contract, the first composer of international reputation to be so contracted to a film studio.

Both Steiner and Korngold came of prominent Viennese families, although of different kinds. Steiner was named after his famous grandfather, Maximilian Steiner, the impresario of the Theatre an der Wien. He was the man who persuaded Johann Strauss, Jr., to write for the theatre. Despite

Leo Forbstein, the director of Warner Bros. Music Department, checking Steiner's score for The Old Maid with music editor Phil Score—surely the most appropriate name ever owned by a film musician.

the general belief, the operetta was not a Viennese invention but a Parisian concoction mostly due to Jacques Offenbach. Although the Viennese flocked to performances of Offenbach's spirited musicals, it bothered them that

Paris should surpass Vienna in anything musical. Strauss, like his father, had done well as a composer of waltzes and little concert pieces, and as a conductor of his own orchestra, but he had steered clear of the stage, reasoning that it had apparently defeated even Schubert and Beethoven. Maximilian Steiner realised this oversight; the first Viennese composer he persuaded to write for him was Franz von Suppe, whose *The Beautiful Galatea, Light Cavalry, Boccaccio,* and *Poet and Peasant* all began their lives at the Theatre an der Wien. Although these were inferior to the operettas of Offenbach, they did well purely on the merit of being Viennese and because of the anti-French sentiment generated by the Franco-Prussian War. Johann Strauss, Jr., badgered by Steiner, decided to try. His first operetta was *Indigo and the Forty Thieves,* and with the highly popular composer conducting, it was an unqualified hit. Next came *Die Fledermaus,* and after it the deluge. There was, however, an odd aftermath to this greatly successful Steiner-Strauss collaboration. When Strauss was fifty-two, his wife died. Six weeks later he became infatuated with a pretty but flighty girl thirty years his junior, Angelika Dietrich. All Vienna scoffed but the handsome middle-aged maestro married the girl and took her to live with him on his estate outside Vienna. The sound of creaking was soon heard in the marriage, and within a few months Angelika left Strauss and went back to what she truly enjoyed—the glitter of the Viennese salons and the admiration of many men. Ironically the man she decided to move in with was her unhappy husband's old friend and benefactor, Maximilian Steiner, whose own son, Gabor, would soon fall in love with, and marry, one of the beautiful chorus girls in his father's theatre. From the union would emerge, on May 10, 1888, a son, their only child, and they would call him Maximilian Raoul Walter Steiner.

The Steiners were a prosperous business family. Gabor owned and managed a theatre, and dabbled in several entertainment enterprises—he was the man who built the Riesenrad, the giant ferris wheel in Vienna's Prater. His wife Marie inherited three of Vienna's leading restaurants from her family. Both parents encouraged the precocious musical talents of their son. They sent him to the Vienna School of Technology, where he showed little interest in anything scholastic. But later, at the Imperial Academy of Music, he was brilliant and completed a four-year course in only one year, for which achievement he was awarded a gold medal. His brilliance was greatly aided by the affluence of his family, who could afford to send him to the best teachers available, including Robert Fuchs and Gustav Mahler. Having a father with a theatre was also helpful. Recalls Steiner: "He produced Offenbach and Gilbert and Sullivan and all the others. When I was twelve he let me conduct an American operetta, *The Belle of New York,* by Gustave Kerker. Kerker happened to be in Vienna at the time and he asked my parents if he could take me back to America with him as a Boy Wonder. My mother told him, 'No, all musicians are stinkers.' And then, as an afterthought about her own problems with her restaurants, 'And that goes for all waiters.'"

Steiner made his first mark on the musical world when he was sixteen. "I wrote an operetta and called it *Beautiful Greek Girl*. I asked my father to stage it and he refused, saying he didn't think it was very good. He had a stage manager named Karl Tuschl, who had just left him to lease and manage the Orpheum Theatre on the Josefstadt. So I took this thing of mine to Tuschl and he thought it was worth doing, perhaps because it seemed like a good ploy to rival Gabor Steiner's theatre with something written by his son. I conducted the opening night, and the production ended up running for a year. Out of that came offers to conduct other shows, a couple of which took me to Moscow and to Hamburg. In 1906 I accepted an offer from the British impresario George Edwards to go to London to conduct Lehar's *The Merry Widow*, and that was the start of eight years in England for me. I conducted all kinds of musicals at Daly's Theatre, the Adelphi, the Hippodrome, the London Pavilion and the Blackpool Winter Garden. Then came the First World War and I was interned as an enemy alien. But artists are luckier than most other people and through the Duke of Westminster, who seemed to be a fan of mine, I got my exit papers to go to America. However, my possessions and my money were impounded, and I arrived in New York in December of 1914 with thirty-two dollars in my pocket."

Max Steiner was now about to commence fifteen years in the American musical theatre. He built a solid reputation as an arranger and orchestrator of musical comedies, and as a conductor of stage shows of everybody from Victor Herbert to Youmans, Kern and Gershwin. His last effort on Broadway was *Sons Of Guns*, which opened on November 26, 1929. Two years previously he had orchestrated and conducted Harry Tierney's *Rio Rita*, and now that Tierney had contracted with RKO to do the film version, he asked the studio to hire Steiner. RKO's head of production, William Le Baron, went to the theatre to see Steiner conduct and he was greatly impressed with the fact that Steiner's thirty-five musicians each played several instruments, which made his elaborate orchestration sound even richer. Obviously, here was a man Hollywood could use. The next day, Le Baron had Steiner put his signature on a contract, and thus began the real career of Max Steiner, Dean of Film Music until his death in 1971.

Steiner's arrival in Hollywood came at a time when the industry was turning out musicals as fast as they could produce them but by the end of 1930 the glut had spent itself. RKO laid off most of its musical staff and Le Baron asked Steiner if he would run the department, and take a cut in salary. Using a ten-piece orchestra, library music and the limit of a three-hour recording session per film, it was all Steiner could do to provide main and end titles, plus whatever "on screen" music was called for. His first original composition for film was *Cimarron*. "At that time there were only about three or four composers in Hollywood and the one they wanted for this picture was busy at Paramount. Le Baron said to me, 'Could you knock out something for this picture? If we don't like it, we'll get someone else to re-do it. Just give us enough for the preview.' The picture was a big success; I didn't get any mention in the credits but some of the reviewers asked who had written the music. I then realised I was on to something."

The real start of Steiner the film composer was *Symphony of Six Million* in 1932. David O. Selznick, then thirty and in the early years of his career as a producer, came to RKO intent on making quality productions. He had bought the Fannie Hurst book and he hired Irene Dunne, Ricardo Cortez and Gregory Ratoff to star in the film version. Selznick was not satisfied with the result of his filming and approached Steiner. "David said, 'Do you think you could put some music behind this thing? I think it might help it. Just do one reel—the scene where Ratoff dies.' I did as he asked, and he liked it so much he told me to go ahead and do the rest. Music until then had not been used very much for underscoring—the producers were afraid the audience would ask 'Where's the music coming from?' unless they saw an orchestra or a radio or phonograph. But with this picture we proved scoring would work."

It was Steiner more than any other composer who pioneered the use of original composition as background scoring for films, although in those early years at RKO, sheer volume of work prevented him from applying the technique to every film to which he was assigned. Mostly the scores consisted of a main title, perhaps a snippet or two during the film, and then the end title. Even within those limitations Steiner could make himself felt. For Katharine Hepburn's first film, *A Bill of Divorcement*, the film ends with she and John Barrymore sitting at the piano playing a Steiner miniature sonata, which leaves the audience feeling they have heard more music than they actually have. This is something at which Steiner quickly became a master—the careful placing of music. That, and an unusual talent for 'catching' things musically—giving a musical fillip to a little piece of action or a human characteristic. He caught Leslie Howard's limp in *Of Human Bondage:* Leopold Stokowski told Steiner he thought this was a stroke of genius. Other people, Aaron Copland among them, considered it in questionable taste. Either way, it was an arresting device and one which marked Steiner's use of music in film. At its best, this 'mickey-mousing' could be very effective—some examples: a dog walking along a corridor in *Since You Went Away;* old prospector Walter Huston scrambling like a goat up a hillside in *The Treasure of Sierra Madre;* Errol Flynn gently loping his horse across a parade ground in *They Died with Their Boots On;* or the harp-celesta counterpointing of the water dripping in Victor McLaglen's cell in *The Informer.* And any number of catchy tunes for comic characters.

Max Steiner in his office at Warners, with a few of his many citations visible.

The film score that brought Steiner to everyone's attention was *King Kong*. "It was made for music. It was the kind of film that allowed you to do anything and everything, from weird chords and dissonances to pretty melodies. When the picture was completed, the studio bosses were very sceptical about it and doubtful that the public would take to it. They thought the big gorilla looked unreal and too mechanical. In fact, they didn't want to waste any more money on it and told me to use old tracks. Merian C. Cooper, the producer, then came to me and asked me to score it to the best of my ability and that he would pay the cost of the orchestra." Steiner took him at his word, he brought in an eighty piece orchestra and ran up a bill for fifty thousand dollars. But it was worth every penny because it was his score that literally makes that film work. As soon as the audience hears that three-note theme—those three massive, darkly orchestrated descending chords it knows it is in for a fantastic experience. The score accents all the strangeness and mystery and horror in the story, it limns the frightful giant gorilla but it also does something else—it speaks for the streak of tenderness in the monster, the fascination and the compassion he feels for the terrified girl he picks up in his huge paw—the music is the voice of the doomed brute.

Steiner became the man the producers ran to when they were in trouble with their films, as if he were a doctor who could heal the afflictions of their children. When *Of Human Bondage* was previewed, it had no score and the producers were distressed to find the audiences laughing in the wrong places. Steiner was called in and asked to clarify the intentions of the film with his music. When John Ford's *Lost Patrol* was viewed by the head men of RKO, they all agreed that the film, admirably directed and acted, lacked a certain tension. They felt more sympathy was needed in order for the audience to sense the plight of a band of soldiers, lost in the desert and being picked off by Arabs who were never seen. Steiner was again brought in to acoustically supply the suspense and 'paint in' the Arabs. Ford took no chances on his next film, *The Informer*, and hired Steiner as the composer before he started production. He even sent his scriptwriter to talk to the composer, which, claims Steiner, is the only time in his film career he has conferred with a writer prior to filming. In this case, the extra interest of the film-makers paid off because it brought them Academy Awards for several areas of their work, including one for Steiner. For most of his Hollywood career, Steiner was probably too busy to be concerned with any aspect of film other than music. The mere scanning of the list of his scores leaves one wondering how any man could have done so much.

In addition to composing scores, Steiner also acted as the arranger-conductor on many RKO musicals. He music directed most of the Fred

Astaire-Ginger Rogers pictures—*Flying Down to Rio, Roberta, Top Hat, The Gay Divorcee,* and his last job for RKO was *Follow the Fleet.* Steiner claims he left RKO because they refused to raise his salary but a more feasible explanation would be the offers made by other studios. Selznick by 1936 had set up his own production company, and the only composer he wanted was Steiner, who wrote the scores for three films Selznick produced in association with United Artists: *Little Lord Fauntleroy, The Garden of Allah,* and *A Star Is Born.* Steiner would probably have worked for Selznick exclusively but he was used to prodigious work schedules and Selznick didn't turn out films very quickly. Steiner then accepted a long term contract from Warner Brothers, with the provision he could work for Selznick when that producer needed him. The first Steiner score for Warners was *The Charge of the Light Brigade* with Errol Flynn leading the noble Six Hundred. Over the years he would score another fourteen of Flynn's pictures, mostly action stories and although he did this kind of work most dexterously—supplying exciting passacaglias for fights and battles —he complained that this wasn't really the kind of movie he enjoyed. What he really liked were the Bette Davis romantic dramas (he did eighteen of them), and the actress said many years later, "Max understood more about drama than any of us."

It's doubtful if any composer in history has worked harder than Max Steiner. In his first dozen years for Warners he averaged eight scores per year, and they were symphonic scores calling for forty and fifty minutes of music each. He would seldom look at a film more than two or three times; then with the aid of an assistant he would break down the sequences he felt needed music and map out the timings. In the case of sequences that needed split second cues, he would have someone make an acute timing sheet. After making a piano sketch of the score he would go over it and mark in all the instructions for orchestration. Only a man with such a torrent of musical ideas could possibly have coped with the volume of work. His peak year was 1939, in which he worked on twelve films, including *Gone with the Wind,* the longest score then written. Selznick had spent two years putting his mighty package together and Steiner was the only composer he would consider, but the problem was Steiner's Warner work load. The scoring was discussed several times but Selznick couldn't get Steiner to agree to a starting date for the scoring. He then let it be known that he might consider Herbert Stothart as co-composer of the score. Stothart, the long-time chief composer at M-G-M and a born Southerner, dearly wanted the assignment, but once Steiner heard of the possibility of another composer being brought in, he doubled his efforts to clear himself for Selznick.

**Max Steiner recording his score for** Gone with the Wind.

Writing the three-hour score of *Gone with the Wind* occupied Steiner for twelve weeks, although it was in that same period he wrote the *Symphonie Moderne* for *Four Wives*, and the incidental music for *Intermezzo*. There are sixteen main themes in the score and almost three hundred separate musical segments. Steiner says he managed to live through these twelve weeks only with medical aid, that a doctor came frequently to his home and gave him benzedrine so that he could maintain a daily work routine of twenty hours at a stretch. He was greatly aided in this Herculean task by a team of five of Hollywood's best orchestrators: Hugo Friedhofer, Bernard Kaun, Adolph Deutsch, Maurice de Packh, and Heinz Roemheld, all of them composers in their own right and all capable of rounding out Steiner's ideas and devices. Obviously, the score would never have been written without these five men. Sadly, the score did not win the Oscar it deserved, although the film won eight for its other various contributions. Bob Hope, as the MC, referred to that particular Academy Award show as "this Selznick benefit." Steiner recalls the excitement of the preview at

Riverside, California: "Selznick and all his executives and aides were beside themselves with anxiety and elation. During the intermission I went out into the lobby, spotted David and some of his entourage and went up to them. I asked them if they had noticed anything amiss in the first half. They looked at each other, puzzled. Selznick shook his head. I then pointed out to them that the entire eleventh reel was missing. None of them had noticed it. I had because I was waiting for my music."

About the producers and the studio chieftains, Steiner shakes his head. "They're amazing people. They seem to think that if they pay you well, they own you. Even Leo Forbstein, who understood the problems of composers, became unreasonable after a few years of being an executive. When I was scoring one particular epic, I fell ill with intestinal flu. One evening, after several days in bed, Leo phoned and asked me if I could come in the following morning at nine and conduct a recording session. I explained that I was flat on my back, under sedation and so weak I couldn't even get up to go to the bathroom. All he could say to this was, 'Max, we gotta have you there.' My doctor was with me so I put him on the phone and he told Leo how sick I was. Afterwards, the doctor handed the phone to me and I said to Leo, 'it would cost me my life to get there at nine tomorrow morning.' There was a long pause and then Leo asked, 'Well, how about one o'clock?'"

Steiner's favourite story of musical ignorance: "When I was at RKO, recording a session, one of their directors came in and asked me if I would record one of his compositions with the orchestra. In this business you never say no. He then gave me a single sheet of paper on which was written the simplest, barest melodic line. He went off and I laid the thing aside. The same afternoon he came back and asked if it was ready. I said, 'look, this would have to be harmonised and orchestrated and . . .' Before I could say anything else, he chimed in with, 'Come on, Maxie, you can do all that later—get the guys to play the piece now.' But that's not as bad as some producer badgering you to write a score as fast as you can so he can take off on a trip. I remember one who did this, and I told him I couldn't possibly have the score completed in the next three days in order to record the following day, because it was a difficult score. He wanted to have a *première* the next week so that he could go to Europe. There was no way to do this and he had to delay his trip. At the *première* he came up to me and said, 'What was so difficult about it—it sounded all right to me.'"

Steiner's career with Warners spanned almost thirty years and included the scores of around one hundred and fifty films—an incredible output. Not unnaturally, there was a fair amount of self-plagiarism and repetition, especially toward the end, but the general level of craftsmanship and the consistent understanding of the musical needs of filmic story telling added up to an astonishing total contribution. The scores are too many to discuss but outstanding, in the minds of Steiner buffs, are: *Dodge City, They Died with Their Boots On, The Big Sleep,* and *The Treasure of Sierra Madre.*

Steiner wrote scores for more than twenty large scale Westerns but *Dodge City* is a fair choice in that genre. Its title music tells the audience immediately that it's an epic of Western Americana, all about empire building and progress. The stately measure tones of the theme, with downward modulations *à la Puccini* (Tosca on the range?) accelerate into upward spiralling scherzos as scenes of a train and a stagecoach racing each other come into view. Then Flynn and his marvellous pair of sidekicks, Alan Hale and Guinn Williams, spot the train carrying their boss, Colonel Dodge. Flynn yells, "Let's pay our respects to the Colonel," and off they gallop, supported by a galloping orchestra. Later, when old Henry Travers looks over a map to figure out where his family might be in their wagon train trek, he says, "I'd say they'd be at Broad Plain by now." And Steiner bursts into an expansive, lilting, loping melody that bespeaks the glorious visual of the wagons and the horses and the cattle making their way across a handsome landscape. Throughout the whole film, whatever the drama or the comedy, the music picks up the picture and carries it. *Dodge City* is, after all, just an entertainment, with no attempt at being serious, accurate or realistic.

*They Died with Their Boots On* was Warners glamourised account of the controversial George Armstrong Custer and his career from his days at West Point to his death at the battle of the Little Big Horn. Again, it's entertainment. Flynn was at his best as the charming, impetuous, glory-loving Custer, with Olivia de Havilland giving her eighth and final performance opposite Flynn. Steiner's love theme for the two is exquisite, perhaps his love theme *par excellence,* and he uses it to almost painfully overscore Flynn and de Havilland's final scene together, where Custer rides off into history, never to return. Since Custer himself had chosen the Irish jig "Gary Owen" as the regimental march for his U.S. Seventh Cavalry, it was reasonable to feature it in a film such as this. The infectious tune is splendidly treated by Steiner in a montage sequence following Custer's introduction to his officers at Fort Lincoln; he and a friend play the melody on the piano, then it is picked up by a small group of soldiers with fifes and drums, then by a bigger group and finally by the entire band on parade. Steiner also uses it in an effective scene of the regiment riding along a crest in the early light of dawn, counterpointing it with the love theme. But the real highlight of this score is the highlight of the film—the final last stand of Custer and his men. Steiner pits his Indian theme against "Gary Owen" in furious, mounting key changes. This is an extraordinary piece of composition and the only way to appreciate its merit is to hear it away from the picture. It is easy to see why Steiner did not enjoy assignments such as this one—the visual is so commanding that the audience is hardly aware, except most subliminally, that music is being employed.

Two of Humphrey Bogart's best films have Steiner scores. *The Big Sleep* is the ultimate "private eye" story, with Bogie as Philip Marlowe, Raymond Chandler's tough, glib detective. Steiner ushers in the mystery and the mayhem with heavy chordal passages accented with chimes; he gives Bogie a cheeky little theme, a wryly romantic one for Lauren Bacall, swirling music for chases in fogs, orchestral flutters for suspense and in that final showdown where Bogie routs the hoods, there are rising modulations punctuated by heavy chords. And when the gunsmoke clears and Bogie and Baby look at each other in that sardonic but enticing way—you know they're meant for each other because there's a gorgeous Steiner theme telling you it can't be any other way.

*The Treasure of Sierra Madre* is a rich, full score but one that has not pleased every film lover. Many say it overplays its role, and others say, justifiably, that it isn't Mexican music, it's Spanish. Criticisms aside, the score is high on the list of Steiner admirers, and in certain scenes it is beautifully effective. The main theme denotes the determination of the plodding prospectors bent on the finding of gold, with variations on the theme ranging from joyful to tragic. In the scene where bandits attack a train, Steiner builds the excitement with massive orchestral figurations, almost a Richard Straussian colouration. A passage of particular power is the one that marks Bogart's fright following the shooting of Tim Holt, and his later panic when he finds the body has disappeared. Steiner almost holds a mirror up to Bogart in these scenes. He also makes Bogart's violent end even more painful: the magnificent Mexican actor Alfonso Bedoya, whose huge mouthful of teeth made him look like a shark when he grinned, comes across Bogart—Fred Dobbs as this shifty, shallow character is called —while the exhausted man drinks at a waterhole. The quietly pulsating music underlines Bogart's fears and the obvious intentions of the bandit to kill him. As Bedoya cuts Bogart down with his machete (Bogart off camera) musical stings match the strokes of the large blade and indicate the butchery. Yet another example of Steiner's "catching" an action.

Steiner also "caught" William Powell in *Life with Father,* with a theme that delineated both the pomposity of the character and the good-heartedness. For Flynn in *Adventures of Don Juan* he provided a cheeky six-note motif that speaks like a trumpet call for the amorous cavalier. Steiner put his finger on the wackiness of *Arsenic and Old Lace* with a bizarre treatment of *There Is a Happy Land, Far, Far Away.* Many times he helped Bette Davis put across her emotional, dramatic problems, notably in *Now*

*Voyager* where she, as an ugly duckling, struggled to get away from a domineering mother and find happiness. That score brought Steiner his second Oscar, and it was one of his favourite scores. He and Davis did well by each other in *Dark Victory*, in which she played an heiress dying from a brain tumor. At the end, her eyesight almost gone, Davis makes her way from her garden to her bedroom, aided by a harrowing cello theme. The music lets the viewer know that this is her last trip.

Steiner, a soft-hearted man who pretended otherwise, was always effective with emotional scenes. In the film that brought him his third Oscar, Selznick's *Since You Went Away*, he poured out a stream of melodious themes for this wartime tribute to the American home front. Oversweet and now terribly dated, the film contained one scene that was made, almost to order, for Steiner. At the railroad depot, Jennifer Jones sees her soldier (played by her then husband, the ill-fated Robert Walker) off as he leaves for the war, never to return. The music underlines the poignancy of the situation and then, as the train begins to move and pick up momentum, so does the music. The girl runs along the platform, almost hysterical. The sequence is an emotional wallop of music, dialogue and photographic effects. What made it even more touching, as Steiner must have known at the time, was that Jones and Walker were, in fact, at the end of their marriage and finding it painful to act together—especially as Jones was being courted by producer Selznick.

According to Steiner, film and music help each other in the way a husband and wife help each other in a good marriage, but neither one can save the other. As for his method: "There is no method. Some pictures require a lot of music, and some are so realistic that music would only interfere. Most of my films were entertainments—soap operas, story book adventures, fantasies. If those films were made today, they would be made differently and I would score them differently. But my attitude would be the same—to give the film what it needs. And with me, if the picture is good, the score stands a better chance of being good."

While Steiner was always a melodist, he also always knew how not to use melody in film scoring. Sometimes, a melody calls attention to itself when it should not. Steiner used catchy themes to point up the main characters in pictures but he was adept at doing something more subtle than that—writing neutral music with chordal progressions and just enough melodic motion to make it sound normal but not enough to compel attention. Steiner looked upon scoring more as a craft than an art: "The hardest thing in scoring is to know when to start and when to stop. The location of your music. Music can slow up an action that should not be slowed up and quicken a scene that shouldn't be. Knowing the difference is what makes a film composer. I've always tried to subordinate myself to the picture. A lot of composers make the mistake of thinking of film as a concert platform on which they can show off. This is not the place. Some composers get carried away with their own skill—they take a melody and embellish it with harmonies and counterpoints. It's hard enough to understand a simple melody behind dialogue, much less with all this baloney going on. If you get too decorative, you lose your appeal to the emotions. My theory is that the music should be felt rather than heard. They always used to say that a good score was one you didn't notice, and I always asked, 'What good is it if you don't notice it?' "

Often complimented as the man who invented movie music, Steiner would reply, "Nonsense. The idea originated with Richard Wagner. Listen to the incidental scoring behind the recitatives in his operas. If Wagner had lived in this century, he would have been the Number One film composer." Asked to criticise contemporary music: "I have no criticism. I can't criticise what I don't understand."

Steiner's last film score was *Two on a Guillotine* in 1965. A miserable, feeble film, its producer accused Steiner of "ruining it." To have ruined such a film could only have been regarded as an accomplishment. It was, however, a weak coda to a mighty career. Steiner would like to have continued scoring but no other producers called upon him. Steiner was by now in his late seventies and his eyesight had failed drastically, something he tried to hide even from his friends. A charming and amusing man, given to terrible puns and very earthy jokes, Steiner could not always conceal his bitterness about an industry that didn't seem to want him any more. Occasionally, the bitterness was justified, as when Twentieth Century-Fox announced their intention of filming *The Day Custer Fell*, later dropped. Steiner called the studio to tell them he would be interested in scoring the film, and the young executive with whom he spoke asked him if he had ever written any music for Westerns.

The Steiner birthday parties were always joyous occasions for his many friends. Steiner, who retained in old age the appeal, and sometimes the capriciousness of a boy, owed his health and welfare to his understanding, patient, charming wife Lee. At his eighty-second birthday party, May 10, 1970, Steiner bedecked himself in all his ribbons and medals and donned a Beethoven wig to greet his guests. One of the guests, Albert K. Bender, who organised the Steiner Music Society (an international league of admirers), responded, "Max, you look better than Beethoven." To which Steiner replied, "I should hope so—he's dead." The following year the Steiner birthday party was attended by only a handful of close friends. Long ailing, the old composer was in too much pain to bear company. In his last months he suffered the agonies of cancer. Finally, on December 28, 1971, his heart stopped. The boy who had sat on the lap of Emperor Franz

Josef had lived to be almost eighty-four. When Max Steiner died, a link with Old Vienna ceased to be and yet another door on the Old Hollywood was closed.

**Erich Wolfgang Korngold.**

The place of **Erich Wolfgang Korngold** in the history of film music is special, possibly so special that it lies aside from the mainstream of consideration. In the twelve years he worked for films, he wrote only eighteen scores and he worked under ideal conditions. Korngold was the highest paid composer of his time; all of his assignments were for expensive, major productions and he worked on a film only if it pleased him. He also worked *with* each of his films as part of the production and his advice on dramatic construction was often heeded. He was, in fact, a "fair haired boy" and while it is easy to claim his film scores as superior to most others, it is also unfair to compare him with film composers who might have produced more substantial scores had they worked under Korngold's conditions.

Korngold arrived in Hollywood in 1934 with a shining reputation. Hailed as a second Mozart, he had astounded the music world with his concert works and his operas. As a teenage composer, pianist and conductor he had the most prominent composers of the day shaking their heads in disbelief. Richard Strauss said: "This firmness of style, this sovereignty of form, this individual expression, this harmonic structure—one shudders with awe to realise these compositions were written by a boy." When Korngold was ten, his father took him to Gustav Mahler for a critical judgement. The boy played from memory a dramatic cantata as Mahler walked up and down reading the score, his pace quickening with growing excitement. At the end he looked at the father and said, "A genius," and made suggestions for education. A few years later, with a pair of one-act Korngold operas playing all over Europe, Puccini remarked, "The boy has so much talent he could easily give us some and still have enough left for himself." That Strauss, Mahler and Puccini should feel this way about the music of Erich Korngold was not surprising because they were the three strongest influences upon it. An analysis of Korngold reveals a Straussian orchestral colour, a Mahlerian feeling, and the melodic concepts of Puccini, all of them somehow melded and dominated by a strong Viennese character—plus Korngold's own personality.

That such a composer should find his way to Hollywood and write exceptional film scores was not surprising. But it was also rather sad that such a composer would fall into a big, soft, comfortable trap and never really emerge from it and return to his former prominence. And it is ironic that his name is kept alive in the minds of many people by his sumptuous film scores and not by his operas and his concert compositions. The Korngold story is indeed sadly ironic, rather like the Horatio Alger saga in reverse—beginning with spectacular success and subsiding into mere general success. His story also points to the furious acceleration of musical development in the twentieth century. As a youth his music was regarded as daring and startlingly modern but by the time he died it was considered faintly *passé*.

Every artist is both aided and hindered by the era in which he lives. Korngold had the enormous fortune to be born into the stimulating musical environment of Vienna at the turn of the century, but the enormous misfortune of coming into the adult phase of his life at a time when the political climate of Europe put an end to his career in the concert hall and the opera houses. He was thirty-seven when he made his *début* in the film world. But for the Nazi *régime* he might have continued writing opera. On the other hand, there were critics who claimed he had already reached his high-water mark, that he had blossomed too soon and spent himself. Who can be sure? Perhaps it was Korngold's true mission to cultivate film scoring and further its dimensions. Certainly he arrived at the ripest possible time. Warner Brothers needed a composer to score their well produced, intelligent, handsome costume dramas. Korngold's concept of a film scenario was its being another form of opera libretto, and it was a theory that worked magnificently with subjects like *Anthony Adverse, The Adventures of Robin Hood, The Constant Nymph, The Sea Hawk,* and *King's Row,* but when the age of filmic historical romance petered away, so did Korngold's interest in film scoring. In 1947, aged fifty, he made the decision to divorce himself from the movies, and return to writing serious music. However, by then the world had changed; he returned to Vienna but his Vienna had "gone with the wind," and neither there nor anywhere else was he able to revitalise his former fame. Hollywood had been very good to him—and bad for him.

The musician most closely associated with Korngold during his film years was Hugo Friedhofer, who orchestrated all but one of his scores. Later Friedhofer would become one of the industry's finest composers— more about him in the following chapter of this book—but he was the only man Korngold fully trusted and relied upon to orchestrate his music as he would have done himself given the time. Says Friedhofer: "I learned and grew from my association with Korngold. I find it hard to speak of him without feeling emotional. He was a warm, witty, humorous man, and he took his film scores as seriously as any other kind of composition. I know there is a tendency in some quarters to be rather derogatory about his music but I don't think that anybody with any spark of feeling can listen to Korngold and not agree that here was a man who knew exactly what he wanted to say and said it beautifully. He was 'all composer' and his work gave a new impetus to film scoring. To be honest about it—we were all influenced by him."

Erich Korngold was born in May 1897 in the city of Brno, then part of Austria but now Czechoslovakia. He was the second son of Dr. Julius and Josephine Witrofsky Korngold, both parents of affluent means. The older brother, Hans Robert, lived five years longer than Erich Wolfgang but, as the novelists might put it—never amounted to anything very much. Possibly the reason for this might be the fact that his father centered all his pride and attention on his miraculously gifted younger son. The father had given his sons the second names of Robert and Wolfgang, after his two favourite composers: Schumann and Mozart. There were times when he regretted the naming. With Erich's fame as the outstanding musical prodigy of the time, the father was often accused of having added the name Wolfgang later, to play up the obvious comparison with Mozart. This was a particularly stinging accusation because Dr. Julius Korngold happened to be Vienna's foremost music critic. He had taken the position of music critic with *Neue Freie Presse* in 1902 and held it until 1934, during which time he duplicated some of the esteem and respect, not to mention the opposites, of his celebrated predecessor, Eduard Hanslick. Thus, Dr. Korngold's pride was mixed with confusion and embarrassment. He could not conceal the boy's talent; nor could he promote it. He also knew that the boy's music would be played by musicians who were out to curry favour, and as a weapon by other musicians who were not in favour.

Erich Korngold showed his precocity at an unbelievably early age. At three he could beat time and at five he was playing four-hand piano pieces with his father. He could also reproduce on the piano any melody he heard, and pick out elaborate chords. By the time he was seven, he was composing. Later, he was put in the hands of teacher-composer Robert Fuchs, and, at ten, on the advice of Mahler, he was sent to study with Alexander Zemlinsky. As Mahler saw it, there was no point in sending the boy to the Conservatory, for his grasp of form and theory, his perfect pitch, and facility with the piano obviated further study. At the age of eleven Korngold wrote his first major work, the ballet-pantomime *Der Schneemann* (The Snowman); first performed at the Vienna Court Opera in a command performance before Emperor Franz Josef, the work was subsequently staged in some forty Austrian and German houses. Other works followed; a trio written the following year was given its *première* with Bruno Walter as the pianist, then came a piano sonata; the Seven Fairy Pictures; an orchestral overture; and a large scaled Sinfonietta. All of them were widely performed, with some people doubting them as the work of a boy and a few actually insinuating the music was really the composition of the father.

In the summer of 1910 Korngold, now all of thirteen and already a *cause célèbre*, vacationed with his family in the southern Tyrol, during which time he and his father visited various famous musicians who formed little summer musical colonies throughout this spectacular area. One of the neighbours was master pianist Artur Schnabel. It was the start of a lifelong friendship. Years later when Korngold was ensconced in Hollywood Schnabel would express amazement at this association of "such a composer in such a line of work." He was always convinced Korngold would "surely give it up," and that he was "unhappy making all that money."

In his excellent biography of Schnabel (Dodd, Mead and Company, 1957), César Saerchinger referred to this first meeting of Korngold and Schnabel and the young composer's second piano sonata, which the pianist introduced to the public shortly afterwards:

There is no doubt that Korngold, at thirteen, was not only a phenomenally gifted composer but that the sonata in question was a remarkable work, well worth performing. Speaking about it nearly forty years later, Schnabel called it "still a most amazing piece." Never afraid of doing the unusual, he decided to play the work in public, and did so during the following season in young Korngold's home town of Vienna, as well as in various other places. Aside from the objective estimate of its merit (which it got) one would have expected only favourable comment on Schnabel's gesture in the Press. There appeared, however, several malicious innuendos regarding his motives—in view of the fact that Korngold senior was at that time the most influential critic in Austria. The gossip that went around is best summarised by the imaginary conversation in which a colleague asks Schnabel whether Korngold's sonata is "rewarding," to which he replies: "No, but his father is." Schnabel paid no attention to the rumours and not only continued to play the work, but he and Flesch also played young Korngold's violin and piano sonata (written in 1912) at their regular recitals in Berlin.

According to his father, Erich Korngold was a normal child when not composing or playing the piano. He was tractable, cheerful and well behaved but almost trance-like at those moments when music came over him. The critics could find nothing childish in the compositions; they reviewed the pieces as being complicated, elaborate and definitely pointed toward the future. Korngold wrote his first opera, *The Ring of Polycrates,* when he was sixteen, and *Violanta* the following year. Both were performed all over Europe, with the latter reaching the New York Metropolitan. Both are one-act operas, the first comic and the second dramatic. *Violanta* caused comment due to its sensuous and rather erotic nature, qualities that perplexed even the young composer. When questioned about the opera, all he could do was shrug and assume that one doesn't have to experience love and passion to describe them. But long after the staging of this opera, in 1916, Korngold would have a chance to become more worldly—he was inducted into the Austrian Army. His two years of military service were in no way warlike. Seemingly, he didn't even have to perform much in the line of drill because he was always being called into the Officer's Mess to play the piano for them. At one point, his Colonel asked Korngold to write a march for the regiment: on hearing the piece, the Colonel expressed his delight but added, "Isn't it a little fast?" to which the composer replied, "Well, yes, but this is for the retreat." It was typical of the humour that marked Korngold and endeared him to his friends.

Among the staunchest of young Korngold's supporters was Bruno Walter, who, at various times and places conducted all the Korngold operas.

After the composer had died in 1957, Walter reflected: "The experience of hearing him play and sing for me the two one-act operas (*Polycrates* and *Violanta*) which I was going to perform at the Munich Opera House will remain unforgettable. One could have compared his interpretation of his works on the piano to the eruption of a musical dramatic volcano, if the lyric episodes and graceful moments had not also found their insinuating expression in his playing."

Korngold also had enemies—Vienna could be vicious as well as charming—mostly musicians who disliked his father. Richard Strauss had been one of his keenest encouragers and had conducted several Korngold compositions but Strauss's affection for the young man cooled with time, probably because his famous librettist, Hugo von Hofmannsthal, despised Dr. Julius Korngold, who in turn was cruel in his critiques of the Hofmannsthal works. In a letter Hofmannsthal wrote to Strauss and dated May 5, 1927, he wrote (in part):

As soon as you have had a little while to settle down, I shall be delighted to tell you the story of the comic opera or musical comedy with which we are going to challenge *Der Rosenkavalier*. We cannot, of course, expect our work, neither in words or music, to soar to the heights of the light opera now said to be coming from the pen of Erich Wolfgang. But then, it is no use asking for the moon.

Korngold's first composition after leaving military service was an incidental score for a production of Shakespeare's *Much Ado About Nothing*, at Vienna's famed Burg Theatre. The concert suite from the score became a popular concert item, and several selections from the score, notably, the Garden Scene and the Hornpipe were often played (and recorded) by violinists Fritz Kreisler, Mischa Elman and Jascha Heifetz. Korngold's most famous work, his opera *Die Tote Stadt* (The Dead City) was presented in 1920, and one assumes that most of its writing must have been done during Korngold's two years in the army. First presented in Hamburg, during the three years Korngold spent in that city as the conductor of its opera house, *The Dead City* is set in Bruges and concerns a widower who is obsessed with the memory of his wife. He falls in love with a young dancer who greatly resembles the dead wife and, during a trance, he kills her. The melodic highlight of the opera is Marietta's *Lute Song*, one of the most performed of all Twentieth century arias. The opera was an immediate and sustaining success all over Europe and it was selected by the Metropolitan in New York as the vehicle for Maria Jeritza to make her American *début*. The German soprano was much in favour in these years, and one of the operas in which she had made her name was Korngold's *Violanta*.

Korngold was also responsible for the Johan Strauss revival during the Twenties. Passionately interested in the music of the Strauss dynasty, he exhumed a number of lost scores and re-orchestrated them. Korngold staged his version of *A Night in Venice* in 1923, and two years later, *Cagliostro in Vienna*. He would later re-score several other Strauss vehicles, as well as operettas by Offenbach and Leo Fall. In 1929 Korngold began a long association with the great German impresario Max Reinhardt, an association that would change the course of his life. However, two years prior to this union with Reinhardt, Korngold had written what he considered his best work, the opera *The Miracle of Heliane*, although it never rivalled the popularity of *The Dead City*.

Reinhardt cultivated Korngold's liking for the theatre. Together they staged a number of musical plays, the most famous being their version of *Die Fledermaus* which, with a completely re-worked score, became *Rosalinda*. Korngold also selected from a large collection of little-known Strauss music and put together an operetta called *Waltzes from Vienna*, which would later become popular as *The Great Waltz* in America. The next year came the similarly constructed *The Song of Love*. Such was the success of these Strauss vehicles, that Reinhardt and Korngold did a similar treatment to the scattered music of Offenbach and staged it as *The Beautiful Helene*. In New York in 1944, Korngold further re-worked the score and called it *Helen Goes To Troy*, which ran for several hundred performances under his baton. Korngold also conducted his score for *The Great Waltz* in long runs in Los Angeles in 1949 and 1953.

By the early Thirties Erich Korngold was operating, so to speak, in full throttle. He was well known, well liked and well off. Part of his time was given to composing chamber music, part to the theatre, part to being a guest conductor and the rest to anything that caught his fancy. At the age of thirty-three he was awarded the title of Professor Honoris Causa by the President of Austria, and he began teaching classes in opera, composition and conducting at the Music Academy of Vienna. This stream of activity was broken when he received an offer from Max Reinhardt, postmarked Los Angeles. Reinhardt had come to terms with Warner Brothers on the production of a film version of his own stage version of Shakespeare's *A Midsummer Night's Dream*. Warners apparently felt at this time the need to produce a film of prestigious value, and with true film-tycoon thinking (find the best and offer enough money) they picked upon the world's most estimable stage director—Reinhardt, although when it was time to start filming, Reinhardt discovered himself saddled with a producer, Henry Blanke, and a co-director, the German-born William Dieterle. However, for his music score, Reinhardt wanted Korngold—not to compose an original score but to take the famous Mendelssohn stage score for *A Midsummer*

*Night's Dream* and adapt it for filming. This interested Korngold, he accepted the generous offer and arrived in Los Angeles in late 1934 with his wife and his two young sons.

*A Midsummer Night's Dream* involved Korngold for half a year. Warners gave Reinhardt the choice of all their players; he chose James Cagney as Bottom (the most striking performance in the film), Dick Powell as Lysander and Mickey Rooney as Puck, and for Hermia he chose a nineteen-year-old beauty who had just played the part in his Hollywood Bowl production of the play—Olivia de Havilland. The film turned out to be more interesting to the critics than the public at large but over the years it has assumed something of the aura of a classic film, forever shown at film retrospectives and Shakespearean festivals. Darkly shaded, dramatic and fantastic, Reinhardt's film is most obviously Germanic in style, and thus a rather odd treatment of a Shakespearean comedy. It is enormously aided by Korngold's scoring: he used all the Mendelssohn incidental music for the stage play and supplemented it with fragments from the *Songs without Words,* and Mendelssohn's *Scottish and Italian Symphonies.* Reinhardt wanted the film, as he described it, "underpainted by the music" and to do this Korngold had to apply the scoring in three different layers, first, by pre-recording some sections (e.g. the Scherzo and the Nocturne) and having the players perform to them; then performing some sections of the score as the actors were being filmed; and finally, by conducting some of the actors in the rhythmic reading of their lines and adding the music later. No film score had ever been so elaborately executed, and it made a great impression in the business.

The acute timing necessary in film scoring is one of its most difficult factors. Korngold had very little mechanical aptitude—he would never employ the click-track device, in which the conductor can hear the predetermined timings of so many bars of music matched to so many frames of film. Even a stop watch confused him. His stop watch was his brain. Korngold's innate sense of timing was a constant source of amazement to the musicians and sound engineers with whom he worked. When he was first being shown around the studio by Henry Blanke, Korngold asked him: "How long is one foot of film?" "Twelve inches," replied Blanke. "No, that's not what I meant. How long is it in time?" Blanke confessed that he had never before thought about it, but called over one of the technicians, who explained that film runs at twenty-four frames per second, with sixteen frames for every foot. Therefore, one foot would take two-thirds of a second. "Ah," cried Korngold, "exactly as long as the first two measures of the Mendelssohn Scherzo," thereby inventing the timing method that he would use in all his scoring. He never used timing sheets, cue marking on the screen, or earphones. If a sequence called for forty-two and two-thirds seconds, he would write a piece of music and conduct it so that it would fill forty-two and two-thirds seconds.

After he had finished with *A Midsummer Night's Dream* Korngold returned to Vienna to work on his new opera, *Die Kathrin* but four months later he returned to Hollywood, having accepted an offer from Paramount to write a film operetta with lyricist Oscar Hammerstein II. It turned out to be the least memorable of Korngold's films. *Give Us This Night* starred Gladys Swarthout and Jan Kiepura, and was highlighted by a short opera as its finale, the first piece of opera originally written for the screen. But the film was so trite and corny that it quickly sank from sight. Years later, when film product was badly needed for television, the programme directors even had second thoughts about playing it on TV. The lovely Swarthout sang beautifully but the atrociously hammy Kiepura sang twice as much and hogged the film. Korngold had been attracted to the idea of scenario as it had been described to him—it took him years to master the English language—but he knew nothing about the Hollywood penchant for re-writing scripts during the production. Hammerstein recalled Korngold saying to him, as the script went from hand to hand, "This thing gets worse from week to week—by the time they film it, it will be useless." He was right.

During the filming of *Give Us This Night,* Korngold was approached by Warners with a request for him to score a film they had just made called *Captain Blood.* Korngold said he wasn't interested, especially in view of the picture he was currently doing. However, Warners kept after him with daily phone calls and telegrams. Finally, he agreed to look at the film—and he was enchanted with its quality. He liked its humour and its romance. After signing the contract, Warners told him he had three weeks to write the score. Korngold now discovered why even the best composers in films need orchestrators. However, three weeks was not quite enough even though working frantically around the clock and Korngold told Friedhofer to use part of a Liszt tone poem in the duel between Errol Flynn and Basil Rathbone. The film was a great success, and a new day in film music. The score reflected all the vitality and the spirit of the adventurous story; it ushered in Flynn as the foremost movie swashbuckler, and it would be the first of seven Flynn films scored by Korngold—both men ideally suited to their assignment. With another fifteen of his films scored by Max Steiner, Flynn would become the best musically supported actor in film history.

With *Captain Blood* a certified blockbuster at the box-office, Warners again pressed Korngold to sign a contract, and on any terms he wanted. Again he refused, but he did agree to supply a few brief scoring passages to *Green Pastures,* a film that was otherwise scored with a choir singing

Negro spirituals. He was charmed by this story of the Bible as seen through the eyes of simple black children in the American South. Korngold scored *The Creation* and *The Flood* and a few other fleeting spots—he did this without a contract and when Warners later asked him what he wanted as payment, he told them, "Nothing, I enjoyed doing it." He also asked that his name not be included in the credit titles, lest it draw attention away from the excellent work done by choirmaster Hall Johnson. He was impressed by this erudite black musician who spoke several languages, including German, and Korngold frequently invited him to dine with him in The Green Room, the restaurant at Warners. He couldn't understand why Johnson politely declined the offers. It was explained to him while having lunch with producer Hal Wallis that none of the cast of *Green Pastures* were allowed in the Green Room because it was restricted and Negroes were not, at that time, admitted—not even the star of the picture, Rex Ingram, who was playing "De Lawd." The black actors ate at the cafeteria on the lot. On being told this, Korngold got up to leave. "Where are you going?" asked the surprised Wallis. Replied the composer in a loud voice, "I'm going down to the cafeteria to eat with God."

Korngold still showed little interest in film music but Warners persuaded him to look at their *Anthony Adverse*. Once more the composer was hooked by the appeal of an epic romance—Hervey Allen's lavish novel set in mid-eighteenth-century Italy, the Alps and France. This, to Korngold, seemed like an opera. In fact, he could only come to terms with a film if it struck him in this manner. The score of *Anthony Adverse* is very much an opera minus singing; it forms an almost non-stop sound fabric behind the picture and threaded with more themes than any other film score. It was, for all those who cared to listen, the most extensive composition ever, until then, developed for a film, and it won Korngold an Academy Award. With this, and much other acclaim, Korngold's appetite for film scoring was increased, although he still feared the idea of becoming known as a "film composer" and he still turned down the contracts that were offered him. He did, however, agree to score two more pictures, both with Errol Flynn—*The Prince and the Pauper*, and *Another Dawn*, the former a charming treatment of the Mark Twain yarn about the son of Henry VIII and the beggar boy who looked exactly like him (played by the Mauch twins), the latter a dreary soap opera.

In scoring *Anthony Adverse*, Korngold came upon a technique that was later used by other composers—that of pitching his music just underneath the pitch of the voices of the actors and surging into pauses in the dialogue. Korngold was also, with this score, the first film composer to write long lines of continuous music, great chunks that contained the ebb and flow of the film's mood and action. The key, of course, is Korngold's conception of film as a form of opera. Once, in conversation with Hugo Friedhofer, Korngold said he thought the second act of Puccini's *Tosca* was the best bit of opera he knew, and he added, "Come to think of it, *Tosca* is the best film score ever written." That view is a clear indication of Korngold's film style.

Discussion of Erich Korngold among those who knew him in Hollywood, always draws forth reminiscences about his sense of humour. At the time he was working at Paramount, there was also an arranger at the studio named Sigmund Krumgold. Their mail was always going to the other. Spotting Krumgold in the commissary, Korngold went up to him and asked, "Siggy, are you getting any of my letters?" Krumgold admitted that a few pieces had come his way. With a dramatic flourish of his hands, Korngold said, "Well, I hope to God they're more interesting than yours," and walked away. The most quoted Korngold quip is this one: at Warners he was always being asked for his opinion on musical matters. Leo Forbstein got him to come into a screening room one day to look at a newly completed sequence of one of their gargantuan musicals. Apparently, it was a scene with hundreds of chorus girls performing elaborate, geometric routines and a huge orchestra playing a complicated, lengthy arrangement. When it was over, Forbstein, obviously proud, asked for Korngold's assessment. He had been in Hollywood long enough to pick up all the superlative adjectives, and he said, "Leo, it's fantastic, colossal, stupendous." Then he leaned a little closer to Forbstein and added, "But it isn't very good."

In late 1937 Korngold returned to Vienna for the staging of *Die Kathrin*. By now, the political climate of Europe was one of growing trauma, and he found it difficult to muster his forces and arrange for the *première*, which was delayed several times, and finally, forbidden by the Nazis. Korngold was not a political person. He seemed oblivious to what was happening, possibly because his was an affluent, happy, almost "dream" world, in which everything had always worked well for him. But he was now persuaded by friends that he should consider leaving Austria until the situation was resolved. This, and the advice of a doctor that his ailing youngest son needed a warm climate, persuaded Korngold to return to California. He bought a house in the Toluca Lake district of North Hollywood, less than a quarter of a mile from the Warner studios, so that he could walk to work. He had, by this time, decided to accept more assignments from Warners but they would have to be on his terms, i.e., that he would have *carte blanche* in scoring a film, that the music could not be tampered with, and that the music would remain his and not the property of the studio. Warners were so anxious to get his name on a contract that they allowed him any condition. The first thing they wanted him to do was score the most expensive production that had so far been done, *The Adventures of Robin Hood*. Korngold looked at it and declined. He thought it was beautiful but had too much action, and that he couldn't do it justice in the short time they wanted the score completed. He wrote out a formal letter of refusal and delivered it to Warners. On February 12, 1938, Leo Forbstein arrived at the Korngold home and began trying to persuade the composer to take the job. He was still uninterested but something else happened that day and it helped change his mind: Austrian Chancellor Schuschnigg met with Hitler at Berchtesgaden. Korngold was deeply attached to Vienna and the news depressed him. After a while he began to talk to Forbstein less adamantly about *Robin Hood* and he agreed to write the score, provided he could do it on a week-to-week basis and drop out if he wasn't pleased with the way the job progressed. Forbstein realised that his mission had been a success. Seven weeks later the score was married to the soundtrack for what is, most probably the *pluperfect* example of the blending of film image and music.

*The Adventures of Robin Hood* is about as good a film of its type that has yet been made. Its script and its direction, its costumes and sets, its action and its pacing leave little to be desired. The casting is near perfection: Flynn at the peak of his appeal as Robin, Olivia de Havilland exquisite as Maid Marian, Basil Rathbone as the magnificent villain Sir Guy of Gisbourne and Claude Rains as the weasel-like Prince John. The music delineates them all as it strides, bounces and lilts along. Highlights: the rout of the Norman column in Sherwood Forest by Robin and his Merry Men—the music builds and builds and then releases as the men jump and swing out of the trees; the gaiety of the music for the banquet in the forest; the heraldic music for the Archery Tournament; the noble theme for King Richard when he reveals his identity to Robin; the gentle theme for Maid Marian when she understands Robin's purpose in being an outlaw: and the elaborately orchestrated march accompanying the outlaws, dressed as monks, as they make their way up the hill to the Abbey for the coronation. Altogether, like the film itself, a never ending delight.

Korngold's next three scores were for more massive historical subjects: *Juarez, The Private Lives of Elizabeth and Essex*, and *The Sea Hawk*. Each called for, and received, lavish musical treatment. All of them were rich subjects for a composer of Korngold's leanings, and had the dialogue been sung instead of spoken, each film might have been an opera. *Juarez* appealed to him because of the story of the Hapsburgian monarch Maximilian and his devoted but tragic wife Carlotta, who lost her mind after her husband was executed by the Mexicans. The doomed pair loved the song *La Paloma,* and Korngold treated it memorably in his score. He helped underline the nobility and the weakness of Maximilian, and he made the rather austere Paul Muni image of *Juarez* more appealing. Whenever it came to ethnic music, Korngold invented his own because he felt properly conceived dramatic music was more effective than the genuine material. In speaking of his score for *Elizabeth and Essex,* he said, "The loves and hates of the two main characters, the ideas expressed by the playwright generally, while taken from history, are symbolical. It is a play of eternally true principles and motives of love and ambition, as recurrent today as three hundred years ago. The characters speak the English spoken today. Why then should the composer use 'thou' and 'thee' and 'thine' if the dialogue doesn't?"

**Erich Korngold, who always sat down to conduct a scoring session, here conducts his score for** The Sea Hawk. **The elderly gentleman in the foreground is his father, Julius Korngold, who attended every session, score in hand. To the right, the composer's son Ernst makes a comment to his mother.**

In his career article on Korngold for *Films in Review* (February, 1967) Rudy Behlmer discussed the score of *The Private Lives of Elizabeth and Essex* and pointed to one of the most interesting aspects of the composer's concept of film scoring: "Korngold continued to experiment with his idea of pitching music just underneath the pitch of actors' voices, which he thought achieved, in the dubbing, an important, albeit a subtle, balance between the spoken word and the music."

*The Sea Hawk* was the last of the Korngold "historical romance" scores. From the first bar of the main title, it speaks of nautical adventure. The music captures the roll of the ocean and the splendour of fully rigged Spanish galleons and English privateers. Again Flynn, the supreme celluloid cavalier, is supported in his *amour* and his heroics by suitably lush and dashing music. When, toward the end, he and his men escape the galleys of the galleon in which they have been imprisoned and take over the ship, they burst into a stirring operatic chorus, "Bound for the shores of Dover." Ridiculous, of course, but so sweeping and rousing—why quibble? The love theme for Flynn and Brenda Marshall is about as close as any composer has come to matching Wagner's *Liebestod*.

Korngold's film music took a different turn with *The Sea Wolf*, a fog enshrouded filming of the Jack London story with Edward G. Robinson giving a masterly performance as Wolf Larsen. The scoring was atmospheric, misty, minor moded and slightly dissonant. Less assertive and more subtle than his previous scores, the music for *The Sea Wolf* is more a favourite of other composers than of Korngold's fans. But then came *King's Row*, the score that brought him his biggest mail—one fan wrote to say he had seen the film sixty times, mostly with his eyes closed. The main title was especially arresting—a bold, almost heraldic statement that undergoes variations during the course of this story of life in a small mid-Western town, circa 1890. The town is rife with psychosis, love, hatred, bitter memories and tender memories, ambition and resolve. And a field day for Korngold. Particularly memorable is the grandmother theme —a lovely melody stated by a cello for the diminutive, charming Russian actress Maria Ouspenskaya. The finale, with Robert Cummings declaiming Henley's *Invictus* to rouse legless Ronald Reagan from his lethargy, with a powerful choir breaking into the lines, "I am the master of my fate, etc . . ." borders on the absurd filmically, but it's a beautiful piece of opera.

Next: *The Constant Nymph*, another of Korngold's most generous scores. Margaret Kennedy's sentimental novel about a Belgian composer who marries a rich socialite instead of the young music student who adores him, gave Korngold ample scope. He later adapted part of the score into a tone poem for soprano, choir and orchestra, *Tomorrow, Opus 33*. This film represents the high water mark in his career as a film composer, the films that followed being of lesser quality and far less successful with the public. *Devotion*, filmed in 1943 but not released until three years later, was a very romanticised and wildly distorted account of the Brontë sisters. The score is sumptuous but largely wasted. Particularly impressive was Korngold's darkly dramatic music for the Yorkshire Moors and the dream sequence in which a masked, mounted knight manifests himself and envelops Emily in his huge black cloak. Korngold's next score (his favourite, even though the film was a failure) was *Between Two Worlds,* a Second World War setting of the play *Outward Bound,* in which a group of dead people are transported to the next world, their past and their characters revealed in the process. Since the leading character in this treatment was a Viennese concert pianist, Korngold had an opportunity to provide a little rhapsody for the piano, which he dubbed himself as Paul Henreid pretended to play.

After the disappointing reception to these two scores, Korngold began having doubts about film scoring as an art. He had been enormously lucky with his first dozen films; now the tide seemed to turn and in fact his next job was a disaster. Warners decided to re-make RKO's 1934 version of *Of Human Bondage* and star young Eleanor Parker in the Bette Davis role of Maugham's cold-hearted trollop and Paul Henreid as the medical student who loves her. Both were miscast, and the film was pedestrian and lacklustre. For once, Korngold's music was painfully obtrusive, a rich symphony hanging on a scarecrow. Korngold was curious to see the previous version after he had finished scoring his own. Coming from the screening room, he happened to spot Bette Davis on the lot and called out to her. The two greeted each other warmly. Then he said, "I've just seen your *Bondage,* and you were wonderful. Of course, after ten years some of the scenes look a little ridiculous." Davis raised her eyebrows at this but before she could reply, Korngold added, "But we, with our new version, are ten years ahead of time—we are already ridiculous."

*Escape Me Never,* made in 1946 and kept on the shelf for two years, was also slightly ridiculous but nonetheless pleasant and certainly easy to listen to. Errol Flynn appeared in his least probable role, as a ballet composer, thus giving Korngold the opportunity to provide an original ballet, and one song called *Love for Love,* which had some popularity beyond the picture. Set in Venice, the Dolomites, and London in the Victorian era, the picture glows with music, and had the theatres been packed with millions of Korngold fans, Warners would have made a fortune. Unfortunately, people who go to films to listen to background scores are a distinct minority.

Korngold's last score was quite different from all the others, in that it contained very little background music. *Deception* is a kind of intellectual soap opera, about a brilliant modern composer-conductor, played to the bravura hilt by Claude Rains, his pianist mistress, Bette Davis, and her lover, cellist Paul Henreid. Davis finally kills the egocentric composer.

**During the filming of** Deception, **Erich Korngold confers with Paul Henreid and Bette Davis, doubtlessly with advice on how to handle his music in this highbrow soap opera about the loves and jealousies of concert musicians.**

Both melodramatic and highbrow, *Deception* is perhaps of most interest to music lovers. The score includes portions of Haydn's *Cello Concerto*, Chopin's *Prelude in E Major*, part of the second movement of Beethoven's *Seventh Symphony* and the first movement of his *Appassionata Sonata*. Korngold also supplied a new composition of his own, a short and brilliant cello concerto, which he later expanded into a complete concert work, his *Opus 37*. This marked the end of his composing for films.

Dr. Julius Korngold died at his son's home in 1945. He had never been very pleased about the association with films and urged his son to return to absolute composition and to opera. In October, 1946, when his Warner contract expired, Korngold refused to renew it. He said at that time, "I shall be fifty next May, and fifty is old for a child prodigy. I feel I have to make a decision now if I don't want to be a Hollywood composer the rest of my life." He also realised that the war had brought a change in public taste in films and the kind in which he had excelled was no longer in favour. His many jests about films masked his true feelings. When he first started scoring, he was greatly enthusiastic about the possibility of reaching millions all over the world; in his last year, he quipped, "A film composer's immortality stretches all the way from the recording stage to the dubbing room." Just before he left Warners, veteran producer Henry Blanke said to him, "Erich, when you first came to us, your music was so exciting and vibrant and soaring—now it doesn't seem to be quite the same." Korngold replied, "When I first came here, I couldn't understand the dialogue—now I can."

The favourite Korngold joke in Hollywood music circles is this one: in his last year at Warners, Korngold ran into Max Steiner, with whom he kept up a bantering friendship. Steiner needled him, "Erich, I've been thinking. We've both been writing music for Warners for ten years, right?" Korngold nodded, wincing at the reminder. Steiner continued, "Well, it seems to me that in this time, my scores have got gradually better and yours have got gradually worse." Korngold beamed, "Maxie, my dear, you're absolutely right. And I'll tell you why—it's because I've been stealing from you and you've been stealing from me."

The remaining ten years of Erich Korngold's life saw him composing a violin concerto, a Symphony, a Symphonic Serenade and several other works, and for almost all of them he mined his film scores for thematic material. The violin concerto, performed and recorded by Jascha Heifetz, is based almost entirely on film themes, as his father had advised him to do. Neither it nor any of his other compositions from this period found favour with the critics, or wide acceptance from the public. He returned to Vienna in 1949 with his wife and stayed for more than a year; he hoped he could revive his former activity and fame, but after a while it dawned upon him that what had happened twenty and thirty years ago was irretrievable. His opera *Die Kathrin* was staged, finally, in Vienna in 1950 but withdrawn after only six performances, torn to shreds by the critics. *Die Tote Stadt* was slated for a Viennese performance but collapsed in a welter of complications during the rehearsals. It was not until ten years after his death that the opera was staged at the Vienna Opera House, warmly accepted by the public but bitterly denounced by the critics as "old fashioned nonsense." However, *Die Tote Stadt* continues to be staged in European opera houses and will likely be one of the few enduring twentieth-century operas.

Korngold made one more contribution to the cinema. In 1954 he was asked by director-producer William Dieterle if he would arrange, conduct and supervise the scoring of the Wagner biography, *The Magic Fire*. Korngold told him, "I'll do it—if only to protect Wagner." The picture was made in Germany and turned out to be a disappointment, although for

Wagner lovers, it held much of interest. Korngold made a remarkable three-and-a-half minute musical montage of the sixteen hours of Wagner's *Ring* cycle, and was later amazed when asked by Republic Studios if he could slice another twenty seconds out of it. The film was, in fact, cut by almost an hour for American release, and butchered in the process. Korngold appeared briefly in the picture, as the famed conductor Hans Richter, and he was heard but not seen in two episodes of Wagner and Liszt playing the piano together—Korngold recorded both tracks. It was often said of him that he might have been a great concert pianist if he had devoted himself to the instrument. He said, "I play only two instruments—the piano and the orchestra, and the orchestra is such a nice instrument." Hugo Friedhofer recalls, "When Korngold played the piano, it *sounded* like an orchestra."

Korngold was an amiable, genial man. He was also vastly fortunate; he was secure and confident and removed from the competitiveness that blemishes the film and music businesses. It was only in his later years that bitterness soured his good humour. He never fully accepted California as his home until the last years when he realised there could never be a return, in the full sense, to Vienna. He spoke caustically about the atonal, anti-sentiment turns in modern composition. Many people regarded him as the last master melodist among the composers of this century, and he asked, "Should I deliberately become an ultra-modernist just because some critics would consider that an advance over what has gone before?" It was Korngold's conviction that the tonal system was inexhaustible—that there were endless melodic and harmonic combinations waiting to be discovered. He compared the process of artistic creativity with nature, a continually renewing source, but he would add, with a twinkle in his eye, "Don't expect apples from an apricot tree."

As if abetting the decline of his career, ill health marked Korngold's last years and robbed him of his energy. He was only fifty when he suffered his first heart attack. In the winter of 1956 he suffered a stroke, and on November 29, 1957, age sixty, he collapsed from a heart seizure and died a few hours later at a North Hollywood hospital near his home, and a mere half mile from the Warner studio. The next day, a black flag—the traditional Austrian mark of mourning—appeared over the Vienna Opera House. The city he loved, the city that had been the generous cradle of the famed *Wunderkind* but had been indifferent to his return, noted its loss. When told of the flag gesture, his widow stared silently for a few moments, and then said quietly, "It's a little late."

# 5
# The Price of Excellence

In the light of knowledge about the circumstances and conditions under which film composers work, we have every reason to be grateful that any good scores have been written. The film composers of the most intelligence and the most integrity often pay a price for their excellence—less fame than their more flashy colleagues and lessening opportunity in a business that has become more and more commercial. Three American composers who fit this odd but dignified *niche* are Bernard Herrmann, Hugo Friedhofer and David Raksin.

**Bernard Herrmann conducting his opera** Wuthering Heights **in 1966.**

141

**Bernard Herrmann** was the kind of composer somewhat feared in the Hollywood of thirty years ago. Young and brilliant, Herrmann had excelled in every avenue of composition—symphonic, vocal, theatrical. He was modernistic and forceful and very critical of film music. He may never have cracked the Hollywood barrier had it not been for Orson Welles, who insisted that Herrmann was the only man to score *Citizen Kane*. That celebrated picture launched several careers but Herrmann might well have gone under had he not won an Academy Award for his next score, *All That Money Can Buy*. In the Hollywood of 1941, an Oscar was tantamount to the keys to the city. For all that, Herrmann kept his distance and scored only one film a year and carried on with his other musical activities. He scored no films between 1947 and 1950 but after that he became more interested in writing music for films and then averaged two or three a year. He might have done more but he was very selective about his pictures, and hardly endeared himself to the producers with his open contempt for their work. George Antheil referred to Herrmann as "my old squawking friend." Herrmann has, apparently, insulted just about everyone in Hollywood and has often stormed out of a projection room and railed at the producer who wanted to hire him, "Why do you show me this garbage?"

Bernard Herrmann was born in New York in 1911, of a non-musical family. While attending public schools he took music lessons from local teachers and at the age of twelve won a prize for a song he had written. At New York University he studied composition, and he continued the study as a fellowship student at the Juilliard School of Music. By the age of eighteen Herrmann was making a living as a musician, he had written a ballet for a Broadway show and he had formed and conducted a chamber orchestra to give concerts of *avant-garde* composers. His career took shape in 1933 when he was hired to compose and conduct music for the Columbia Broadcasting System. He was conspicuously successful with CBS, both for creating musical backgrounds for their dramatic and documentary programmes and for conducting his concert pieces with the CBS orchestra. Herrmann was thus one of the leading figures in this heyday of American radio and it led him into a profitable association with another young genius, Orson Welles, Herrmann scored many of the famous Welles broadcasts.

While he was, and is, an advocate of modern music and open to any style or school of musical thought, Herrmann has never typed himself. "I count myself an individual. I hate all cults, fads and circles. I believe that only music that springs out of genuine personal emotion and inspiration is alive and important." Herrmann qualifies as the personification of what a composer should be—educated, knowledgeable, as respectful of old forms as he is interested in new forms, and deeply personal; all this in addition to being gifted with great musical ability. But Herrmann, somewhat like Richard Wagner, is a little difficult to accept on a personal level. He speaks little about himself but is often unkind in his estimates of other musicians. One of his close friends says, "With Benny for a friend, you hardly need a hair shirt." Those who know him say that the rough manner of the man hides a warm heart, but the important thing about Herrmann is that his depth of character is part of his skill in expressing himself deeply in music. The quality of his film music and the imagination and invention he brings to scoring tends to put him aside from other film composers—where he no doubt prefers to be. Typical of Herrmann is his lack of interest in belonging to the Academy of Motion Picture Arts and Sciences, which he despises.

Bernard Herrmann's first film score is an extremely interesting one, which is not surprising in view of the long apprenticeship scoring hundreds of radio programmes and the prior association with Orson Welles. In scoring the picture he received a luxury denied most Hollywood composers—he was present during the entire production and often made sketches during the shootings of the sequences. His music accurately reflects Welles's and Mankiewicz's story. The opening scoring is sparse and ominous, and varies from faintly romantic to dry and dramatic as the character of Kane is revealed. Herrmann uses music suggestive of the period—waltzes, ballet, opera, a newsreel episode, etc. The orchestration of the score is unusual in that it continually varies. This is an interesting point since Herrmann is the only major film composer in Hollywood who does his own orchestrations. He later adapted this score into an orchestral suite and titled it *Welles Raises Kane*.

Herrmann's next score was quite different from the previous one. For *All That Money Can Buy* he wrote some superlative Americana, dexterously employing a number of New England folk melodies. The score is full of charm and humour, and it was immediately apparent to the music circles of Hollywood that a man who could write this kind of score, as well as the *Citizen Kane* kind, was a man to reckon with, or not to reckon with, as the case may be. Again Herrmann worked the material into a suite; known as *The Devil and Daniel Webster* it has been frequently performed. Both this suite and the previous one have been recorded by Herrmann.

Orson Welles called upon Herrmann to score his next film, *The Magnificent Ambersons*, but this time Welles had nowhere near the same freedom he had with *Kane* and RKO edited and cut the picture. It gave Herrmann scope for more turn-of-the-century Americana and allowed for his penchant for waltzes. The lack of success of the film no doubt strengthened Herrmann's resolve not to become known as a film composer and he returned to New York for more conducting and more composing. Even now, long established as one of the true craftsmen of film scoring, Herrmann bridles at the term "film composer." "America is the only country in the world with so-called 'film composers'—every other country has composers who sometimes do films."

In 1944 Bernard Herrmann was brought to Hollywood again, this time by Twentieth Century-Fox to score *Jane Eyre;* yet another association with Orson Welles, although here merely as an actor (Rochester) and not as the writer-director-producer. Herrmann's music mirrored the sombre tragic-romantic story lines with murmuring bass figures suggesting the malevolence and the mystery of Thornfield. Herrmann is, among other things, a fervent Anglophile and he is attracted to most things English. His only opera is *Wuthering Heights* and it contains many passages from *Jane Eyre,* along with themes from his score for *The Ghost and Mrs. Muir.*

Herrmann next scored a minor classic of its kind, *Hangover Square,* which starred the memorable Laird Cregar as a composer with intermittent amnesia who is given to brutal murder during his sanity lapses. The film is especially interesting on the musical level because the composer is in the process of writing a piano concerto and his drastically fluctuating state of mind affects his composition. The actual concerto, completed by the mad musician as his burning house falls about him, is one of the most interesting virtuoso pieces ever written for a film. Dark and dazzling, it was too cerebral a work to become widely popular.

Herrmann wrote sparingly for films in his first ten years in the medium, never more than one film a year. He was, at this time, still active as a conductor for radio and concerts in New York and it was only the attraction of a particular film that would bring him to California. He was also judicious in choosing subjects that were varied and that could be scored in various ways. For *Anna and the King of Siam,* Herrmann based his score on authentic Siamese scales and melodic fragments. "I tried to get the sound of Oriental music with *our* instruments. The music made no attempt to be a commentary on, or an emotional counterpart of, the drama but was intended to serve as musical scenery."

Herrmann considers his score for *The Ghost and Mrs. Muir* (the 1947 feature, not the TV series) as one of his best efforts in film music, as well as being his most romantic. It told an odd kind of love story between a young widow living in a seaside house and the ghost of a sea captain. It was obviously a story that greatly appealed to Herrmann because his accompanying music was tender and charming. This from a man who in person appears anything but tender and charming, but as Aaron Copland comments, "If it's in the music, it's in the man."

In 1951 Herrmann scored one of the first of the major science fiction films, *The Day the Earth Stood Still.* It was an experimental score, ahead of its time, in which he suggested electronic music without using any electronic instruments. By this time Herrmann was too well respected for his film composition to be able to resist the increasing demands for his services. Now he was producing two and three scores a year, with an inevitable decline in the general choice of jobs. Among the more interesting are *The Snows of Kilimanjaro,* and the films Herrmann has scored for Alfred Hitchcock. *Kilimanjaro* was one of the few successful attempts to put Hemingway on the screen, and Herrmann's music had much to do with that success. His music commented on the African scenery and was especially effective in the flashback sequences where the hunter—played by Gregory Peck in an idealisation of Hemingway himself—lies dying of an infected wound and muses on incidents in his life. The love theme from this score was later extracted and titled "The Memory Waltz," a delicate piece of music which Herrmann says is symbolic of Hemingway's recollections of his youth in Paris.

Herrmann became associated with Alfred Hitchcock in 1955 when the master of suspense and macabre comedy asked him to score *The Trouble with Harry,* which was too short on suspense and overly macabre in its humour to find favour. Herrmann fared better the following year when he handled the music for *The Man Who Knew Too Much,* although his own scoring was somewhat overshadowed by Doris Day's singing of *Que Sera, Sera* and the fact that the finale of the film called for a dramatic cantata called "Storm Clouds," written by Arthur Benjamin. The cantata was performed in London's Albert Hall and conducted by Herrmann himself—his one screen appearance so far. Again this was a film in which the music was involved with the story: it tells of the assassination of an international figure during a concert, with the assassin, obviously musically educated, firing the lethal shot at the moment of a loud cymbal clash.

The Hitchcock film with which Herrmann is perhaps most associated is *Psycho,* a stunning example of subtle musical horror. The bizarre, blood curdling moments of bloody murder are accompanied by loud, high, bird-like shrieks made by pitched violins, and they are probably the finest examples in cinema history of music being able to chill an audience to the marrow. However, the best of the Herrmann-Hitchcock scores is *Vertigo,* a landmark in film scoring and a sadly under-appreciated one. This 1958 film, handsomely set in San Francisco, has James Stewart as a detective named Scottie Ferguson and Kim Novak as a woman of mystery named Madeleine. Page Cook, in his career profile of Bernard Herrmann for *Films in Review,* made this comment on the *Vertigo* score:

The credit music, in an invention of major thirds, accompanies some dizzy optical effects, and the prelude begins with a huge basso ostinato upon which a solid horn figure startlingly appears. We then hear, for the first time, the melody, written in the key of D Major, which

**Bernard Herrmann with Alfred Hitchcock during the scoring of** Vertigo.

is the clue to Madeleine's obsession about her dead grandmother. The melody's first use grows in intensity—the orchestration is quite bizarre—and achieves a grim crescendo, which leads, after a harrowing drop, to a sustained note in the double bass. The harmonies are abstract but never cacophonic.

For the chase at night over the rooftops, following the credits, there is a vibrant movement culminating in drum reverberations as the detective falls to his death. To depict Scottie Ferguson's acrophobia Herrmann uses a sharp discord based on an augmented triad. Madeleine's theme is first heard as Scottie spies her in a cocktail lounge, and, as she approaches him and then moves away, it grows and dims. There are no sounds on the soundtrack save this music. It's cinematic and extraordinarily effective. This theme is superbly used in the scene in which Madeleine pleadingly asks Scottie if he thinks she's insane.

The key of the score—the note D—is sombre when Madeleine gazes at the portrait of Carlotta, whose spirit, Madeleine believes, is slowly possessing her. The nightmare sequence —i.e. Scottie's dream of Madeleine and Carlotta—is scored for timbrals, castanets and snare drums (Carlotta was of Spanish-Mexican descent). The entire movement grows into a fantastic array of orchestral timbres, which end as Scottie awakens.

The story line in *Vertigo* is involved and mysterious, and Herrmann's subtle score helps both the air of mystery and final resolving of the complicated parts. The excellence of this score paradoxically points to a problem in writing excellent scores—that one viewing of such a film is not sufficient to really be able to appreciate what the composer has done.

In 1958 Bernard Herrmann delved into another kind of film, the fantastic-exotic. He scored *The Seventh Voyage of Sinbad*, followed the next year by *Journey to the Center of the Earth*, and over the next few years: *The Three Worlds of Gulliver, Mysterious Island,* and *Jason and the Argonauts.* All these films allowed Herrmann rich orchestral palettes and scope for musical imagination. These scores called for a kind of Rimsky-Korsakov texture, which Herrmann gave them, along with wit and charm. He has often said that the great inducement to writing film music, aside from the money involved, is the opportunity to experiment. However, composers, like actors, tend to get type-cast and after five fantasy films Herrmann decided he had fully explored that particular mineshaft and declined similar offers. He returned to Hitchcock in 1964 and scored the not very popular *Marnie*, giving another discreet score for another story of a woman of mystery.

The failure of *Marnie* at the box-office had a direct bearing on Herrmann when Hitchcock made his next film, *Torn Curtain*. Hitchcock contracted to make the film at Universal Studios but when he made known his intention to hire Herrmann for the score, he was advised against it. Hitchcock protested. The studio then lowered the boom and pointed out to him that his past few pictures had not done well and that they wanted a composer whose score for *Torn Curtain* would be more exploitable. Hitchcock gave way and agreed to accept John Addison, but as it turned out, neither the score nor the film itself were exactly exploitable.

Hollywood assignments, as they had for most of the veteran composers, became fewer for Herrmann. In 1966 François Truffaut offered him the job of scoring his ambitious filming of *Fahrenheit 451*. Herrmann was curious to know why Truffaut, who was a friend of many young jazz composers, would choose him instead of them. Said Truffaut, "Because they would give me music of the twentieth century, you'll give me the twenty-first." Herrmann scored the film somewhat differently than Truffaut specified, playing down the hard, emotionally, dry futuristic concept of "things to come." *Fahrenheit 451* was a failure but Truffaut was gracious enough to send the composer a note saying, "Thank you for humanising my picture."

Page Cook says that Herrmann was reticent with him at the time he was writing his article but that after the publication the composer became somewhat more confiding. Herrmann has been called many things worse than reticent but his idiosyncrasies are taken in stride by those who realise his musical values are unquestionable. No musically discerning person has reason to cavil. In correspondence with Cook, Herrmann revealed some of his contempt for the turns taken in scoring films in the late Sixties: "Everybody's looking for a new sound, which means taking an old sound and jacking it up and amplifying it till it hurts your ears. There are no new sounds, only new ideas, and they don't come along very often. I've been extraordinarily lucky to have worked with men like Welles and Hitchcock. If I were starting now I'd have no career in films."

Bernard Herrmann bitterly resents the lack of attention paid film music by the press; if worthwhile scores were intelligently reviewed and assessed it would have a beneficial effect on the medium. "It's because there's no critical attention to movie music that it is left to producers—who are musical ignoramuses. I can't understand how a producer of a sophisticated film will pander in the score to the lowest common denominator."

Pressed for his philosophical point of view regarding composing, Herrmann says, "I am not interested in music, or any work of art, that fails to stimulate appreciation of life, and, more importantly, pride in life."

*    *    *

The case for **Hugo Friedhofer** is simply put by his friend David Raksin: "I think he has a better understanding of film music than any composer I know. He is the most learned of us all, the best schooled, and often the most subtle." This viewpoint is general in the world of film scoring and yet Friedhofer's is a name that has never caught the fancy of the movie-going public, despite the excellence of his work over a long period of time. To explain this lack of fame Raksin proffers this: "Virtue may be its own reward, but excellence seems to impose a penalty upon those who attain it. Composing something that isn't a repetition of what's been done before, cultivating differences from others, seeking out what is special, requires extra effort, extra time, and a little more indulgence from producers. Those who want scores 'not good but by Thursday' often prefer to promote men whose qualification is that they deserve it less."

Hugo Friedhofer arrived in Hollywood in July, 1929. He has composed

Hugo Friedhofer (right) with conductor Lionel Newman at a recording session at Twentieth Century-Fox.

the complete scores of some seventy feature films and contributed sections to the scores of at least as many more. Indeed, he has worked as a collaborator, adapter, arranger, orchestrator and utility composer on more films than he can remember. It's doubtful if any other musician has had quite the degree of involvement with film music as has Friedhofer. In the highly specialised field of orchestration he is regarded as The Master. He orchestrated more than fifty of Max Steiner's scores, and he was the only man Korngold fully trusted to touch his music—he orchestrated 17 of Korngold's eighteen film scores.

The terms "adapter" and "arranger" tend to confuse the public, not unnaturally since the terms often intertwine. To adapt is to tailor a piece of music composed for another purpose, e.g., a part of a symphony, and make it fit a scene. To arrange is to change the clothes of the music—a sonata can be arranged into a concerto, or something written for certain instruments in a certain range can be arranged for other instruments in other ranges. Arranging often allows a musician more scope than adapting. In the case of Morton Gould making a five-minute orchestral arrangement of a Jerome Kern song, that almost constitutes re-composition. The skilful and imaginative work of Hollywood's best arrangers has never been widely appreciated. These men quite literally took the tunes of song writers and built them into compositions. So many of the song writers, gifted with melody though they may have been, were incapable of making even a respectable piano score, let alone an orchestration. As Friedhofer puts it, "Having been witness to what has been accomplished in the art of transmuting the baser metals into pure gold by such arrangers as Ray Heindorf, Conrad Salinger, Herbert Spencer, Eddie Powell, Earle Hagen, Maurice de Packh, Leonid Raab and others, I can't help wondering if film musicals would ever have gotten off the ground without their blood, sweat and tears."

Friedhofer was born in San Francisco in May, 1902, where his cellist father was also born. However, the father studied music in Dresden and it was there he met his wife, also of a musical family. Friedhofer, who had majored in art, dropped out of school at the age of sixteen and took a job as an office boy. Later he worked in the designing department of a lithograph firm, and at nights studied painting at the Mark Hopkins Institute. His father had started him on the cello when he was thirteen but it wasn't until five years later that his interest in music began to predominate over his interest in painting. Once he had chosen between the two he studied seriously and within two years he was able to earn his living as a musician —casual engagements at first, then steady work in movie theatres, two years with The People's Symphony, which had been set up in opposition to the San Francisco Symphony, and, in 1925, a berth with the orchestra of the Granada Theatre, which Friedhofer describes as "one of that decade's most ornate film cathedrals."

It did not take Friedhofer long to realise that he had more interest in what the other instruments were doing collectively, i.e., in orchestration, than in being a performing cellist. And so, concurrent with his various jobs as a cellist, he studied harmony, counterpoint and composition with Domenico Brescia, a graduate of, and fellow pupil with Respighi at the Conservatory in Bologna. Brescia later became head of the music department at Mills College, a post he held until his death in 1937. Years later, as a well employed film musician, Friedhofer picked up his studies of musical form with Schoenberg and composition with Ernst Toch. In 1944 he also spent periods of study with Nadia Boulanger, the celebrated French teacher and the musical mother of so many American composers, at the time when she was living in Santa Barbara, California. Friedhofer feels a composer should never stop studying, although he cringes at the name dropping of his famous teachers. "I have an aversion to the types who try to impress you with the fact that they sat at the feet of this or that Great Master. I'm only interested in what they themselves have done. The woods are full of no-talent characters with degrees from this or that diploma mill. Ravel failed to win the Prix du Rome three times, despite the fact that his music was being performed and applauded concurrently with his bad status at the Conservatoire. Stravinsky, outside of a couple of years with Rimsky-Korsakov, is completely self taught. In the last analysis, all a teacher can do is point out the road, after that you walk by yourself."

Friedhofer eventually was able to put aside his cello and pick up work as an arranger. A violinist friend, George Lipschultz, who had become music director for Fox studios in Hollywood, now offered Friedhofer a job as an arranger. The first film on which he worked was the musical *Sunny Side Up*. He stayed with Fox for five years until it merged with Twentieth Century, at which time Friedhofer fell out with the new management and took to being a free-lancer. Looking back on that busy period, he reflects, "My activities as an arranger, composer and orchestrator were so intermingled that a catalogue is out of the question—not that posterity will be any the poorer as a result. Frankly, considering all the work I've done in films it's a wonder I'm not blind or paralysed or both. I give thanks for the stamina bequeathed me by my peasant forbears."

The next plateau of Friedhofer's career came in 1935 when he was hired by Leo Forbstein, the head of music at Warners, as an orchestrator. Under Forbstein's astute command Warners maintained the most formidable music department in the industry. Concurrent with Friedhofer's arrival at the studio was the contracting of Max Steiner and Erich Korngold. Steiner's first score for Warners was *The Charge of the Light Brigade,* and Korngold's first for the studio was *Captain Blood*. Both scores were orchestrated by Friedhofer, who performed the work so well he became typed as the principal orchestrator for these two giants. He had hoped, in joining the company, that he would become one of the celebrated team of Warner composers but in the eleven years he spent at the studio he was assigned to only one picture as a composer, this being *Valley of the Giants* in 1938, the title of which seemed somewhat descriptive of his predicament. Forbstein realised that Friedhofer was a brilliant orchestrator and paid him well. "Forbstein was no musician to speak of, but he was an excellent executive and a good businessman, and he organised that music department so well it could practically run itself. We were all cogs in his well-oiled machine. Forbstein had the complete confidence of the Warner brothers, and it was *the* place for a musician to work. We had a fifty piece staff orchestra, which we augmented to seventy for the bigger scores, and Forbstein was fortunate in not having individual budgets for the films, as was the case elsewhere. The studio gave him an annual allotment of money and he used it well. As for me—working conditions were good, and I suppressed my creative ego until I could do so no longer."

In between his Korngold and Steiner assignments Friedhofer, with Forbstein's approval, was able to occasionally do a job for another studio. In 1937, on the advice of Alfred Newman, Friedhofer was hired by Samuel Goldwyn to score *The Adventures of Marco Polo*. His first full-length score is a fine piece of work and it was well received by the music community of Hollywood but it still didn't change Forbstein's mind—he already had superb composers on his staff. What he needed was this able orchestrator who serviced Korngold and Steiner so well. Steiner had himself been an orchestrator and he knew the value of a good man in this laborious but essential aspect of scoring. He would indicate in his sketches the effects he wanted and leave it to Friedhofer to fill in. Steiner, in his first ten years for Warners, averaged something like eight scores a year, and the success of this huge volume of work is partly attributable to Friedhofer. Friedhofer was one of the several musicians who worked for Steiner when he was scoring *Gone with the Wind*, and sections of that long score were written by Friedhofer, developing Steiner material and interjecting a few fragments of his own.

The need for the orchestrator in film music is obvious, and snobs who sneer at film composers not being able to orchestrate are being absurd. A composer like Korngold would hardly have used an orchestrator had it not been a matter of time. Steiner wrote his almost three hours of music for *Gone with the Wind* in a twelve week period, while at the same time writing the *Symphonie Moderne* for *Four Wives*. When Friedhofer wrote the score for *The Best Years of Our Lives* he himself employed an orchestrator, and he has orchestrated few of his own scores since then.

Friedhofer claims a musician either has a knack for orchestration or he hasn't. A similar thing can be said for the whole art of film scoring. Friedhofer can look at a film and know immediately what it needs musically. He also has the ability to place himself musically in any surroundings, and, without actually quoting local material, simulate the musical colour of an environment. There's an Indian mode to his score for *The Rains of Ranchipur*, and an entirely different kind of Indian music for the tasteful and intelligent Western written and directed by Delmer Daves, *Broken Arrow*, one of the first such pictures to deal with American Indians on an understanding, humanistic level. Friedhofer's score for *The Bandit of Sherwood Forest*, in which Cornel Wilde played the son of Robin Hood, came from a study of medieval English music. "I knew I couldn't do anything like Korngold's *Robin Hood* and expect to get away with it. His approach had been rich and operatic so I had to go the other way and be fairly austere and more historical. I used some old English melodies; one of them was the song *Brigg Fair*, the same one Delius had used for his orchestral rhapsody. Of course, I got letters panning me for having stolen from Delius. One has to be philosophical about things like this. I tend to go along with Virgil Thomson's advice: 'Never make the mistake of over-estimating an audience's taste, but don't under-estimate it either.' "

There is almost no kind of film Friedhofer has not scored in the past forty years. The film for which he won his Academy Award (he has also been nominated for eight other scores) was *The Best Years of Our Lives*, and it is a particularly tasteful kind of Americana. The film itself was an intelligent treatment of American servicemen returning home after the Second World War and it was done without so much of the cloying sentiment and patriotism that marred so many American films of this kind. "I got the film because once again Sam Goldwyn called Al Newman and asked who should be the man for the job—I think Goldwyn still somehow thought Al was working for him. This was years after Al had been head of music at Fox. Anyway, Goldwyn took his advice without question and I got the job even though William Wyler and others didn't want me. Wyler was a very confused man about music—he was also hard of hearing. He had great trouble hearing the lower frequencies of music, and when he did hear them, he hated them. He obviously disliked my score very much, in fact, so did many people around the Goldwyn studio, and it wasn't until after I'd won an Oscar for it that they started talking to me again. It was a difficult score because of the three disparate story levels—disparate but connected, and I had to find a common denominator. Somehow I managed." *Managed* is putting it modestly; *The Best Years of Our Lives* is a score that bears the closest examination.

Friedhofer's score for *The Young Lions* is as good as anything ever written for a war film. The title music for this picture is especially impressive, a minute and a half of very business-like martial music. The upper line of brass instruments carries the melodic figures while the lower is a chorus of drums playing a relentless, repetitive rhythm. It has that inexorable quality suggestive of the modern war machine moving like a juggernaut. Friedhofer in this, and similar films, never indulges in flag waving, what he says in the music is that war is ugly and non-glorious.

One of the themes in *The Young Lions* was written twenty-five years previously. It's the theme for Mai Britt, who played the wife of the army captain who is Marlon Brando's immediate superior. At one point in the story Brando visits her in Berlin to tell her about her injured husband—he finds her more interested in him than the news about her husband. "I racked my brains for something suitably decadent for this woman but with no luck. One night I awoke around three in the morning with this theme surfacing from my subconscious. It was something I had written in 1933 and discarded, knowing then that it was far too modernistic to be acceptable to the musically Neanderthal people for whom I was working. So, in the middle of the night, I searched frantically through old manuscripts and after a couple of hours I found this thing. Miraculously I didn't have to change a note, as originally conceived it was just the right length for this scene with Britt and Brando. All I did was hand it to the orchestrator. Eddie Powell looked at it and said, 'Isn't this kind of way-out for 1942?' I reminded him, as gently as possible, that Strauss's *Salome* was written in 1905, and that by 1910, Schoenberg was doing things which made my little ditty sound like something out of Carrie Jacobs Bond by Charles Wakefield Cadman. He agreed. Moral: don't throw anything away, and, by God, I never do."

Friedhofer's most charming score is contained in *The Bishop's Wife*, a Goldwyn picture of 1948, in which Cary Grant appears as a kind of blithe spirit, materialising in answer to the prayers of a beset young bishop, David Niven, whose diligent efforts to raise money for a new cathedral are bringing him to the verge of an estrangement from his beautiful wife, Loretta Young. Grant, as Dudley, is a genial chap who performs all the required miracles but provokes jealousy on the part of the bishop when his wife apparently falls in love with their philanthropic guest. This is a situation Dudley clears up before he departs into ether. Friedhofer's music for this story is humorous and delightful, he uses a classical *concerto grosso* form for the opening music and sparks it with the cheeky, earthy sounds of a saxophone for Dudley, the handsome, celestial visitor with the winning ways.

Completely the opposite of the music for *The Bishop's Wife* is Friedhofer's score for Billy Wilder's *Ace in the Hole*, which the composer considers one of his most satisfying assignments. The film was none too well received by press reviewers, possibly because it put the Fourth Estate in a very poor light. Kirk Douglas plays a newspaperman of shallow character and thin values who arrives in a small New Mexico town to work as a reporter, presumably having lost better jobs with better papers. He is assigned to cover a rattlesnake hunt but spots a journalistic opportunity when he discovers a man trapped in an old Indian excavation. Rather than rescue the man, he keeps him there in order to string out his exclusive reportage of the situation. Says Friedhofer, "It was a gutsy story and it got to me. I felt I could commentate on this miserable character, this exploitation of his, and the morbid curiosity of the people who traipsed to the scene, everybody cashing in on it. It had the kind of gallows humour that Billy Wilder is prone to, and which appeals to me. However, he was upset by the fact that I hadn't written a schmaltzy score, or at least something Wagnerian, since that's his favourite composer. When we were recording, he said, 'It's a good score, but there isn't a note of melody in it.' I replied, 'Billy, you've had the courage to put on the screen a bunch of really reprehensible people. Did you want me to soften them?' He got the point. In general, you have to be careful with musical characterisations because the person on the screen—as in life—is not always what he seems, he may be smiling on the surface but snarling underneath. The music should point to the qualities behind the image."

Friedhofer's greatest technical problem in scoring came with *The Sun Also Rises*. He felt *en rapport* with the Hemingway story and he was able to communicate musically the sense of turning the clock back a generation. His opening, in particular, has an enormous sense of nostalgia, the feeling of something *lost*. The problems concern the second half of the film, which takes place in Pamplona during the annual bullfight festival. What we see and hear is a mosaic of events—street parades, celebrations, carousing, bullfights—calling for a cascade of music of various kinds. Friedhofer worked with composer-orchestrator Alexander Courage on these sequences. "Alex is an *aficionado* of Spanish bullfight and festival music and we worked for two weeks on a sort of road map of themes, a layout of cross fades. Very interesting and very difficult."

One of the films that gave Friedhofer particular scope in scoring was *Boy on a Dolphin*, a romantic, exotic story filmed in the Aegean Islands and beautifully photographed by Milton Krasner. The film contained more than usual footage allowing for aural description—mountains, a harbour, a monastery, the Acropolis, cafés, street scenes and several long sequences of diving for ancient treasure. "The nature of the film called for music written in an idiom which has been current for approximately fifty years. In other words it is music essentially romantic and impressionistic in style. Anything in the nature of *avant-garde* experimentation would have been

**Hugo Friedhofer (left) with orchestrator Edward Powell during the recording of Friedhofer's score for** Soldier of Fortune **on Stage One, Twentieth Century-Fox in 1955.**

a shocking intrusion, completely out of harmony with the film itself. Some austere souls might even call it 'lush,' with no intention of using that adjective in a complimentary sense. I won't waste my time in vehement protestations. Southern Europe, and particularly the Mediterranean area, is hardly an Arctic wilderness." Friedhofer's score for this film also made use of Greek folk music although with no attempt on his part to establish absolute authenticity. "The countries bordering the Mediterranean have been swapping cultures for centuries now, and to determine what is purely regional, and what has been borrowed, would take years of delving into the subject. With only ten weeks in which to write the music for *Boy on a Dolphin,* the best I could hope to achieve was a stylisation which would be theatrically effective, rather than a completely truthful recreation, which might very well have turned out to be dull no matter how authentic."

Queried about his style, Friedhofer squirms and denies he has striven consciously for a personal style. Some ears detect a certain Hindemithian quality, certain suggestions of lineal dissonance. Friedhofer thinks of himself as being in the mainstream of modern music without being "far out." He was schooled in the German masters, grew up in the jazz-impressed Twenties, and he is particularly fond of Spanish, Mexican and Latin music, although he doesn't know why. "Maybe there was a Phoenician in the woodpile away back. Or maybe I felt my flat-footed Teutonic genes could stand an infusion of Mediterranean sunshine."

Friedhofer's affinity for Mexican music is part of his larger interest in Mexico, where he hopes to retire once done with the Hollywood scene. This interest is apparent in his vigorous score for the Gary Cooper-Burt Lancaster romp *Vera Cruz* (1954). The score points to something Friedhofer feels keenly about—the frequent use of Spanish-type music in films about Mexico. One of the few Steiner scores he dislikes is *The Treasure of Sierra Madre,* even though it's one of the composer's most popular. He criticises it for not being truly Mexican. "Read Prescott and you'll quickly latch on to the idea that our neighbours south of the border aren't exactly enamoured of Cortez and his crew. Actually, the folk music of Mexico has, to me at least, a strong aroma of Old Vienna, on which has been superimposed a curious rhythmic vitality. The Moorish influence, which is such a marked characteristic of Spanish music is not at all noticeable in the Mexican folk-idiom. Art in Mexico is strongly nationalistic and largely derived from the pre-Hispanic heritage. Listen to Chavez's *Sinfonia India* and Revueltas's *Sensemaya*—Spanish flavoured they are not. Furthermore, if you want to make yourself unpopular in Mexico, try speaking Spanish with the Castilian lisp on the sibilants. The natives will either laugh contemptuously or beat the hell out of you. The best film score by a North American in the Mexican idiom, for my money, is Alex North's *Viva Zapata!* Alex lived in Mexico for a while; consequently, he knows the difference. I found out the difference through research and through having been resident there for nigh on four months while composing and recording the score for *Vera Cruz.*"

As Friedhofer sees it and hears it, it isn't the function of a film score to be wholly autonomous. "In this respect it differs from music written for concert hall presentation in much the same way that design for a stage setting differs from an easel painting. For example, a film score conceived with as much detail, or as richly textured as the *Fourth Symphony* of Brahms (we should live so long) would not be a good film score, regardless of its merits as music. Being inherently self-sufficient, it would be constantly drawing attention to itself at the expense of the drama it was intended to enhance. I don't mean to imply that music for a film should be as consistently bland and unobtrusive as the so-called 'mood music' which accompanies the rattle of dishes and the buzz of small talk in a coffee shop. To the contrary, it is my belief that the ideal film score is one which, while at all times maintaining its own integrity of line, manages at the same time to coalesce with all the other filmic elements involved; sometimes as a frame, at other times as a sort of connective tissue, and in still other (although naturally rarer) instances, as the chief actor in the drama. Other than this, it would be foolhardy to make any sort of sweeping statement as to what film music should or should not be. The problems confronting the film composer are never the same twice, and require in every instance another solution. Every film that comes along constitutes a problem and a challenge—unless one is completely bogged down in the morass of one's own *cliché.*"

In the perpetual war between composers and producers Friedhofer feels he has fared fairly well, and that he has had less music scrapped than many of his colleagues, "Possibly because I was chicken, and gauged the calibre of my man beforehand." He sympathises with producers because their job requires them to be omniscient. "The omniscience of producers isn't taxed as much in the fields of writing, photography and acting as it is in music, which seems to be a closed shop to them. In many instances they are forced, in order to save face, to assume a profundity about music they don't possess." Film music, claims Friedhofer, must not be compared with concert music—its purpose and therefore its texture is different. Producers, like the public, are unmindful of this. On the other hand he is not overly sympathetic to composers who complain about not having enough time. "The composers of the baroque period also had to turn out scores whether they felt like it or not. They, too, had no time to second guess. When Papa Haydn got another order from Count Esterhazy he first knelt in prayer, then spat on his hands and wrote another masterpiece." However, the film composer is much less likely to turn out a masterpiece because his music is determined by the nature of the film, and the technique obliges him to curtail material he might otherwise like to expand. Asked to explain his own *modus operandi*, Friedhofer says with characteristic bluntness, "I write 'em as I hear 'em. When I walk into the studio I'm not an artist so much as a plumber."

\* \* \*

**David Raksin. (Photo by Sergis Alberts)**

**David Raksin** is a musician of substance—unfortunately substance beyond the taste of many of the film-makers for whom he has worked, and over the heads of most moviegoers. He is thus caught in the valley of despair familiar to film composers, between the peaks of ignorance and indifference. Raksin, however, is a man of forceful personality, neither reticent nor modest by nature, and he is too creative to give way to despair. When not working on films, he writes and conducts concert works and contributes much of his time to music education. Raksin has for some years conducted a class in film music at the University of Southern California, and he has written scores for the theatre workshop plays of that and other universities.

Raksin is also an outspoken man and it is likely that his honesty has injured his career. About the trade he has practised for more than thirty years, he says: "The stuff we do is sometimes good, sometimes bad, and sometimes lost. Sometimes you work on a picture that's worth doing, most of the time you don't. But at least you are composing *all the time*, and to me that's a marvellous thing. I get paid for doing what I'd be doing anyhow. And when we work for people of some sophistication and intelligence, who are not inclined to underestimate the public, we do work which amounts to something. All too often, the music is too good for the film. The frequency with which this happens is more an indictment of films than a compliment to composers."

Raksin was one of the few musicians to turn up in Hollywood in 1935—he was then twenty-three—with the specific ambition to be a film composer. Most of the musicians in the industry at that time were men who had drifted into films from other musical avenues, some of them at first reluctantly, like Alfred Newman, and some, like Miklos Rozsa, who had to be persuaded. Raksin was indoctrinated at an early age; his father was, for an extended period, a conductor of scores for silent films at the Metropolitan Opera House in Philadelphia, in the days when that huge edifice was used as a movie theatre. Raksin senior sometimes augmented the supplied scores with bits of his own composition, and on Saturdays he would take his son to the theatre with him. "I would sit alongside him in the orchestral pit as he conducted with a baton with a battery-lit tip on it. I was fascinated. I liked the whole idea, even then I was impressed by what 'picture music' was able to do to people, by its contribution to the emotional effect of a film, and I was heard to say that was what I wanted to do when I grew up."

Raksin's father also operated a music store, and Raksin worked in it while attending the Central High School in Philadelphia, where he played in the school orchestra, edited the school magazine and taught himself to play the organ and percussion instruments. He studied piano with a teacher and learned about woodwinds from his father, who was an accomplished clarinetist. On the side, twelve-year-old Raksin organised his own dance band, which played at private parties around Philadelphia, and by fifteen he was a fully qualified member of the Musicians' Union. Raksin earned his tuition at the University of Pennsylvania by playing in dance bands and the orchestra of WCAU—the CBS radio station in Philadelphia. At Penn he studied composition under Harl McDonald, then head of the music department, and participated in practically all the university's musical activities. He also compiled an extensive glossary of jazz terminology.

At twenty-one and armed with a degree in music, Raksin went to New York and played in, and arranged for, various dance bands, including Benny Goodman's. At one point, conductor Al Goodman bought from Raksin an arrangement of Gershwin's *I Got Rhythm* and when played by Goodman and his pop concert orchestra in a broadcast, it brought more offers for arrangements and eventually a contract with Harms, one of the mightiest of the music publishing houses. Raksin was with Harms for two years when a call came from Hollywood. Alfred Newman, who had had Raksin recommended to him by Eddie Powell and Herbert Spencer, two of Hollywood's top arrangers, needed someone to work with Charlie Chaplin on the score of *Modern Times*. Newman would conduct the score but hadn't time to arrange Chaplin's music. Raksin's job was to make musical logic from the humming and whistling of Chaplin. He soon began to argue with the comedian, who fired him after ten days. Newman looked at the sketches for the score Raksin had concocted from Chaplin's ideas, and he persuaded Chaplin to take Raksin back. The comedian agreed and the job spread out over a period of five months, a rough baptism but one which enabled Raksin to confirm his ambition to compose for the screen. Looking back on the session with Chaplin: "He was an instinctive musician. He had, partly based on his background in the English music halls, a certain conception of the way music should go in his films. He knew what he wanted and he knew better than anyone else what was best for his films. But he couldn't write down the music that came to his mind because he had never learned how. Charlie and I would sometimes fight like tigers but I felt his film was too good for anything but the best and he came to respect this. He is a man for whom I have the utmost personal and professional regard."

David Raksin's recognition as a composer of first rank came in 1944 with his score for *Laura*. All through the late Thirties and the early Forties he had worked at various studios on a large number of films, sometimes as the composer, sometimes as an arranger and contributor to scores assigned to other composers. They were the years in which he learned his craft. *Laura* was not designed by Twentieth Century-Fox as one of their

**Charles Chaplin, Mr. and Mrs. Arnold Schoenberg and a young David Raksin at the Chaplin Studio in Hollywood in 1935.**

mightiest pictures; that it turned out a minor classic was a happy accident and due also to the flair of its director, Otto Preminger. Neither was Raskin's music given any promotion by the studio. It wasn't until the picture was in the theatres and requests by the thousands came into the record stores asking for a recording that the studio and the publishers realised the value of the music. With this public appetite, the publishers quickly decided to turn the theme into a song and presented Raksin with an array of assorted lyrics, all of which he turned down. Recalls Raksin, "They were aghast at my lack of appreciation. The conversation went something like this:

Publisher: Who are you to turn down these lyrics?
Raksin:    Who do you have to be?
Publisher: You keep up that attitude and we may decide not to publish the thing at all.
Raksin:    Well, it could be worse.
Publisher: How?
Raksin:    You could publish it with those lyrics.

"Anyway, I knew what I wanted and that was a lyric by Johnny Mercer, the Flying Wallenda of lyricists. I gave the melody to him and he went off to meditate, or whatever marvellous thing he does, and the rest is history."

*Laura*, as a song, is among the half dozen most recorded pieces of music; its popularity never seems to wane. As used in the film, the melody is a motif for the principal character, a girl who has been murdered by a jealous lover, an acidly witty writer played in bravura style by Clifton Webb. A detective is assigned to the case, Dana Andrews, and he gradually falls in love with the girl's image, mostly from staring at a beguiling portrait of her. By varying the theme, Raksin makes it speak for the detective's strange obsession—the image of the beautiful girl haunts him, irritates him and moves him to anger at the killer and a determination to solve the crime. The Raksin score is one of the foremost examples of the power of music on film. Frequently asked whether or not it was a melody that came easily to him, he replies, "It came quickly, once it came, but I had worried greatly about whether such a melody would come at all. I had from Friday until Monday morning to turn up with something immortal, and after all, you don't do anything immortal every day."

The value of *Laura* to Raksin, aside from the obvious monetary one, was as an argument to use against producers who would consider his scores too hard to understand. He could point to *Laura* as proof of his ability to create melody but that it wasn't the kind of composition to use in the film under discussion. "It's an odd thing, but people make pictures with all kinds of actual or implied violence, and yet they cannot understand the equivalent of that in music. They are a century—and in cases of extreme intelligence, a quarter of a century—behind in understanding what music has to offer."

Raksin's contributions to the art of scoring range from the melodic appeal of the theme in *The Bad and the Beautiful*, one of the longest melodic lines ever invented for the screen, to the dry, dissonant lines of *Al Capone*, a score full of subtly inter-related material. Possibly none but musicians actually hear the inter-relationships but the subliminal effect on the viewer is one of helping to tie together the disparate bits and pieces of the visual. Music can give a film a sense of unity and there are scenes in *Al Capone* that would not have worked as well without that aid. Raksin can be cerebral, as in *Force of Evil*, and *Whirlpool*, and he can be charming, as in *Forever Amber*, and *The Unicorn in the Garden*.

One of Raksin's treasures is a letter from James Thurber, which reads, in part: "I am not a music maker but I enjoyed your music for the unicorn and remember with affection the recorder that spoke up when the unicorn appeared. It sounded exactly right for unicorn." Thurber was referring to

Raksin's score for the delightful UPA cartoon, *The Unicorn in the Garden*. The recorder mentioned is the English straight flute, which was an inspired choice to describe an animal as odd, whimsical and forlorn as Thurber's unicorn.

The score for *Forever Amber* called for a seventy-six piece orchestra and almost two hours of music. The lavish film was a disappointment but Raksin's music, fortunately available to those with the 78 rpm album he made at the time, makes for enchanting listening. Aside from its value to the picture, the score is an exercise and a study in period music. "It was an absolute joy to do. Some people have said it sounds rather satirical, perhaps it is but it was a gentle satire because I love that period of music. The purists like to point out that it doesn't sound very English. I can only point out that the music of the court of Charles the Second was greatly influenced by the French. I aimed for a kind of mock-Lully, mock-Scarlatti sound, but again, a loving kind of mocking."

Raksin has had his share of poor pictures on which he was expected to work wonders. The capable professional is able to manufacture musical sounds appropriate to requirements, but as Raksin explains, "Ersatz emotion is much harder to disguise than real music is to write. It's easier on one's conscience to be compassionate than to simulate compassion, and consequently, more practical. Many films present in themselves challenges that arouse the composer, but when you cope with one that doesn't provide emotional or intellectual incentive, you must provide them for yourself. In *Forever Amber*, the Great Fire of London was presented almost as an interlude between beds; I tried to play it for the affliction it really was. I may experiment with musical forms and devices. In one film I used a twelve-tone row whose first five notes spelled out the name of the film's hero, which was otherwise not revealed until the last few seconds. The head of the music department asked what had prompted me to be so daring, and I replied that it was in the hope that the producer would come running out of the theatre after the preview crying, 'Fire that man, he gave away the secret of the picture in the main title.'"

Writing music for films is possibly more fraught with pitfalls and frustrations than most other professions. It needs a tough-minded man to survive the sometimes brutal decisions that affect the scoring. David Raksin recalls that while working on the score of *Carrie* he had a scene near the end of the film in which he was able to write a piece six and a half minutes in length, a piece that carried the visual story. The producers decided to cut the scene to forty-six seconds. There was another production decision on that film that was even harder for the composer to appreciate. "Carrie has left Hurstwood (Laurence Olivier) and goes her own way to fulfilment. Your re-introduction to Hurstwood—in the original print of the film—takes place in a horrid turn-of-the-century New York flophouse. We had a long dolly shot through the flophouse—all you hear are sounds of men who have awoken drunk, coughing, retching, spitting. The camera moves into this tiny cubicle in which you see this wreck of a man who was once so beautiful. Director William Wyler said he wanted the music for this scene to be 'towering.' I said, 'Willie, there's nothing I can do to approach the image you have on camera, and you know damn well that if I did, you'd have to squeeze the music down in order to hear all this coughing and spitting. What I have to do is think of something very meagre. I don't know what but give me a little time.' Well, I thought about it and came up with an idea: when you first saw Hurstwood he was the manager of a swank restaurant in Chicago and looked stunning in his morning coat and striped trousers. You saw him through Carrie's eyes and he was a sort of demi-God. Off screen there was a little orchestra playing a period waltz. I used this waltz as an association for Hurstwood and it made certain transformations in the film. Now I took a celeste and had them tape the bars, so that it would sound like a doll's piano. I played the waltz on this thing in a halting way, as a child would. The notes were dull and non-reverberating. It meant little when we recorded it but when we put it in the film the effect was absolutely hair-raising—all of a sudden you felt as if your skin was crawling. Everyone thought it was a 'tour de force.' But the producers decided the scene was too harrowing and the whole thing was cut."

Some years later, Raksin suffered an even keener disappointment when his score for *Separate Tables* was rejected by the producers as being too modernistic, too contemporary—in other words, far too cerebral for their own tastes. Raksin simplified his score and incorporated, as he was ordered to do, a rather tepid title song written by Harry Warren. He feels the change in the score weakened the film, that it altered some of the emphasis on the characters. Raksin has several times used a scene from *Separate Tables* in his film composition class at the University of Southern California. He illustrates it in two ways—first with the score as it was heard in the released film, and then the scene as he had originally scored it. The scene involves Rita Hayworth attempting to inveigle the affection of her former husband, Burt Lancaster. The original scoring was contrapuntal, an "edgy" kind of music to suggest the odd relationship between the characters on scene—the woman using her wiles on a proud man trying to resist. The producers insisted the scene be scored romantically. On one occasion in his classroom, Raksin says he asked his students for the comparative effects of the two pieces of scoring—the romantic and then the other. One girl put up her hand and commented, "The second time, there were more close-ups." She had missed the device but got the message. The romantic scoring certainly matched the vamp image of Hayworth but the more subtle music pointed up the uncomfortable intimacy of the scene.

Raksin has been unlucky with some of his assignments, not merely in having to score inferior pictures—that's the plight of composers in general—but in working on films that deserved much better reception than they received from the public. Two cases in particular: *Too Late Blues* and *Will Penny*. *Too Late Blues* was made by John Cassavetes in 1961, and starred Bobby Darin and Stella Stevens in a story about jazz musicians. The failure of the film killed the proposed recording of the score, a great pity in view of the artistry involved. Raksin created a dozen pieces exploring the various kinds of jazz, all of them tuneful and entertaining and played by the best musicians money can buy. The score is highly regarded among musicians, and as a signal event in scoring, producer Martin Poll requested Raksin to use several of the *Too Late Blues* pieces in his score for *Sylvia*.

*Will Penny* is an unusual and an exceptional Western. Beautifully photographed in colour by Lucien Ballard, it is one of the few films to depict the cowboy for what he was—a working man on a horse doing a rough, grimy, lonely job. It also pointed out that the cowboy was often an illiterate and probably none too well adjusted, socially or personally. Raksin had scored other Westerns; his music for *Smoky* and *Jubal* are tuneful but without the tinge of melancholy that is apparent in the *Will Penny* music. Says Raksin: "There's something about the grandeur and the loneliness of the Western landscape that appeals to a composer's innards. Most composers like scoring Westerns because of the opportunity for descriptive music, and the opportunity for the music to be heard, due to the long, relatively silent sequences where it can assert itself. *Will Penny* required a special kind of expressive music to delineate the title character, an over-the-hill cowboy who knows there's nothing much left for him. I got the idea for a melody—after much worrying—when I watched Charlton Heston doing a scene. I was suddenly struck by the poignancy of it. The theme emerged full blown in my head. Bill Stinson, the head of the music at Paramount, liked it and commented that it had a Slavic quality. I said, 'Yes, I'm thinking of calling it *On the Steppes of Central Utah*.'"

Several scenes in *Will Penny* bear aural scrutiny. In particular the scene where Donald Pleasence, as a mad, renegade, frontier preacher has just had one of his sons killed in a gunfight by Penny. In a rage, he delivers a series of biblical imprecations, "An eye for an eye, etc. etc.," and the accompanying music is a set of variations on a twelve-tone row derived from the main theme. The music punctuates Pleasence's fearful speech, and its odd dissonance helps promote the impression of madness. At the end of the film, Penny, a basically warm-hearted but inexpressive man, realises that he loves a widow and her son and that they want him, but he also realises that it is too late in his life for him to adjust to such a change. In declining their love he condemns himself to continued loneliness. Raksin scores this scene in a way that makes it both radiant and touching, and articulates in a way the characters themselves cannot. The music *says* what is on their minds and in their hearts.

David Raksin is occasionally criticised by his colleagues for writing music that is too involved and that he would perhaps land more assignments if he were willing to simplify his scoring, in short, stress his gift for melody rather than his interest in subtle sonorities. But Raksin is a man not much prone to bending. In the late Thirties and during the years of the Second World War when Arnold Schoenberg was living in Los Angeles and available as a tutor, Raksin was among the composers who went to him. "I wanted to learn from a man with such overall grasp of form in music, or larger form, which has always been a problem for me. I never believed that by filling in the cubes and other structures of a sonata form that I could compose music. There's a time in your life when you think there's some magic thing somebody can teach you that will let you by-pass the sweating and suffering. There isn't. But a wise man can tell you when not to feel guilty."

Film music, feels Raksin, could and should occupy a kind of middle musical ground, between the poles of popular and serious music, as well as being a meeting ground for both. As for the tired old dictum that film music is not supposed to be heard: "That's like saying breathing is only useful when you don't know you're doing it. Film music is utilitarian, but so are a lot of things and some of them are quite beautiful in their own right. A teapot is made for a purpose but it can also be a work of art."

Raksin is long inured to the disdain in which Hollywood is held by some, and the peculiar kind of snobbism expressed toward the composing of film music. "I've lived here so long I've learned that the blanket-indicters can't tell the difference between what is good and what isn't unless they're told. They lump people of talent and hacks together without bothering to discover the many different forms of aspiration and realisation. I think they do themselves out of something."

# 6
# Americana to the Fore

Odd as it may seem from this distance, the composers who found it most difficult to establish themselves in the so-called Golden Age of Hollywood were the Americans of serious musical background, those who can be referred to, vaguely and for lack of a better term, as "longhairs." The reasons are mostly historical.

The concept of film scoring in the early years of sound in California was influenced for the most part by the kind of music that had been used in conjunction with silent films. A tradition had grown up from the use of popular classical music, which was basically of the romantic-symphonic school of the late Nineteenth century. It was a style more germane to European composers. It was also the general *universal* taste in concert music, and the Hollywood studios were, after all, turning out product with an eye on the world market. This was a period, too, when hardly anyone thought in terms of *serious* American music, the evidence was overpoweringly of the other kind.

In a broader sense, the choice of music in Hollywood films of the Thirties was part of the rather rapid growth of music in America since the turn of the century. There then began a ground swell of American music—work songs, Negro spirituals, minstrel shows, burlesque, ragtime, blues, dixieland jazz, and a growing body of publishers of popular songs and dance music. The American musical theatre was long in gestation but it suddenly burst and blossomed abundantly after the first World War with a wave of confidence and enthusiasm. All of a sudden it seemed as if all the bright, vital young men of music were in New York and ready with bags full of songs. In 1919, George Gershwin knocked out a bouncing, irrepressible song called *Swanee*, whose energy and appeal seemed to symbolise the whole landslide of American music that follows: Gershwin, Vincent Youmans, Richard Rodgers, Irving Berlin, Arthur Schwartz, Harold Arlen, Cole Porter, Sammy Fain, Harry Warren, Jerome Kern, Jimmy McHugh and others all shot up like meteors in the Roaring Twenties. This—to the whole world—was American music, and what happened in New York had a direct bearing on what happened in Hollywood.

The style was set in the East, and those Americans who were interested in writing serious music for the concert hall, or for original American opera and ballet were a sadly unappreciated minority. The musicians who gravitated toward the film studios of Hollywood were, even though they may have had classical training, men who had made an impression in theatrical or popular music forms.

George Antheil.

One of the few cerebral American composers of the Thirties to establish himself in Hollywood was **George Antheil**, which surprised everyone because Antheil had made his name writing quite iconoclastic music. He was a darling of the Parisian intellectuals and his concerts drew packed audiences in the serious music salons of Paris. Jean Cocteau hailed him as a genius. In 1927 Antheil created a great deal of noise with his *Ballet Mécanique:* the work was scored for anvils, electric bells, car horns, sixteen player pianos and an airplane propeller, plus orchestra. Said Antheil at the time, "My idea was to warn the age in which I was living of the simultaneous beauty and danger of its own unconscious mechanistic philosophy." Unfortunately, the notorious composition blemished his career, it became the one thing with which his name became identified and he regretted it. Antheil grew more conservative with time and his first major scoring job in Hollywood was not for some weird effort but for Cecil B. DeMille's epic Western *The Plainsman.* His music for the sequence in which Gary Cooper, as Wild Bill Hickok, is tied to a stake and tortured is much more modernistic than anything that had previously been written for that kind of picture but DeMille was intrigued by it and decided to give Antheil another historical pageant to score, *The Buccaneer,* much to the surprise of the other musicians then working at Paramount. Antheil's music for *The Buccaneer* served the picture beautifully, it was clearly music composed by someone of taste and skill yet he also did what the lesser composers at the studio would have strived for—to write a score with good tunes and rousing emotions. Antheil felt at the time that he was on shaky grounds. DeMille assigned him to write the score for *Union Pacific* but when he came to play his themes for DeMille he found all the other composers and arrangers at Paramount sitting with DeMille. Much as DeMille liked the music he was a man who could be swayed and Antheil could tell from the dour expressions on the faces of the other composers that he had been counted out. *Union Pacific* finally emerged with a patchwork score done by no less than four Paramount composers.

George Antheil left Hollywood in 1939 and went back to writing absolute music. He had assumed his career scoring pictures had died an early death but he returned in 1946 to score an interesting and very unusual Republic film, *The Specter of the Rose,* and then remained in California until he died in 1958. Ironically, his once brilliant reputation as a composer of symphonic, operatic and chamber music diminished and the last decade of his life was spent in film scoring. He wrote interesting scores for several of the films Humphrey Bogart made for Columbia, notably *Knock on Any Door,* and *In a Lonely Place,* and in 1952 Antheil became associated with Stanley Kramer, first scoring two of Kramer's smaller scale films, *The Sniper,* and *The Juggler* and ending with the large and overly weighted spectacle *The Pride and the Passion,* unfortunately the only one of Antheil's score issued on a disc.

Antheil, like most of the educated musicians who found themselves part of the glitter of Hollywood, was always critical of films and film music but he once said, "I think this is one of the few so-called art colonies in the world which actually works." He also spoke for all film composers when he wrote in his book *Bad Boy of Music,* published by Doubleday, Doran & Company, Inc. in 1945:

Hollywood music is very nearly a public communication, like radio. If you are a movie fan (and who isn't?) you may sit in a movie theatre three times a week listening to the symphonic background scores which Hollywood composers concoct. What happens? Your musical tastes become molded by these scores, heard without knowing it. You *see* love, and you *hear* it. Simultaneously. It makes sense. Music suddenly becomes a language for you, without your knowing it. You cannot see and hear such stuff week in and year out without forming some kind of taste for it. You do not have to listen to a radio program of stupid banal music. But you cannot see your movies without being compelled to listen.

In this special regard I sometimes wonder greatly at music critics. They take infinite pains with the molding of public taste, at least insofar as the concert hall and the symphonic radio program is concerned, but they absolutely ignore the most important thing of all, the background movie score.

\* \* \*

The place of **Virgil Thomson** in the annals of American film music is one of, deservedly, veneration. It's also unique in that he has written only six film scores, with just one of them for a theatrical feature—*The Goddess,* made in Hollywood in 1958. Thomson's esteem in this medium rests upon his work for three documentaries, *The Plow that Broke the Plains, The River,* and *Louisiana Story.* He re-worked the scores for these films into concert suites, and they have each been widely performed and recorded. Each is a monument of film music.

Thomson, born in Kansas City, Missouri in 1896, has been a vital force in American music, not alone as a composer but as an author and a music critic. From 1940 to 1956 he wrote critiques for *The New York Herald Tribune* and his columns had considerable bearing on American musical matters. In 1936 he was asked by the Resettlement Administration of the government to score their documentary, *The Plow that Broke the Plains.* Produced by Pare Lorentz, the film powerfully dealt with the glory and the desolation of the Great Plains, the narration begins: "This is a record of the land, of soil rather than people . . . the four hundred million acres of wind-swept grass lands that spread from the Texas Panhandle to Canada . . ." The film outlines the history of the region, the growth of the cattle empires, the coming of the railroad and the immigrants, and the turning of the land into farms and vast fields of wheat. The story

**Virgil Thomson, extreme right, at the recording of his** Louisiana Story **suite. To the left of Thomson is recording engineer Robert Fine. Seated are Helen Van Dongen, conductor Eugene Ormandy and producer Robert Flaherty.**

builds and builds, and then crashes—the stock market disaster of 1929 and the Depression adversely affect the Great Plains, but not nearly so devastatingly as the fantastic drought of the mid-Thirties. The ruined settlers of this immense man-made dust bowl fought their barren lands until their stock, their machinery and their homes were finished. Then, like their ancestors, they packed up and moved further West—not in covered wagons but in old motor vehicles. Thomson's music for this documentary reflects the joy and the despair, the grandeur and the desolation in every frame. The score is epic Americana, it involves hymnal passages, blues, and settings of folk melodies, in addition to his descriptive passages for pastoral scenes and human activity.

A year later Virgil Thomson was again approached by the government, this time the Farm Security Administration, to supply music for another documentary produced by Pare Lorentz, *The River*. The river in question was the Mississippi and Thomson gave it a tonal setting that again mixed original composition with folk themes. The concert suite derived from the score is in four movements and it fairly closely follows the progression of the music as it was used in the film. There are four movements: *The Old South* is a broad musical subject, evocative of the area and its history. *Industrial Expansion in the Mississippi Valley* describes scenes of new factories and the new way of life they bring, scenes of town life, Saturday night celebrations, etc. *Erosion and Floods* is a slow movement, poignant and slightly dissonant; and the *Finale* is mostly bright and optimistic. The four movements constitute what is virtually a symphony, and the composition is a masterly example of the use of colourful scoring in a documentary of great scope and skilful construction. However, it's well to bear in mind that few films of any kind allow for quite that musical scope. It also points to the difference in scoring documentaries and feature films. It is easier in most documentaries to maintain musical forms than in theatrical features, the one often allows for elongated lines and the other often does not.

*Louisiana Story* is even more of a musical subject than Thomson's previous vehicles. Made by the late Robert Flaherty in 1948, the film takes place in the Bayou region of Louisiana, among the French speaking residents of the area, the Acadians or "Cajuns" as they call themselves. *Louisiana Story* is much more an atmospheric than a dramatically narrative picture and Thomson had ample opportunity to use music freely. Interestingly, and exceptionally, the recording of the musical track for the film was made by forty-one members of the Philadelphia Orchestra conducted by Eugene Ormandy. The story line is a simple one: it tells in the main of a young boy and his adventures in the Bayou swamps, and his wonderment at the coming of modern machinery—an oil well crew with drilling rigs and bulldozers—into his backwoods domain.

Thomson derived two orchestral suites from his score for *Louisiana Story*, one is a slightly expanded version of his original, descriptive music, and the other is a group of his charming settings of melodies native to the region. The latter suite, the most popular of the two, is titled *Acadian Songs and Dances*. Thomson selected the tunes from Irene Therese Whitfield's collection of *Louisiana French Folk Songs*. Since the tunes in that collection are composed only of bare melodic lines, Thomson could use his taste and skill to bring them to orchestral life. This he did not only deftly, but delightfully. This "Cajun" music is what Thomson used to describe the activities and life style of the people of the Bayou. The other suite is divided into four movements: *Pastorale,* the opening music of the film, describes the boy as he glides through the swamps in his little home-made canoe, noticing the plantlife, the birds and the swamp animals. Later it describes the manoeuvres of the amphibious oil-drilling buggies. *Chorale* is the music that accompanies the boy as he plays in a tree top with his pet raccoon, and then as he watches the oil barge approaching. *Passacaglia* describes the boy's adventures robbing an alligator's nest of its eggs, and *Fugue* is the chromatic music that accompanies the boy as he fights to land an alligator he has hooked with his fishing rod.

Thomson's score for *Louisiana Story* won him the Pulitzer Prize for Music in 1949. The music for the film repays listening on every level—as an example of film composition, as skilful orchestration and as a fascinating treatment of indigenous musical material. Aside from their functional value, these three documentary scores by Thomson attain that utmost criterion of film music—the ability to stand by itself unquestionably when divorced from the film.

*      *      *

Neither Aaron Copland nor Virgil Thomson have in any way implied a lack of respect for the film as an outlet for musical composition, in fact, their appreciation of the possibilities in scoring films is particularly keen. Thomson's conception of scoring is that it supplies a warmth to the figures on the screen, giving them a communicable sympathy they might otherwise not have and that good scoring can bridge the gap between the audience and the screen. Copland has emphatically stated many times that he considers the sound film, along with the invention of radio and recording, as comparable to the advancement in human comprehension as that brought about by the printing press. In the wake of the discovery of radio, the phonograph, and the film came new listening audiences, audiences in addition to those at concerts and operas. Copland has always looked upon the cinema as a serious challenge to composers and he makes a most important point, "The cultural level of music is certain to be raised if better music is written for films."

**Aaron Copland.**

**Aaron Copland** was a well established and respected composer when he first turned his attention to film scoring. In 1939 he supplied the music to a documentary, *The City,* a freely flowing impression of contemporary American life which was presented at the New York World's Fair. Copland later extracted and re-wrote two sections of this score for his concert suite *Music for Movies.* The titles given to the movements are self explanatory: *New England Countryside,* and *Sunday Traffic.* The same suite also contains two movements from Copland's next film score—his first done in Hollywood—*Of Mice and Men.* In writing this score Copland claims he deliberately kept away from overlush scoring, the kind that was quite common on the screen at that time—1940—the kind that often defeats its own purpose by being overemphatic. For *Of Mice and Men* Copland wrote music that was suggestive of California ranch life and since John Steinbeck's story concerns itinerant farm hands, some of the melodies have a simple, folksonglike character, the kind the workers themselves might have whistled. The two sections of this score Copland uses in his *Music for Movies* suite are *Barley Wagons,* and *Threshing Machines.* The first piece has a pastoral quality, as the wagons move across the fields, and the other is a fairly obvious piece of sound picturing done in a rhythmic, happy style.

Shortly after scoring *Of Mice and Men* Copland was contracted to provide music for more Americana, perhaps the definitive example, Thornton Wilder's *Our Town*. The major theme of this score was also included in the *Music of Movies* and titled *Grovers Corner* but both the theme and other sections of the score were later fashioned into a short suite, much performed and several times recorded. The first five notes of the main theme make a melodic statement that beautifully pinpoints Wilder's story, the theme is simple, subjective and the whole score has a misty quality that delicately underlines the poignancy of the film. Copland indicates the atmosphere of the little town, the gentleness of life at this time and place, the sadness, the remoteness. In short, Copland's score for *Our Town* concedes to the primary consideration of film music—that it be entirely appropriate to the visual.

Copland's next score came three years later, for a now almost forgotten film called *The North Star*. Produced in 1943 by Samuel Goldwyn, it was one of Hollywood's rare cinematic tributes to the Russians and their war efforts, probably the reason why the film has virtually vanished. It was, however, the film that demanded more from Copland than any other film on which he has worked and it kept him busy for half a year. Aside from the background score, Copland wrote a number of songs and dances, all of which covered a huge emotional canvas of war, love and comedy. The chief problem was one of style, "I wasn't sure how Russian the music should be. It was something of the same problem that Shostakovitch would have had if he had been asked to supply a score for a movie set in the United States." Copland wisely decided that since the American actors weren't speaking with Russian accents he wouldn't overdo the Russian tone of his score. But the picture was not well received and Copland had his first taste of something with which his Hollywood colleagues were very familiar —that it is impossible to pour a great deal of time, hard work and creativity into a dud film.

Copland did the score for a documentary produced in 1945 by the United States Office of War Information. *The Cummington Story* required Copland once more to underscore life in a rural New England town but this time the theme was a contemporary one and made a plea for tolerance. Copland did not appear on the Hollywood scene until six years after *The North Star*. In 1949 he composed what is possibly his *magnum opus* among film scores, *The Red Pony*. The film was an untypical choice for Republic studios since they specialised in purely programme pictures, largely Westerns, and it is to the credit of the producers that they turned out a thoroughly good film in *The Red Pony*. Obviously they realised that the film would not be a blockbuster and that it might as well be done properly. Having purchased the rights to a story by a master American writer, John Steinbeck, they decided to hire another American master to write the score. It was, however, no long-shot gamble—Copland's music for *Our Town* was the kind of score (and film) that is lauded outside of the United States since it depicts a rather idealised concept of Western American life—the young boy growing up on a horse ranch—that has a universal appeal.

Shortly after completing the score Copland decided to adapt it into a concert suite and as such it has become one of his most popular pieces. "Steinbeck's *The Red Pony* is a series of vignettes concerning a ten-year-old boy called Jody and his life in a California ranch setting. The story gets its warmth and sensitive quality from the character studies of the boy, his grandfather, the cowhand Billy Buck and Jody's parents. The kind of emotions that Steinbeck evokes in his story are basically musical ones since they deal so much with the unexpressed feelings of daily living. In shaping the suite I recast much of the material so that, although all the music may be heard in the film, it has been reorganised as to continuity for concert purposes."

The suite from *The Red Pony* has six movements and they each highlight the main facets of the film. *Morning on the Ranch* suggests the sounds of daybreak and the simplicity of country life. *The Gift* depicts the boy's surprise when his father gives him a pony and his pride in showing it off to his friends. *Dream March* and *Circus Music* describe the boy's daydreams—his imagined adventures as a knight in silver armour and as a ringmaster. *Walk to the Bunkhouse* points up the boy's admiration for Billy Buck who, as Steinbeck put it, "was a fine hand with horses." *Grandfather's Story* underlines an old man's anecdotes about his days as a young man crossing the plains in a wagon and his bitterness in lamenting what he considers the disappearance of the spirit of the Old West. *Happy Ending* re-states the gentle folklike themes of the opening score but this time in a bolder and happier vein.

Copland's score for *The Red Pony* is that ultimate in writing for films—music that perfectly does its job yet lives and breathes and thrives even when divorced from the picture.

The film for which Aaron Copland won his Oscar is *The Heiress* (1949), which fact has an ironic twist to it. After Copland had recorded the score and returned to New York, the front office at Paramount—and producer-director William Wyler must have been the main voice—decided to remove Copland's title music from the picture and replace it with an arrangement of the song "Plaisir d'Amour," which was also featured in the course of the story telling. Copland wrote to the press disclaiming responsibility for that part of the score. Just how much this damaged the picture is hard to tell; certainly it ruined Copland's intentions of setting the tone and character of the story. His original title has a marked tragic-dramatic mood, suggestive of the complicated life of the young woman who is thwarted by a domineering father and cheated by a shallow lover. The title music for a film is the one spot in the score where a composer can employ strictly musical form and summarise the content of the film. Copland in this instance, like the heiress herself, was thus badly cheated. It was a brutal professional insult yet it was one with a strange rebound—this is the only occasion of a composer winning the coveted gold statuette of the Academy of Motion Picture Arts and Sciences for a score minus its title overture, which is the only part of a score the majority of filmgoers ever consciously hear.

Copland's music for *The Heiress* is especially interesting in that it reveals his research into music that was current in New York in 1850. He chose several pieces of the period, including Gossec's *Gavotte*, Ketterer's *Queen of the Flowers*, and several little dance pieces of unknown authorship. To this he added a number of pieces of his own composition cast in the same *genre*. The score is on two levels—foreground music and background, with both helping to tell the story. It is also the only Copland film score in which he has used the operatic device of giving the principal characters a musical motive and then varying the motif according to the shifts in the revelations of the story. Copland mostly disapproves of the leitmotif device in film scoring but he felt it was necessary in *The Heiress* since the story is a series of character studies, principally the main character of the woman whose personality moves from innocence and timidity through love and disappointment to bitterness and reclusiveness. Copland declined to concertise the score, feeling that, eloquent though it might be in the picture, it didn't lend itself to divorcement.

The fact that Copland had won an Oscar and that he was by now quite clearly the foremost American composer made little impression upon the Hollywood producers. Copland has not worked in a Hollywood studio since *The Heiress*, and it was not until fifteen years later that he scored another film. This was a film made in New York by Jack Garfein and starring his then wife Carroll Baker. Its title—*Something Wild*—fairly describes this not very successful picture, telling as it does about a young girl raped in a Brooklyn park and then imprisoned by a brute of a garage mechanic. A none too convincing "beauty and the beast" story, the most interesting things about *Something Wild* are in glimpses of New York and the opportunity it gave Copland to write a musical accompaniment. Rather than allow the score to pass into oblivion along with the film Copland wisely re-wrote it into a compelling symphonic suite, *Music for a Great City*.

Asked why he has scored so few films in the past twenty years, Aaron Copland smiles philosophically and says, "It's simple. They don't ask me."

Copland has also been frequently asked whether or not he likes writing film music, the implication being that it is possibly somewhat degrading for a serious composer to be thus employed. With that implication comes another—that a composer of stature writes for films mainly because of the high pay. Copland squashes this argument immediately. "I would do it even if it were less well paid and moreover, I think most composers would, principally because film music constitutes a new musical medium that exerts a fascination of its own. Actually, it is a new form of dramatic composition and it opens up unexplored possibilities, or should." What bothers Copland about writing for films is its being taken so much for granted by most moviegoers. "Five minutes after the termination of the picture they couldn't tell you whether they had heard music or not. What is lacking here is a proper attitude—one's appreciation of a work of art is partly determined by the amount of preparation one brings to it, and since the majority of movie patrons are undoubtedly musical to some degree, they should be encouraged not to ignore the music; on the contrary, I would hope to convince them that by taking it in they will enrich both their musical and their cinema experience. Hopefully, some day the term 'movie music' will clearly define a specific musical *genre* and will not have, as it does have nowadays, a pejorative meaning."

An American composer greatly respected by the Hollywood music community is **Alex North**. A mild mannered, quietly spoken and completely unpretentious man, he is referred to by the younger composers as The Boss. North is a composer of depth and substance and his music is less obvious than most film scoring. He is the kind of musician who thrives in a community of intelligent film-makers but is likely to be lost and neglected among lesser people. North won an Oscar nomination with his first score in Hollywood, *A Streetcar Named Desire,* in 1951 and went on to score films as varied as *The Member of the Wedding* and *Spartacus, The Rose Tattoo* and *Cleopatra, Who's Afraid of Virginia Woolf?* and *The Agony and the Ecstasy.*

Alex North was born in Philadelphia of Russian parents, and Russia had a part in his musical education, although in a rather bizarre way. As a youngster in a poor family North won a scholarship to study the piano at the Curtis Institute of Music, which led to his winning another scholarship to attend the Juilliard School of Music in New York. It was a four year course in composition but North's financial predicament made the going tough. "To support myself I learned to be a telegraph operator and I worked from six in the evening until two in the morning, and then went to Juilliard during the day. After three and a half years of this my health

Alex North.

descended to the breaking point." In his desperation North hit upon a wild idea. The Russian government was at this time—1934—in dire need of skilled artisans and they were openly inviting engineers, scientists, technicians and doctors to work in the Soviet Union, all expenses paid. North went to the Soviet agency in New York and allowed them to assume he was a telegraphic engineer. "I wanted to go somewhere where my musical education could be subsidised. I was attracted to the idea of studying in Russia, partly because I idolised Prokofiev. The Russians probably thought I would re-work their telegraphic system for them but after a couple of weeks in Moscow I was put to sorting nuts and bolts. They were about to send me home but they were intrigued when I said I was a composer and wanted to study music in Russia. They auditioned me at the Conservatory and I got in. I was there for almost two years; I had picked up a little Russian from my parents, who were born in Odessa, but I had an interpreter who came to the classes with me. But I gradually got homesick for American music. I remember one night playing a recording of Duke Ellington's *Mood Indigo* and breaking into tears. As a kid working in Atlantic City I used to go to the Steel Pier and listen to Paul Whiteman, Coon Sanders and Ted Weems. I soaked up all kinds of jazz, and suddenly it hit me in Moscow. I had to go home."

Back in New York in 1936 North studied with Ernst Toch, then a refugee from Germany. When Toch went to Hollywood to score films he encouraged North to send his compositions to him. "He was a beautiful man. He would comment on my music, correct things and send them back. It was a great help." North also came into contact with Aaron Copland who was helpful in getting North work, writing music for contemporary American ballet companies. "My first functional music was for modern dance. I wrote for Martha Graham, among others, and I joined the Federal Theater Project, along with many other unemployed artists. I wrote music for their plays and this led to offers to score documentary films for commercial companies. Some years later I got to scoring films for the government, for the State Department, the Health Department, the Agriculture Department, etc. All in all about eighty such films, and it was hard going because these things, running from fifteen to thirty minutes, called for wall-to-wall scores—you started at the beginning and went non-stop to the end. It was a lot of experience."

North got to Hollywood through the influence of Elia Kazan. He had been working in New York with Kazan and Arthur Miller writing incidental music for the play *Death of a Salesman*. After staging the play and being greatly impressed by North's music, Kazan went to Hollywood to set up the filming of *A Streetcar Named Desire*, at Warners, where he plugged for North to get the score. Kazan wielded some power at that time and it took a fair bit of it to persuade Warners to bring an unknown (to them) New York composer into that august music department.

North's score for *A Streetcar Named Desire* is a landmark in the history of Hollywood music. It was a considerable departure from current concepts in scoring; it was, in fact, the first major jazz orientated score and its impact was instantaneous. Richly coloured with the sound of New Orleans jazz, the music wailed and stung, it pointed up Brando's coarse Kowalski and tinged the delusion and despair of Vivien Leigh's Blanche. "I tried to simulate jazz, to get its essence rhythmically and harmonically and apply it to drama. It was tailored. Some years previously I had done a similar thing when Benny Goodman commissioned me to write him a jazz concerto for clarinet and orchestra. It was introduced by Leonard Bernstein at New York City Center. The object was the same—to simulate jazz in a classical structure."

Alex North feels that jazz has been abused by "pop" musicians and sadly neglected by most serious contemporary American composers: "Jazz is by far a more authentic indigenous ingredient of American music than the folk music which is expressed in mountain ballads and cowboy songs which are, for the most part, of English and Scottish derivation. True, jazz has become commercialised to the degree where it has lost its freshness and spontaneity, but the jazz form should not be snubbed by composers because of its occasional maudlin wanderings into Tin Pan Alley. An attempt should rather be made to extract the essence and spirit of jazz and to project it with all the resources of craftsmanship at one's command to produce an end product which will have artistic integrity as well as emotional impact."

North's next major score, also with Kazan, was another with which he felt musically comfortable, a film in which he could use his own musical interests. This was *Viva Zapata!*, the story of the Mexican patriot Emilio Zapata. "I went to Mexico in 1939 when the Federal Theater Project folded. I went there with Anna Zokolow and her ballet company. I stayed there two years and I was able to sop up their music. I met and studied with Silvestre Revueltas, to my mind the top Mexican composer, more interesting than Carlos Chavez because his roots were more indigenous to Mexico. He had a more earthy personality than Chavez, he would conduct in a blue denim shirt whereas Chavez would appear in full evening dress—I'm not knocking Chavez, he was a more social man and had to be in order to hold his position as Mexico's foremost conductor. But Revueltas was a marvellous person—I would go to his classes and he might take his four or five students and go to a bistro and hold the class there. What I learnt from him was invaluable when it came to score *Viva Zapata!* because it's important when you write music based on the elements of another country's music to be able to feel it. I was also very fortunate with this film because Kazan hired me from the start of the production—he and I often wandered around our Mexican locations together, going from village to village. I would jot down little tunes I heard peasants humming or singing. This really was a luxury, this is ideal for a composer because you can work directly with the director and get to know exactly how he feels about the story. It doesn't happen very often."

*Viva Zapata!* contains some excellent musical moments. One occurs in the sequence where Brando is arrested by four mounted policemen and led out of his village with a rope around his neck. As this happens, a man picks up two stones and taps them together as a signal—other men in the village pick up stones and tap them in acknowledgement. A simple musical statement arises from this cadence of tapping stones. A group of villagers follow Brando and the policemen and as the group move across the fields and into the hills, small groups of men trickle into a growing stream of men silently and passively walking alongside and behind Brando. The music grows in scale and intensity as the numbers of men increase, and it reflects their purpose and their pride. Eventually it becomes a full statement as both the men and the policemen realise the situation. The music stops as the chief policeman halts his men, dismounts and takes the rope from Brando's neck. The sequence to this point has been devoid of dialogue; it's a long pictorial sequence, impressive in itself but made magnificent by the use of music.

Another of the musical highlights of *Viva Zapata!* came about through the insistence of Kazan. "In the scene near the end where Brando is to be assassinated, the sound effects men prepared their track, the sounds of horses and soldiers, but when Kazan heard the music for the scene he told them to hold back, that he didn't want to hear horses or footsteps, that he wanted the music to carry the scene up to the point where the massive fusillade of shots cuts Brando to pieces. This was unusual because the emphasis is almost always placed on realism in terms of sound in films. Music and sound effects are too often in conflict, with the music losing. I prefer to have one thing or the other. I have sometimes suggested that sounds be used in favour of music but the attitude of producers seems to be that they are paying you to write music, so go ahead and write it, it can always be thrown out later. This attitude results in many films being over-scored, and this is unfair to the composer because he has, or should have, a knowledge of what is dramatically right."

Alex North's musical preference in films is for small subjects, those that are intimate and personal. For all that, he has been assigned some of Hollywood's weightiest epics—*Spartacus, Cleopatra, The Agony and the Ecstasy,* and *The Shoes of the Fisherman.* "What I try to do in these cases is to personalise the films as much as possible, to concentrate on the character relationships, *Cleopatra* was interesting because I was working for Joe Mankiewicz, who is a musically sensitive man. This was another exceptional experience because I was able to go to Rome and watch them shoot. Usually the composer is brought in at the end of the picture so that they don't have to pay him from the start. Mankiewicz felt differently; he wanted me to be there and amalgamate my ideas. I was able to do some research on music of the period and I tried to simulate the musical sounds of what I thought might have prevailed at the time."

Mankiewicz was pleased with the North score for *Cleopatra*. Alluding to one point he remarked, "As the muted trumpets scream, in Antony's name, for honourable death, they scream an anguish which cannot be written, in a voice no actor can project."

North feels that writing for huge spectacles is difficult for him because he likes to identify with the film and its characters. "Spectacles call for writing that is objective in character. I prefer to be subjective. I like to say something that has to do with myself personally and mould it so it fits the content of the film. I write best when I can empathise. When you can't do that, then you have to fall back on technique and write programmatic music. Each picture calls for its own solution. I remember being stunned when I looked at *The Agony and the Ecstasy*. It was so pictorially vast. How can you illustrate with music anything so magnificently illustrative as the ceiling of the Sistine Chapel? I did a lot of research into music of the Renaissance period, particularly Gabrieli. I listened and I listened and I arrived at a concept. I decided to stay close to that style and interject my own manner of writing."

North had to return to more or less the same location some years later to score *The Shoes of the Fisherman*, an expensive, earnest, but unsuccessful picture. Again a broad palette, calling for musical depiction on modern Rome and, almost in contrast, melodic ideas with modal style for the more intimate moments of the Pope and his loneliness. The theme for the Pope posed a problem for North because the producer insisted on a Russian theme, inasmuch as the Pope in this story was Russian. "I resisted this; the dramatic theme of the picture seemed to me to be much broader —it had to do with a possible clash between Russia and China, the possible devastation of the world. But the composer is an employee and I did write a Russian theme for the Pope. I thought it was wrong and I still do. I don't think it means much dramatically when you see the Pope, when he is alone and troubled and you hear a simple Russian theme. However, your own ideas don't always prevail, you must compromise."

A favourite score of North's is the one he wrote for *The Rose Tattoo*. Although set in the South, the principal character is a Neapolitan woman, played to the hilt by Anna Magnani. "This is what I mean by an intimate story. A woman of great personality. I could colour the music in a Neapolitan fashion and the performance allowed for humour, lightness and pathos. It gave me a great range musically to say what I had to say. Another film I enjoyed scoring was John Ford's *Cheyenne Autumn*, unfortunately a flop but a film with admirable intentions. It dealt with the tragic migration of Indians and their hardships. I felt great sympathy with the story—I had an emotional reaction to it. That's one of the joys of writing functional music, if you can identify with your subject. This was especially interesting because it allowed me to study Indian music. It's not a case of using the music *per se*, it's a matter of letting it seep into the recesses of your mind so that when you sit down to write, the subconscious is permeated with the sound and the style of that music."

One of Alex North's finest contributions to film scoring was his music for Mike Nichols's excellent screen version of *Who's Afraid of Virginia Woolf?*, with Elizabeth Taylor and Richard Burton giving full force to Ernest Lehman's scenario based on the Albee play. North is a rather diffident man by nature and his initial reaction to many films is one of self-doubt. This is uncommon among Hollywood composers, especially in a man with such command of interpretive music. He told Nichols that the picture was so intense and so full of brilliant dialogue that it hardly needed music. Nichols didn't agree and hounded North to come up with a musical solution. "I thought I would try a jazz approach but I was soon unhappy with that and threw out the idea. Maybe a twelve-tone score would work? No, that was too abstract for so personal a story. The solution came from my own rather romantic concept of the man-woman relationship, and I decided on a quasi-baroque feeling, one that would play against the picture and suggest that these people basically had something going for them despite the fact they were haggling and fighting—a common problem in society today. The obvious thing to have done was to write *schrecklich* music (cruel, fierce) to go along with the hysteria and the violent situations, but I thought something rather pure would work. I wanted to get to the soul of these people and suggest they were really meant for each other. Frenetic music would have tipped the scales too much in one direction. You have to let the scenes play themselves."

Perhaps much of what Alex North has done in films is too subtle to be widely appreciated, but he is not a musician to compromise with musical values. "What a composer does may not be obvious to everyone but that's part of art, that's part and parcel of creativity—making a statement that has to do with yourself personally."

\* \* \*

The most dynamic and the most prolific Hollywood composer of the late Fifties and throughout the Sixties was **Elmer Bernstein**. In 1970 he took over the presidency of The Screen Composers Guild, succeeding David Raksin, thereby adding yet another duty to an already busy schedule. Bernstein, a man of enormous energy and vitality, has the good fortune

**Elmer Bernstein.**

to be gifted with a sense of melody as well as a sense of drama, and film scoring has thus been a very profitable as well as satisfying career for him. Almost thirty of his scores have been issued on recordings, more than any other composer. Some of his themes, particularly those for *The Man with the Golden Arm, Walk on the Wild Side,* and *The Magnificent*

*Seven* are among the most quoted examples of film music. The criticism may be levelled that his overall output is somewhat uneven but this is true of all film composers who write for a vast number of pictures. This was true of Steiner and Tiomkin; the strain of writing four and five major scores a year is possibly too much for any composer. Bernstein, given a worthy vehicle like *Summer and Smoke, To Kill a Mocking Bird,* and *Hawaii* has proven himself to be a master of the medium.

Bernstein's interest in composition grew from his study of the piano. His affinity for the piano was apparent at an early age and by the time he was twelve he knew he wanted to be a concert pianist. His piano teacher noticed that the boy was always improvising and rather than discourage the tendency, as some piano teachers are wont to do, this teacher was wise enough to seek a qualified opinion. Bernstein, at thirteen, was taken to see Aaron Copland, who was sufficiently impressed to send the boy to one of his own pupils, Israel Sitkowitz. The teenage years were spent in a formal study of composition, while maintaining the study of the piano. Bernstein later studied piano with Henrietta Michelson at the Juilliard School of Music and afterwards composition with Stefan Wolpe and Roger Sessions. His budding career as a concert pianist was interrupted when he was inducted into the army in 1943.

It was through his military service that Bernstein was introduced to the art of scoring incidental music. Due to his knowledge of American folk music, something for which he had acquired an early taste and something that would come in very handy in Hollywood, Bernstein was assigned to writing orchestral arrangements of folk songs like *Blue Tail Fly,* and *Sweet Betsy from Pike* for Major Glenn Miller and the Army Air Force Band. Out of this came the chance to score a dramatic radio programme for the Armed Forces Radio Service. That was the hook. By the time Bernstein got out of the service he had written something like eighty scores for radio. Despite the whetted appetite for scoring, he found no opportunities for such in Civvy Street and he then decided to resume his career as a concert pianist. The experience with the Armed Forces Radio Service came to someone's attention in 1949 and Bernstein was asked to write the music for a presentation of the United Nations Radio Wing, a documentary about the armistice the UN had effected in Israel. Henry Fonda was the narrator and the programme was also carried by NBC. From this came an offer from writer-producer Norman Corwin to score one of his impressive radio programmes, which in turn brought an offer from a Hollywood producer.

Elmer Bernstein began his Hollywood career in 1950 scoring two undistinguished films for Columbia, *Saturday's Hero,* and *Boots Malone.* By his third score, *Sudden Fear,* it was fairly obvious to the composer himself and to those who employed him that he had found a natural *niche*. His music for *Sudden Fear*, a Joan Crawford melodrama, revealed characteristics that would mark his work in this medium—the use of some of the more exotic instruments and the use of solo instruments like the piano and the flute, and smaller groupings, a thinning out of the concerted form that was prevalent at that time.

Bernstein is, among other things, one of the most articulate of film composers.

THOMAS: How did the musical atmosphere of Hollywood in the early Fifties appeal to you?

BERNSTEIN: Greatly. It was exciting and intriguing. Bear in mind that the veterans were still operative—Steiner, Tiomkin, Newman, Herrmann and John Green were here and highly productive, Alex North had made a big impression, Franz Waxman was in full flower, so to speak. It was a kind of golden age—a golden age plus. I say "plus" because we could look to the future with great hope at that time. Film music was a burgeoning art.

THOMAS: What attracted you to picture scoring?

BERNSTEIN: I found it very exciting to be given a musical problem, solve the problem and then hear the results almost instantly. In the past, writing symphonies was a long, laborious process and even if the composer was lucky enough to get a performance he might not ever hear the piece again. With film music you can write something and quickly find out if it functions in the situation. You know immediately if you've won or lost and I've always found that very stimulating. People continually refer to the limitations of writing film music; actually, the limitations are not that severe. Every form has its limitations—if you write opera you are limited by the range of the human voice; if you accept the challenge of writing a three-part fugue you have to keep within the framework of a three-part fugue. Most composers become annoyed at this harping on the so-called limitations of writing film music—you could hardly call Prokofiev's score for *Alexander Nevsky* a limited composition, or Vaughan Williams's for *Scott of the Antarctic*. I don't hear much limitation in Korngold's music for *The Adventures of Robin Hood*. But I can understand why people nowadays might think this way because there has been a change—largely for the worse—in scoring due to commercialisation, promotion, the record business, etc. Let us say that *theoretically* film scoring is an open form of composition and that it *has done*, occasionally *still does*, and *always should* give a capable composer ample opportunity. The film is a marvellous medium of composition—composers have done things in films they couldn't get away with in any other medium. For a while—in that Golden Age—the best film composers were a kind of vanguard. Leonard Rosenman's twelve-tone score for *The Cobweb* in 1958 comes to mind—millions of people heard that music and were affected by it yet how many of them would have wittingly gone to hear a twelve-tone composition in a concert hall?

THOMAS: Are you concerned about the snobbism displayed by so many critics and music lovers toward film scoring? The stigma that seems to go with the job?

BERNSTEIN: There is a stigma, yes. It's because we're attached to Big Business and an industry whose morals are, rightfully, suspect. That's a problem and you learn to live with it. Haydn was attached to the Ester-hazy Court—that was *his* problem. As for the critics, you have to realise that they themselves are basically entertainers and they are writing to amuse rather than to analyse. I enjoy reading them. What we have to bear in mind is that few of us are qualified to criticise anything.

THOMAS: Why is it that the Hollywood composer comes in for heavier criticism than the film composers of other places?

BERNSTEIN: Simply because this is, or was, the major centre of film production, turning out an enormous amount of product and it was possible for a composer to work here and make a very good living without having to write for any other medium. This was not the case in London, Paris or Moscow, where working composers worked for the theatre, the stage, the concert hall and occasionally the film studios. Once a composer had estab-lished himself in Hollywood, especially if he was contracted to a studio, he hadn't time for much else but composing film music. It was therefore easier to draw a bead of criticism on him, but what the critics often over-looked was that such a composer had distinguished himself elsewhere before he took to the road to Hollywood.

THOMAS: Don't you also have to come to terms with the public? You can write a splendid score but it's likely to be only that simple four-bar theme that they will remember.

BERNSTEIN: That's a sore point. Yes, it's true and the composer has to learn to respect this because it is his job to communicate and if he can reach out and touch them with a four-bar theme—provided it is in keeping with the character of the film—so much the better. There are, of course, composers who look down their noses at this, but they most often are the ones who can't come up with an attractive four-bar theme. But here again, you must be careful. Sometimes music in a picture can do its emo-tional thing best when you don't have a melody. It's a tricky business—

a melody can call attention to itself. You have to be careful how you use melody in film scoring—the melody must be an absolute extension of what is taking place on the screen. For example, in *The Man with the Golden Arm* the main character, Frankie, was a man who wanted to be a jazz drummer, so I there tried to make that broad jazzy theme speak for his ambition, and by giving it a sad quality it also implied his frustration. He was a tormented man, a narcotics addict, and there are sounds in jazz— blues, wails, trumpet screeches—that are perfect for expressing anguish. The truly fascinating thing about scoring films is that it allows for any kind of music.

THOMAS: What are your views on the use of jazz in film scoring? *The Man with the Golden Arm* is considered a landmark in jazz scoring, and you've used that kind of music in pictures like *The Rat Race*, and *Walk on the Wild Side.*

BERNSTEIN: Out of respect for the field of jazz and the many gifted people who work in that field, I must say I've never considered myself to have written a jazz score. I've written scores that have used certain elements of jazz. In the case of *The Man with the Golden Arm*, I used the rhythmic elements, I used certain of the harmonic limitations that are inherent in jazz but I never gave that free rein to the players which is the thing that becomes jazz. So it was really a score that used jazz to colour it. It's extremely difficult for jazz in the pure sense to become a film score because one of its greatest assets is its improvisitory quality, whereas a film score is one that must be very carefully thought out. However, there are times in scoring pictures when the kind of primitive excitement that is created by jazz can indeed be an asset.

THOMAS: It's odd how jazz is used mostly in films with connotations of sleaziness—crime, juvenile delinquency, drug addiction, etc. It hardly speaks well for jazz.

BERNSTEIN: It doesn't speak well for jazz at all. One of our great problems is divesting ourselves of prejudices. We're born into a society that has inherited all sorts of prejudices—racial, religious and even musical, and this one concerning jazz, like most prejudices, has its roots in truth or reality at some point. There's no question that at the time of the origin of jazz it was something that grew up in a rather sleazy atmosphere. But that was a long time ago and the prejudice has no relevance in contemporary terms. However, it is a subtle prejudice and I find myself fighting it within myself. The times I've used jazz to colour my music have been in films with sleazy atmospheres—*The Man with the Golden Arm* was about narcotics, *Sweet Smell of Success* dealt with some very unsavoury characters in New York, and *Walk on the Wild Side* was largely set in a New Orleans house of ill repute. So I'm guilty, although I don't think it's necessary to use jazz in this way. It's simply something that is very difficult to avoid.

THOMAS: Let's talk about another kind of Americana, the turn-of-the-century, small southern town milieu that Tennessee Williams conjured up in *Summer and Smoke*. Was that much of a musical problem for you?

BERNSTEIN: *Summer and Smoke* posed great problems in composition because it was a story with very delicate balances. It's the story of a minister's daughter who is tremendously afraid of love and life in general, and her love for a young doctor who has lived a worldly life. The music had to reflect the effect they have on each other—she converting him to the realisation that there is something within all human beings beside their own pleasures, and he opens up the door for her in the sense that she realises she is a woman. But it was something that happened too late for her. Obviously, the emotional balances of a thing of this sort are very delicate, and the problem of the music was to portray something of the inner turmoil of these characters without stepping on the delicacy of the film or overshadowing it. I tried to write tenuous, shimmering music for the relationship of the two main characters, within the broader framework of the period and the southern locale, with the overall music tinged with a folksong-like quality. Again, it's a matter of colouring your music.

THOMAS: You re-visited the South some years later with *To Kill a Mocking Bird*, although it was a very different kind of story, this one being mostly about a young boy and girl growing up in a small town. Your title melody was a simple piano statement, to my ears a very wistful kind of Americana.

BERNSTEIN: I remember that very well because it was difficult to do. The biggest problem was to make the initial decision about the musical evaluation of the picture. You have to decide what the music must do. Sometimes it's obvious. It was easy with *The Magnificent Seven* because the image was active and muscular. But *Mocking Bird* was a more complicated story. Here you had two children with a father but no mother in a rather isolated community which is suffering from a racial disturbance. The father is a respected attorney. And there is also an eccentric neighbour of whom the children are afraid. What was the element to be discussed in the music? I decided to focus on the kind of particular and peculiar magic that is the imaginative world of a child. There's an unsophisticated mysticism about a child's imagination and it's a marvellous thing. Simplicity was the keynote—the score starts with just the right hand playing a simple melody, and I tried to orchestrate simply, with bell-like, harp-like sounds.

THOMAS: I was turned on immediately I heard that melody.

BERNSTEIN: Well, it sounds egocentric to say it but I think you reacted that way because the music was right. It was one of those cases where I was fortunate enough to hit on exactly the right thing to do. And if you do something in any art form that is exactly right, everybody knows it instantly. It's very hard to fool people. They can be confused, but if something feels nice and right, they react to it instantly.

THOMAS: Isn't that the secret of film scoring—appropriateness?

BERNSTEIN: Yes, but the roads to appropriateness, like the roads to hell, are paved with good intentions. Also, stylistically, what is appropriate changes from time to time. For instance, in the Thirties and Forties the writing of symbolic music was very popular—music which immediately tells you where you are, so to speak. And it was something at which Max Steiner had no peers. These are things which you would not do today because people want more sophisticated ways to create the same effect. And, of course, we are living through an anti-feeling period. It's a cool age, people don't want to be that emotionally involved, to be touched. Today a love scene scored with a beautiful melody for strings is likely to be scoffed at.

THOMAS: How about another film music problem—scoring pictures of scenic magnificence? How do you approach so pictorial a subject as *Hawaii*?

BERNSTEIN: That was an interesting problem of another kind. I knew that part of the problem was to create something of the euphoric feeling we associate with the South Seas, although the real problem was that the music we associate with Hawaii is strictly twentieth century. What we now know as Hawaiian music isn't really Hawaiian at all, and it certainly had nothing to do with Hawaii of the nineteenth century. I recall a similar problem working on *The Ten Commandments*, in particular working the music for an Egyptian dance. We know what instruments they used but Lord knows what they played on them. In doing my research for *Hawaii*, I found the Hawaiians of the period had no melodic instruments at all, except for a little nose flute that would produce about three notes. They had a lot of percussion instruments like gourds and small drums, and they had chants, basic two or three note chants rocking back and forth between those notes. I used that characteristic in the score, in fact, the overture starts that way on the bass marimba. Well, from those meagre resources I had to create a whole cloth, and it was almost pure invention. I must say it's one of the scores of which I'm proud, and I was especially pleased to have Hawaiians tell me it sounded Hawaiian to them. I'm very fond of Hawaii and I suppose I was able to get that feeling across in the music.

THOMAS: Isn't it the composer's job to sympathise with a subject? To make some kind of appeal?

BERNSTEIN: The job of the composer is really very varied. You must use your art to heighten the emotional aspects of the film—music can tell the story in purely emotional terms and the film by itself cannot. The reason it can't is that it's a visual language and basically intellectual. You look at an image and you then have to interpret what it means, whereas if you listen to something or someone and you understand what you hear—that's an emotional process. Music is particularly emotional—if you are affected by it, you don't have to ask what it means.

THOMAS: Film music is almost an idealisation of the visual image?

BERNSTEIN: Yes, even with a subject as kinetic as *The Magnificent Seven*, the moment you translate into music the scene of horsemen riding over the plains it becomes an emotional accompaniment to the action. That's part of the fun of being a film composer, that you are reaching people at a subliminal level, where they are relatively defenceless. That's an exciting thing because you can make people feel a certain way, even though they may not understand why they feel that way. Film music does its job best when it deals with what is implicit in the picture, not what is explicit. And this calls for a special attitude from the composer toward the concept of listening on the part of the audience—he must expect them to listen to music in a different way than if he were writing for the concert hall. However, being musically implicit presupposes that you have a film with certain depths—sometimes a film is so simple-minded nothing is implicit, it's all explicit—and that's the hardest kind of film to score because you find yourself being so straightforward you have to strain to avoid being dull.

THOMAS: Suppose this was a classroom of film music students: how would you illustrate, from your own work, this business of writing music that is implicit?

BERNSTEIN: I would pick a score I wrote in 1956 for a film called *Men in War*. This posed a fascinating problem. It was a simple story of a be-leaguered platoon in Korea—they can't get back to their lines—they're moving through enemy territory—the men are tired, nervous, etc. It was a good picture but yet another war film. What was there to say? Then something struck me: the men were moving through beautiful wooded countryside with death and danger on every side. Nothing I could write could make the danger any more obvious than it already was on film. What I decided to do was comment on the beauty of the surroundings, the hidden beauty of the woods, the birds—the pastoral feeling . . .

THOMAS: You wrote *against* the picture.

BERNSTEIN: Right. I wrote what was implicit, and something you might not have noticed without the music. That to me is the best use of music in a film because it gives another dimension, something it might not otherwise have had. If you can allude to something more than is seen on the screen you can make a valuable contribution to a film.

THOMAS: This is something that doesn't seem too obvious to many film producers. Isn't there a gulf between producers and composers?

BERNSTEIN: You can't live in this community and work at writing music for films without realising that the accent is definitely on the "pop" song and not on the art of scoring. One has to censor oneself, to watch out for the tendency to please the producer rather than produce a good score. It's to be hoped that there are enough serious producers—those who are dedicated to making fine pictures, who will eschew the "easy way out" of looking for the "hit" song—the supposed "easy way out." The reason I say "supposed" is that with all the best intentions in the world that is probably the most difficult thing to do.

# 7
# And then came Mancini—and Others

It was sometimes said of Arnold Schoenberg that the worst thing about him was the misguided enthusiasm of his disciples. A similar thing might be said about **Henry Mancini**. Mancini brought a fresh sound to film scoring in the late Fifties, a sound more in tune with the times, one that took advantage of new instrumentation and modern recording techniques. Mancini's deft sense of orchestration and his enviable gift for melody quickly made him the most sought-after musician in Hollywood. Unfortunately, that success persuaded all too many producers that the modern, "pop" sound was what films now needed—a persuasion heavily endorsed by the music publishers and the recording companies. To take the Schoenberg analogy a step further: on one occasion a young admirer told him that composers all over Europe were embracing his theories and using his twelve-tone form of composition. The great composer was not unduly impressed by the news. He nodded at the young man and asked, "Yes, but are they putting much music to it?"

As Mancini sees it there is nothing wrong with finding new ways of scoring providing they turn out to be appropriate, and by 1970 the use of songs and rock music had become prevalent, and, for the most part, inappropriate. "We've become a nation of followers when it comes to fashionable trends. Scoring *The Graduate* with a string of songs by Simon and Garfunkel was an excellent device for that particular film, but it set off repercussions, just as I did myself with the use of jazz in *Peter Gunn*. For years after that, jazz was used in films for which it wasn't suited. Now, everything is geared to the swinging youth scene. Sometimes it works well, sometimes it doesn't. As for integrity—we have the music departments thinking about the record album even before the picture is scored! It's the kind of thing where the tail is wagging the dog. I don't think the craft of film scoring is being furthered by this particular development."

Mancini is among the most adroit instrumentalists ever to work in films. His book *Sounds and Scores* is a course in orchestration, widely used by teachers. His own instrument is the flute, an affinity that is apparent in

**Henry Mancini.**

his films. The Mancini recording orchestra always calls for piccolo, C-flute, alto-flute and bass flute. He used the bass flutes effectively in dramatic segments of *Peter Gunn*. In *Mr. Lucky*, the TV series that followed *Peter Gunn*, Mancini often pitched the Hammond organ, as the principal voice, against a string section. In the opening scene of *Breakfast at Tiffany's* he had an amplified harmonica playing the "Moon River" melody as Audrey Hepburn gazed into the windows of Tiffany's by the dawn's early light. The combination of the instrument and the lonely image of the distinct and fragile beauty of Hepburn was incongruous but it worked perfectly.

This imaginative use of instrumentation is perhaps Mancini's major contribution to scoring. In *Experiment in Terror* he employed two auto-harps, one strumming the background for the other, which picked out the notes of the theme. This odd effect was used chillingly for each appearance of the film's asthmatic villain, played by Ross Martin. In scoring the African adventure romp *Hatari!* Mancini asked to have the studio piano slightly de-tuned in order to give an eerie quality to those sections of the score pertaining to the mysteries of the strange landscape. In the same picture, Mancini came up with one of his most popular themes, the one for the baby elephants. In the scene where Elsa Martinelli takes three little

**Henry Mancini.**

pachyderms down the road to the lake to give them a bath, Mancini has a calliope play a boogie-woogie rhythm as a high E-flat clarinet plays a perky tune. The music here is very much "foreground" and being aware of it makes the scene more enjoyable. "I don't believe in this theory of music in films not being noticed—it must be noticed in its place. In this elephant sequence, as in the opening of *Breakfast at Tiffany's* if I hadn't made myself felt I wouldn't have been serving the picture. You have to be felt at certain points. Where there is no dialogue, no sounds, just the visual—you'd better say something interesting. I don't know who started this theory of the best film music being that which you don't notice, but it isn't true."

The concern with orchestration continues to mark Mancini's film scoring. In 1970 he produced two scores of widely different nature. For *The Hawaiians,* a continuation of the filming of Michener's *Hawaii,* Mancini found, as had Elmer Bernstein before, that there was barely any native Hawaiian music. However, this section of the epic story did deal with the Oriental influence on the islands and this was the opportunity Mancini seized upon. To get an authentic, ethnic flavour he used a number of ancient Chinese and Japanese instruments and hired several experts to play them. Included in the score were extended passages for the Cheng (a Chinese zither known to have been in existence for five centuries), the Hsun (a Chinese ocarina), the Hichiriki (the Japanese oboe), the Santure (an oriental cymbalum), plus kotos and the Chinese flute. This score is possibly the most interesting thing about *The Hawaiians*. Mancini shortly afterwards went to England to record his music for *Salem Come to Supper* (*The Night Visitor*), a thriller shot in Denmark in the dead of winter. For this he used an orchestra of only seventeen pieces: twelve woodwinds, in threes, and five keyboards—an organ, two pianos and two harpsichords, with one piano and one harpsichord tuned a quarter-tone flat, giving a quarter-tone scale between the pianos and the harpsichords. Mancini felt this was good for setting the mysterious atmosphere, the winter scene and the chilling characters in the film. A large orchestra was unnecessary.

The assumption might be that a man as abundantly endowed with music as Henry Mancini might have been born humming, and crawling to the piano while still in diapers. The assumption would be false. "I was forced into music by my father. He started me on the piccolo when I was eight, and I was later railroaded into the Sons of Italy band in my home-town—Aliquippa, Pennsylvania. It was always Dad's prodding and persistence that made me practise. He and my mother were Italian immigrants. At the time he came over the American Dream was still 'on the charts' so to speak—I don't know where it is now. But he was enamoured of the idea that his son wouldn't have to go into the steel mills and work as he did. He loved music and played the flute, and he made many sacrifices to send me to teachers and schools. I would never have had any interest without him, and I didn't start to enjoy music until I became interested in arranging. I then studied with Max Adkins, the conductor and arranger at the Stanley Theatre in Pittsburgh, and a new world opened up for me. After graduating from the Aliquippa High School in 1942, I enrolled at the Juilliard School of Music in New York but after a year there, Uncle Sam nabbed me for the service."

Mancini spent three years in uniform. With his release, he joined Tex Beneke's newly formed "Glenn Miller" styled orchestra as a pianist-arranger. Out of this job came Mancini's meeting with the woman who became Mrs. Mancini—singer Ginny O'Connor, then a member of the Meltones, Mel Torme's group. "It was through Ginny that I started with film music. She and a singing group were hired to appear in a short film at Universal and I was offered the job of arranging the music for it. I hit it off with Joe Gershenson, the director of music at Universal, and he asked me to do some work on an Abbott and Costello picture called *Lost in Alaska*. It was supposed to be a two-week job but I ended up spending the next six years at Universal. That was where I served my apprenticeship: I worked on everything from *Francis the Mule* and *Bonzo the Chimp* to *The*

*Glenn Miller Story* and *The Benny Goodman Story.* The best thing I did was the score for Orson Welles's *Touch of Evil.* I must have worked, in some capacity or another, on about one hundred pictures. I had no control over what I did. I learned all the stock situations. I did all the *cliché* things and got them out of my system."

The six years Mancini put in at Universal formed an apprenticeship of enormous value, the like of which is no longer available. The lack of similar training periods is something to regret. Scoring is a delicate and intricate job, and the studios cannot provide the training since they no longer support large musical staffs. Sadly, this situation applies to many other areas of the entertainment industry, and fledgling artisans have fewer outlets in which to learn while working.

During his years at Universal, Mancini also spent time studying composition with famous European exiles Mario Castelnuovo-Tedesco and Ernst Krenek, but, "I found that for what I wanted to do, there was no real training other than actually doing it. I feel sorry for the young composers coming into the business now because they are expected to be good immediately. They're also expected to come up with hit songs, which tends to persuade them the picture is secondary. In my own case, the successful songs have been secondary considerations—they were all written specifically to *serve* the picture. I'm happy that they emerged from the scores and became popular but I can honestly say they weren't written that way."

Mancini's six years with Universal came to an abrupt end—he was laid off. The rug of security was pulled out from under him and he was upset by this, unemployment was a new experience for him. It turned out to be the turning point in his career. Producer Blake Edwards had devised a television idea, about an elegant private detective, and he needed a composer to score it, a composer who would have to accept the budget limitations of the show. While coming out of a barber shop, Edwards ran into Mancini and casually asked him if the job appealed to him. It did. *Peter Gunn* ran for three years and launched both Edwards and Mancini into the upper echelons of their respective trades.

Mancini's treatment of the *Peter Gunn* scores was an innovation; it was heralded as a new sound in film music, although he claims he was unaware at the time he was breaking new ground. He was too busy to notice. "I had to make do with an eleven man orchestra, that's all we could afford. That's how the unusual instrumentation came about—the use of the bass flutes, etc.—I had to pull away from the old string tremulo business. There's a certain direction movie music must take in order to stay alive, the large orchestra playing all the time is outmoded, and I was forced into this realisation by doing *Peter Gunn.* The melodic approach is still valid, the Tchaikowsky-like melody is still wanted and needed, but the treatment of that melody has to be different, it has to be in keeping with our times. And we can do much more now, we have a vast instrumental world at our disposal and constantly evolving recording techniques."

According to Mancini, the Hollywood studios brought about their own downfall by turning out type products, too many of the same kind of pictures, draining ideas and talents. "In my years at Universal, the studio was packaging around fifty films a year, mostly made by the same people. Musically they tended to a sameness. Your thoughts became moulded into thinking that the thirty-five piece studio orchestra was the only means of scoring. Only occasionally would you go beyond that concept, and that was to increase the orchestra, not to decrease it. The general musical concept was one of bigness, lushness. The large orchestra was always used as a canvas. I think one of the reasons the *Peter Gunn* music caught the ear was its sparseness—the economy of the scoring. Up until then, economy had not been a major factor in film-making in California. It had been a super-rich industry, it was a mentality geared to abundance."

The Mancini experience also points to something that is not generally known about the Hollywood studios: that they were spiritually conservative. By the late Fifties the methods of film-making in Hollywood were already becoming old fashioned and much of the equipment was ancient, although kept in excellent running order. This lack of investment in newer ways and means was largely due to the impact of television on the film industry a decade earlier. The Fifties were years of decline, years in which the television habit replaced the theatre-going habit. With their income nowhere near what it was prior to TV, the movie chieftains flailed around for ways to keep up profits, even to the extent of selling their film libraries to TV, thus creating their own toughest competition, and renting their facilities to television production companies. All the studios were abundantly equipped but little thought was given to technological progress.

Recalls Mancini, "The quality of the recording in the film studios was way behind the quality in the studios of the various recording companies in Hollywood. There was a lethargy in the studio music departments. The record companies were using jazzmen and guys coming off the road from dance bands. The film studios used jazz musicians with great reluctance, only if they had a score that called for jazz. They had the idea these men couldn't read music, they thought they would be lost when faced with classical pieces. Well, they eventually found out the classical pieces were the easiest for these fellows—they read anything, play anything. Most of the men I used in scoring *Peter Gunn* were formerly with the great bands, and if it can be said that I had any influence, I think it was this—using good musicians to give personality to the music and having those musicians well recorded. Initially, this was a great problem. We recorded *Peter Gunn* at Universal, and when I told the engineers I wanted a microphone put on the drums, one on the piano and another on the bass, they looked at me as if I was crazy. This was 1958 and they still thought in terms of a single mike hung over the orchestra. I wanted people to be aware of musical detail in scoring. I didn't consider this exactly revolutionary because the record companies had already created a fresh, 'alive' sound. But it took the film studios years to catch up."

The *Peter Gunn* scoring definitely had an effect on the use of music in other TV and feature films but Mancini shies away from overstressing the importance of his influence. "There's a horrible tendency to pick upon one man and brand him as a trendmaker. These things get all out of proportion. For example, the Beatles weren't aware they were doing anything vastly different. I think they got more kick out of reading about what they were supposed to be doing than they did in doing it. They couldn't believe people would take a record of theirs and interpret it into great meanings, with significance for future generations. I've talked about this with Lennon and McCartney—they were amazed. I did a hundred segments of *Peter Gunn* and all I could think about was getting the stuff done, getting it on and getting to the next one. You do what you have to do and the discussion comes later."

Music comes easily to Henry Mancini and he writes quickly. Film scoring to him is a full musical palette and it seems to present no frustrations. "I'm strong in the belief that a person has to have a point of view, a conviction. I'm convinced of the value of music on film, but my point of view is that it's only one part of a group effort. The legitimate composer has to answer only to himself; the film composer is a different animal, he must know where he fits in the scheme of filmic things. I'm constantly asked about what it takes to be a film composer and I reply, 'A sense of drama.' I can't stress that too much, it's as important as the ability to compose. The ability to become part of something—to be able to help the picture and not get in its way. I know there's a lot of talk about film being an art. Actually, what we have here are a number of crafts having the ability to create art. We are craftsmen, and we become artists if what we do is good enough. But I confess I feel that art has been attained rarely on the screen."

Film-making, especially in Hollywood, is fraught with an evil called "type casting," in which a man can become glued to that part of his talent that seems to shine best. This is apparent in the case of many popular actors, but it also applies to composers. Mancini has had to fight against his own success as a man highly capable of writing light and amusing music. Many of his films have been purely entertainment assignments—comedies and romantic romps. Occasionally he has shown the deeper side of his talent with pictures like *The Days of Wine and Roses* and *Wait Until Dark*. During 1969 and 1970, Mancini picked up three expensive vehicles, all allowing for a wide range of composition: *The Molly Maguires*, *Sunflower*, and *The Hawaiians*. Unfortunately for him, all three were box-office disappointments. He feels, as do many, that *The Molly Maguires* is his best score. Aside from the romanticism and the humour that is generally apparent in his music, there is also a hint of sadness, and this aspect is noticeable in *The Molly Maguires*. The story is set in the Pennsylvania coalfields in the 1870s and the emphasis is on tragedy. Mancini's score is a perfect complement to the imaginative photography of James Wong Howe, a genuis with lighting and shading. The atmosphere is one of ugly beauty, and Mancini's main theme, played by an accordion, immediately speaks of remoteness and a wistful sadness.

Mancini's image as an inventor of entertaining music is fostered by his secondary career as a recording artist. He is, by far, the foremost Hollywood composer-conductor in terms of his activity in the record world. His dozens of LP albums contain a large portion of the music he has written for films but he also records the music of other film composers. Mancini is an affable and seemingly modest man, and apparently little afflicted with the kind of competitiveness and ambitiousness that marks many musicians in his genre. Bronislau Kaper tells of Mancini calling him and saying how much he admired the love theme in Kaper's *Mutiny on the Bounty*, and that he would like to record it. Mancini did record it, and at a time when the Kaper score had been nominated for the Academy Awards in competition with a Mancini score.

Mancini may possibly have contributed to his own type casting, since he elects not to record his more dramatic pieces of scoring. He thus plays into the hands of the critics who regard him as a lightweight. But his thinking, in terms of his career in the record business, is soundly commercial, and the degree of success negates arguments. In addition to his three Oscars, Mancini holds a dozen Grammy awards, and endless nominations. His views on recording film scores: "Most soundtrack albums are not commercially successful because they are not recorded specifically for the ear. Background music is geared solely to create dramatic impact on a watching audience. When a score is plucked from a soundtrack and transferred to an LP, the odds are momentous that the recording will be less than satisfying. I re-record for the album. Tight control is needed for the actual scoring of the film, but in the album session I loosen up on the baton and let the boys have more freedom because that's what produces the extra spark an album needs. You can't get that extra spark from a movie or television soundtrack score because it's not supposed to be there. Composers are paid to build their music around the stories—not the stories around the music."

Despite the increasing use of light, commercially aimed "pop" orientated music in Hollywood films in the wave of Mancini's success, several young composers of more *avant-garde* persuasion managed not only to invade the colony but to establish considerable success. In particular: Leonard Rosenman, Jerry Goldsmith and Lalo Schifrin. Their success tends to negate the lament for the decline of serious music in film scoring, although, on examination, it becomes obvious that they are men who would survive in any musical society because they are as knowledgeable about jazz and electronic music as they are about the more cerebral kind of contemporary concert composition. If film scoring has a future, as it must, in spite of the epic ignorance and bad taste that swamps the industry, it will lie in the hands of this kind of composer.

**Leonard Rosenman** owes his *entrée* into the film world to the interest and persuasion of Elia Kazan, and he doubts if he would have gained recognition without this invitation. Rosenman, born in New York in 1924, had studied composition with Roger Sessions, Luigi Dallapiccola and Ernst Bloch and his musical sights were set on the concert platform. He did some theatre music in New York and he was a resident composer at the Tanglewood festivals, where his chamber works were performed. Rosenman also received a Koussevitsky commission to write an opera. As with almost all serious modern composers, Rosenman's income from composing had to be supplemented by teaching. One of his piano pupils was the young actor James Dean. When Dean was chosen to star in *East of Eden*, he suggested to Kazan that Rosenman might be the man for the score. Rapport was quickly established between the director and the composer. Rosenman asked that he be present during the entire filming, since he knew nothing about film making and would prefer to make his sketches during the filming rather than afterwards. Kazan then explained that he considered this the preferable way of working.

Rosenman's score for *East of Eden* contains a broad and melodic main theme which was, and still is, pleasing to the ear of the general public, but the tone of the scoring is sparse and close in style to Alban Berg. The theme for Dean is spoken by woodwinds—two bassoons and two clarinets—and clearly conveys the loneliness of the Steinbeck character. The final scene of the picture—the death of the father—is one of the longest musical cues ever recorded, running almost ten minutes. All the main characters come together in this scene and Rosenman uses it as a musical chart, with the main themes in counterpoint as a comment on the conflicting characters. "Kazan and I worked together to fit the music to the film. This is not the

**Leonard Rosenman.**

general practice because it's too expensive—and the studios don't care about music anyway. But I couldn't have done the job otherwise because I hadn't learned enough. I was very green. I remember going up to a little man at a desk in the music building at Warners and asking him, 'Do you know what a click track is?' He said, 'Yes, I invented it.' The little man was Max Steiner."

Flushed with the success of his initial score, Rosenman chose to be even more daring on his next project, *The Cobweb.* "The film was directed by Vincente Minnelli, a man of taste and imagination, and produced by the very literate John Houseman, who later left the industry and is now in charge of drama at the Julliard. I told John I wanted to go all out and do a piece in my own style, and he gave his consent. The setting of the picture is a mid-West psychiatric clinic, where the staff seem almost as psychotic as the patients. The place is thrown into a tizzy over a seemingly trivial incident, the hanging of new drapes in the clinic's library, which initiates a mess of conflicts and jealousies. Those of us working on the film came to call them The Drapes of Wrath. What I wrote was the first twelve-tone film score, non-thematic except for one main motif to denote the madness of the place. To my surprise the score was liked by the M-G-M music department and actually recorded. I was beginning to think everything I'd heard about Hollywood was untrue."

Rosenman and Alex North had more to do with bringing the sound of serious mid-twentieth-century music to Hollywood than any other composers, although Rosenman's success has not matched North's. Their introduction of new techniques opened up the development of scoring, which had been almost entirely influenced by the romantic symphonists of half a century before. Picasso once said, "Every time somebody innovates something, somebody comes along and does it prettier." This is always likely to be the problem with film music, but the important thing is for the gates to be open to innovators.

The Rosenman scores never lack for musical interest, even though the enthusiasm for them is something less than widespread. For John Frankenheimer's first film, *The Young Stranger,* Rosenman agreed that a romantic musical approach was valid, but rather than apply the usual Tchaikowsky tinge, he studied the songs of Hugo Wolf and gave the score a slightly different flavour. For Lewis Milestone's stark film about the Korean war, *Pork Chop Hill,* Rosenman unearthed a two thousand year old Chinese lullaby and adapted it into an oddly harmonised march, in a score that was otherwise non-martial. For *Fantastic Voyage,* he talked the producer out of using jazz—the producer wanted to have the first hip science fiction film—and suggested that the first few reels be scored only by electronic sounds, with music appearing on the track only after the miniaturised scientists arrive inside the human body and discover its wonders.

In 1970 Leonard Rosenman produced two scores for films of strange and different characters: *Beneath the Planet of the Apes,* and *A Man Called*

**Leonard Rosenman.**

*Horse.* The picture about the apes has a rather cacophonous sound, with piercing brass chords over shrill strings, all suggestive of a nightmarish world. At one point Rosenman supplies a march for a gorilla army, and it is a satiric comment on the moronic, cruel mentality of the animals. He parodies the mutated humans with mocking distortions of the hymn "All Things Bright and Beautiful." For *A Man Called Horse,* Rosenman not only used genuine Indian music but he employed a choir from the Rosebud Sioux of South Dakota. The score is rife with rattles, whistles, drums and chants, and possibly a little too authentic for most moviegoing ears. Certainly, no one with any interest in the culture of North American Indians could fail to be impressed by the sincerity of the film or the composer's perhaps rather odd amalgam of *avant-garde* techniques and primitive music.

Rosenman is not at all sentimental about film music. "It has all the attributes of music—melody, harmony, counterpoint—but it is something less than music because its motivating pulsation is literary and not musical. Unlike other mixed media forms, such as opera, the composer has no control over the text, over the *mise-en-scène;* he is writing to a circumscribed form. The challenge for me is extra-filmic, it's a question of dramaturgic talent. Either a person is talented dramaturgically or he isn't—you can have a marvellous composer write a score and it might not fit. You're dealing with two arts that are very similar—sight and sound—both move in time and both require memory for the perception of organisation. For instance, you may feel the re-emergence of the theme in Beethoven's Eroica is thrilling, but that's because you remember what it is at the beginning. If you conceive of the Eroica as a series of isolated musical events, it isn't thrilling. The same thing in film—if the villain finally gets punched in the nose its thrilling, because this is Reel Twelve and he's had it coming since Reel Five.

"The film composer has to bear in mind that we are a visually oriented society. In fact, it's biological: more of our brain is given over to vision than to hearing. Film music must be an analogue to the action of the film, and likewise, the film should become an analogue of the dramatic action of the music. This is the value of a director and a composer working together in the construction of the film."

Rosenman has continued his career as a composer of absolute music, although since working for films he has found it more difficult to get performances in the concert hall. This is doubly irritating because he has generally been regarded in Hollywood as something of an interloper. He is, or tries to be, totally schizophrenic about his concert music and his film music, although he candidly admits he uses the cinema as a musical laboratory. "I think Mozart and Beethoven would have given their eye teeth to write for films, because of the opportunity it gives to write something and hear it played the next day by fifty or sixty crack musicians. These are the optimum conditions in which to study orchestration, and to try out musical ideas."

Rosenman looks upon the musical ignorance of film-makers as both good and bad, good in that they are not qualified to interfere and bad in that they do not understand the functions of music. "They tend to think of music in literary terms. When I was scoring part of the TV series *The Defenders,* the producer said, 'I want music that describes the law.' That's a literary idea—music can't describe law. Richard Strauss came as close as any composer in being able to communicate pictures but five people listen to *Ein Heldenleben* and they have no idea what it's about, you'll get five different stories."

Since composers are a mystery to producers, they are also repositories of blame. One of the most common cries in Hollywood is the squeal of a producer that the composer has ruined his film, although this cry never seems to arise from well made pictures. "I was asked by a producer at

Universal to re-score the opening episode of their TV series *The Survivors*. One of my colleagues had done a good job but it was a terrible film, impossible. The producer felt that my changing the musical concept would improve the film. When a picture is really bad, no composer can save it."

Rosenman has an optimistic nature and he is grateful to have worked in films, although he regrets certain things about it. "Unfortunately, in America we have this weird opinion that if a composer writes for films, he can't write good music. This isn't true in other countries. I'm a better composer now than I was before I started film scoring, yet before I started in films I had less trouble from the critics than I do now. Recently, a chamber piece of mine was performed at a concert, a quite serious composition, and a critic said, 'It sounds like Alfred Newman.' Everyone's entitled to be a snob but this man must either have fallen asleep or been deaf. All you can say to these people is what Brahms said to Hanslick when that august critic told him his first symphony sounded like Beethoven's tenth—'Anybody can see that.' However, I think this kind of snobbism will disappear in a generation. Film art is growing fast—this is the technical mythology of the twentieth century and the kids taking film courses today seem to have—pray to God—open minds."

*        *        *

Just as Rosenman's success as a modern "longhair" belies the seeming take-over of the Hollywood music scene by "pop" musicians, so **Jerry Goldsmith**'s full employment throughout the Sixties gives doubt to the laments about lack of work among the film composers. The decade was, in truth, a slim one for most of the long established composers, firstly, because fewer feature films came out of the studios and secondly, because many of the scores went to the more popular musicians—even pianists like Erroll Garner and Peter Nero were handed assignments as film composers, not to mention many lesser musicians. Goldsmith, on the other hand, averaged four and five pictures a year, just as the veterans had done in the heyday of the big studios. This was partly luck and partly being able to impress producers with a remarkably wide range of compositional talent.

Goldsmith, rare among film composers in that he was actually born in Los Angeles, majored in music at the University of Southern California and studied with pianist Jakob Gimpel. In 1950 he took a job with the music department of the Columbia Broadcasting System's West Coast headquarters in Los Angeles, not as a musician but as a clerk-typist. The musical ability was soon apparent to his employers and Goldsmith did his first chores as a composer and conductor for CBS radio programmes.

**Jerry Goldsmith.**

By the late fifties he was well ensconced as a composer of television scores. By the age of thirty, Goldsmith had established a reputation for being not only inventive and imaginative but fast and dependable, a combination of qualities no film studio could overlook in a bright, new composer. By now he had written dozens of scores for *Playhouse 90*, *The Twilight Zone*, *Gunsmoke*, and *Climax;* his work for *Thriller* and *The Man from U.N.C.L.E.*

had brought him Emmy (TV Oscars) nomination, and his theme for *Dr. Kildare* was a hit.

The first Goldsmith film score to catch critical attention was *Lonely Are the Brave*, itself a remarkable film. With a script by Dalton Trumbo and a convincing performance from Kirk Douglas as a contemporary cowboy out of place in the modern world, Goldsmith underscored the picture gently and discreetly. His sensitive orchestration pointed up the poignancy of a stubborn, free-spirited man unwilling to bend to the Twentieth century. Even a bar-room brawl was lightly scored with percussive instruments. Certainly, the musical touch was different, and very welcome. The film was not widely successful when first released in 1961 but over the years it has insinuated itself as a minor American classic, and one sought after for showings at university film courses.

Goldsmith also wrote a similarly quiet and subtle score for John Huston's *Freud*, but the failure of the picture to win public approval also failed to bring the composer the recognition he deserved for scoring a difficult and convoluted subject. The first wide recognition of Goldsmith came not long after when he scored a minutely budgeted film shot in a few weeks on location in Arizona—*Lilies of the Field*. The picture was the kind of longshot winner producers dream about. It made a star of Sidney Poitier, whose winning performance as a good hearted drifter was greatly aided by Goldsmith's infectious use of an old "clap hands" spiritual.

A film characteristic that had long been prevalent—mickey mousing, i.e., a man slips on a banana skin and the music slips with him—has been almost totally avoided by Goldsmith. His scoring tends to be subjective, and he says, "The function of a score is to enlarge the scope of a film. I try for emotional penetration—not for complementing the action. To me, the important thing about music in film is *statement*. I can't describe how I arrive at the decision to make a statement, I simply feel it and react to it. But I do know you have to be very careful with what look like obvious moments for music. It's easy to be wrong, and a scene can be changed by the weight of music, which is something many film-makers still don't seem to understand."

Goldsmith gives the impression of being diffident. He seems to take little pleasure in discussing his scores, a few of which he refuses to discuss at all. If pressed to reveal those that he liked, he will usually mention *A Patch of Blue*. He feels his music made a contribution, which is a modest evaluation. The film was a touching story of a blind girl desperately in need of human contact, and her friendship with a black man, Sidney Poitier. Everything the girl can't say or can't see is conveyed by the music, and the scene in which the girl and Poitier playfully thread beads is a masterpiece of scoring—as the beads drop in ones and twos, Goldsmith delicately places little percussive noises in the light orchestration of piano and bass strings to coincide with the beads falling on the thread. Even Goldsmith allows, this was "pretty good."

John Frankenheimer's *Seconds* was a bizarre and terrifying picture. It outlined a futuristic story of a man deliberately undergoing extreme plastic surgery in order to pass himself off as dead and then continue with a second life. Goldsmith treated a disturbing and horrifying visual in a directly opposing manner; and in writing an orderly and almost serene score, somehow came up with a perfect counterpoint. The music was everything the film wasn't, and only an imaginative composer could make such a method work.

Goldsmith is one of the less verbal of the Hollywood composers, most of whom speak freely, and sometimes volubly, about their work. He is the kind of composer who manages to do brilliant things yet finds it difficult to explain why or how he did them. His comments on the general lack of appreciation of his line of work are likely to be terse, "The fact that certain composers have been able to create first-class music within the medium of film proves that film music can be as good as the composer is gifted." Goldsmith is especially irritated by the lack of response from responsible critics. "You read reviews by top reviewers of films that not only had remarkably interesting scores, but films whose effectiveness was absolutely enhanced, and frequently created by the music, yet the reviewers seem unaware that their emotions and their nervous reactions to the films have been affected by the scoring. This is a serious flaw. Any film reviewer owes it to himself, and the public, to take every element of the film into account."

Goldsmith also feels, from watching old pictures on television, that films could do with much less music, but rightfully and tastefully placed. His own score for the almost three hours of *Patton* totals only thirty-five minutes, but the judicious placing of it seems to suggest a much wider musical coverage.

Goldsmith takes advantage of the newer technology of soundtrack recording; having worked in films since the advent of stereo and multi-track methods, his scoring utilises isolated musical sounds, directions and fades, reverberations, delayed sounds and reversed sounds. In *Planet of the Apes*, arid sounding string scales flutter across the screen when the astronauts first come upon the Forbidden Zone, and later when the gorillas attack, blood-curdling trumpeting spits out from the soundtrack and instantly communicates the fear and confusion of the astronauts.

In *Sebastian*, Goldsmith deftly counterpoints the ancient against the modern. The story has Dirk Bogarde as a crack British cryptographer, working amid banks of fantastic computers and decoding machines; yet

**Jerry Goldsmith conducting his score for** Planet of the Apes. **Goldsmith is said to turn a little ugly if the session doesn't go the way he wants.**

he is also a man "turned on" by Bach, which gave Goldsmith opportunities to use Bachian fugal passages with contemporary rhythm accompaniments. In short, baroque form in discotheque style. The scoring for this "mod" picture also uses some of the newer musical instruments, such as the varitone trumpet—this can actually play in two octaves at the same time, which, if nothing else, afford marvellous expressions for schizoid musicians. The *Sebastian* score brings up a point: should films be scored with electronic music? The answer is negative. Film scoring must always be emotional. The composer is safe, until the day someone invents a computer with a heart and soul.

Another exceptionally interesting Goldsmith score is *The Blue Max*. The film is a rather long-winded account of a German aviator's personal rise and fall during the First World War. Goldsmith went to London to score the film and there found the producers had pre-tracked the film with Richard Strauss's *Also Sprach Zarathustra* to give him an idea of what they wanted. "I admit it worked fairly well but my first reaction was to get up and walk away from the job, but I couldn't. Once you've heard music like that with the picture, it makes your own scoring more difficult to arrive at, it clouds your thinking. Later, as an inside joke, I included a snippet of the Strauss in the score—and some critic pounced on me for stealing. You can't win."

Page Cook, in his review of *The Blue Max* score for *Films in Review*, made this analysis:

The opening music begins as Bruno Stachel (George Peppard), in the trenches, enviously watches a squadron of planes pass over him. A solitary horn for this leads into the film's main theme, which alerts our mind to Stachel's aspirations. This theme is natural material, full of conflict within a relatively simple outline. It's developed with some stunning orchestral effects that simulate the sensations of being air-borne. Stachel's nature is perfectly caught in Goldsmith's music for Stachel's first "kill." It's an exciting re-working of the main theme, with brilliant woodwind coloring. There's ordinary music for Stachel's affair with a countess (Ursula Andress) but earlier, when she tries a cat and mouse seduction, the main theme is used as a waltz—mockingly. The grim side of war is effectively indicated by the fine passacaglia which accompanies the retreat of the German army. The final scenes are heightened by tense music, first as Count von Klugermann (James Mason) asks Stachel to take up the experimental plane, and second, when Stachel is performing stunts in the air, unaware of his inevitable crack-up. The finale music, though far from subtle, is a grand finish.

Goldsmith's finest score, so far, is for *Patton*. The film is one of the most incisive examinations of warfare, particularly on the command level—brilliantly photographed and directed, with a stunning and deeply perceptive performance from George C. Scott as the famed and controversial American general. Patton was a complicated and contradictory man—proud and profane, ferocious and religious—a medieval warrior in the Twentieth century, who believed in reincarnation. Goldsmith captures the man in music; the jaunty main theme, a catchy tune in breezy martial tempo, denotes this soldier's joy of battle, his absolute belief in himself. Whenever Patton thinks of war, as he does when he looks across the scene of some ancient battleground in Africa and says, "I was here," the sound of archaic trumpets cry out in triplets and fade away, as if passing through the man's mind. The *Patton* score is a major film achievement.

As Goldsmith sees it, the real problem of film music is foisting art upon commerce. The composer who can't come to terms with realising that he is part of a big business enterprise had best avoid the medium. As for the limitations and restrictions people assume to be the bane of the film composer's life, "Working to timings and synchronising your musical thoughts with the film can be stimulating rather than restrictive. Scoring *is* a limitation but like any limitation is can be made to work *for* you. Verdi, except for a handful of pieces, worked best when he was 'turned on' by a libretto. The most difficult problem in music is form, and in a film you already have this problem solved for you. You are presented with a basic structure, a blueprint, and provided the film has been well put together, well edited, it often suggests its own rhythms and tempo. The quality of the music is strictly up to the composer. Many people seem to assume that because film music serves the visual it must be something of secondary value. Well, the function of any art is to serve a purpose in society. For many years, music and painting served religion. The thing to bear in mind is that film is the youngest of the arts, and that scoring is the youngest of the music arts. We have a great deal of development ahead of us."

\* \* \*

The film composer of the future is very likely to be a man like **Lalo Schifrin**—a man who is almost as interested in film as in music. Schifrin is a student of film. He took a film course at a university in his native Buenos Aires and studied every facet of its history and its construction. He conceives of a film as a kind of human body, "The producer is its lungs, the director is its brains, the cameraman is its eyes and the composer is its ears, and we should not be aware of any one detail too much. The music shouldn't overplay any more than an actor should overact but neither should it be so subtle it is almost non-existent."

Lalo Schifrin is also typical of the younger contemporary, and futuristically minded, composer in that his musical *modus operandi* includes a thorough classical education, a love of jazz and all kinds of improvisation, and the ability to understand and use electronic instruments and machinery. This enviable combination of skills caused Schifrin to be the Hollywood composer most in demand by the late Sixties, especially in television scoring, where producers are always looking for spectacular and distinct musical cues to arrest attention to their credit titles and opening sequences. This particular ability is highly sought after in the keenly competitive world of commercial television programming. Schifrin has scored many "pilots," the sample films with which the producers hope to inveigle sponsors and networks into running as series. Among the TV series that have been conspicuously aided by Schifrin's inventiveness are *Mission Impossible, Mannix, The Young Lawyers,* and *Medical Center.* In all these TV scores, Schifrin cleverly combines sound effects with music. All these series are contemporary subjects, and since noise is part of modern life, he utilises it in his scoring, even to the point of a musical motif arising from a sound effect. In the main title of *Medical Center,* Schrifrin uses a Moog Synthesizer to imitate the sound of a wailing ambulance siren. The wail increases in pitch and moves in harmony right through the orchestration.

Schifrin, born in 1932, is the son of the man who was thirty years the concert master of the Buenos Aires Symphony Orchestra. His uncle was also the first cellist of the same orchestra. "I was steeped in classical

Lalo Schifrin. (Photo by William R. Eastabrook)

music. Buenos Aires is spiritually a European city, there are no siestas, and the repertoire of our orchestra was basically the same as those of London or Paris. Only occasionally did they play a Latin American composition. My father was very academic in his thinking—I remember string quartets being played in our house on the week ends—my early musical training was of this kind, and I was almost asphyxiated by it. This was 'the establishment' to me and I rebelled against it. When I was sixteen I discovered modern American jazz and became addicted to it, especially the work of Thelonius Monk, Charlie Parker and Dizzy Gillespie. Jazz was the strongest influence on me because it was my own discovery, it helped me find myself. My early musical training was very severe, and jazz helped me to realise that music is alive. Later on, when I matured, I discovered that there wasn't all that much incompatibility between classical music and jazz. Jazz is very old technically and the more I studied it, the more I wanted to play well. To really understand jazz, you have to understand harmony and counterpoint—which brings you back to the classics."

Born into a totally musical milieu, Schifrin finds it difficult to pinpoint his beginnings as a composer. "I wasn't aware of the difference between composing and arranging and orchestrating and playing music—it was all part of the same thing to me, although I do remember writing a sonatine for piano when I was about fourteen." He began his formal study of composition in his late teens with Argentinian modernist Juan Carlos Paz, and later at the Paris Conservatory he furthered the study with Olivier Messiaen. On returning to Buenos Aires at the age of twenty, Schifrin started to write music for the theatre and television. His first film score was for an Argentinian art short, and modestly scored for one violin, one viola, one cello, two saxophones and one tympani.

Schifrin's second major interest in life as a young man in Buenos Aires was film. "I was a member of cinema societies and we studied all the classics, all the works of the masters, and all the good new films from everywhere. Being musically inclined I became aware of the use of music in film, and I would sometimes go three or four times to a film to hear the score. I did this with *Viva Zapata!* and was amazed at Alex North's music. I liked Georges Auric's scores, and Prokofiev's *Alexander Nevsky* was one of the strongest influences on me. I thought, and still do, that Rozsa's *Ben-Hur* was great. Kaper's score for *Lord Jim* is incredible."

The turning point in Lalo Schifrin's young life was the arrival of Dizzy Gillespie in Argentina on a U.S. State Department tour in 1957. Schifrin went to meet his idol but when Gillespie heard the young man's music, he offered him a job. Schifrin proceeded to the United States a year later, once he had cleared the hurdles of immigration, and signed up with Gillespie as an arranger. His reputation grew with the Gillespie tenure, especially with his arrangements for *Jazz at the Philharmonic,* which included his Suite for Trumpet and Brass Orchestra (Gillespiana). Schifrin went on to do similar work for Count Basie, Stan Getz, Jimmy Smith and Sarah Vaughn, but gradually became tired of all the travelling this work involved. What he now wanted was a base from which to work—all the signs pointed to Hollywood, where, with his shining recommendations from some of the world's greatest jazz musicians, he had little difficulty finding work. Schifrin owes his entry into the Hollywood music world— a world populated by the brightest talent money can buy—to the late Stanley Wilson, then head of TV music at Universal. "I started scoring segments of *The Alfred Hitchcock Show, The Kraft Theatre,* and *The Vir-*

*ginian.* These were all kinds of shows—comedic, mystery, Western. It let me get used to the methods of syncronisation and the very sophisticated technology of scoring. It was a paid apprenticeship."

Schifrin scored two low budget feature films during the time he was working in television: *Rhino* and *Joy House*, neither of them memorable in any way but useful when the time came for getting his first major film assignment, *The Cincinnati Kid.* The film studios, ever cautious about using the composers who were creating new sounds in TV scoring, were more inclined to hire Schifrin when they learned he had scored a few features. *The Cincinnati Kid,* made in 1965, marked the real start of Schifrin's career as a film scorer. With this and several other films dealing with the American scene, his knowledge of jazz and the roots of American music, gave him a definite edge on some of the local composers. Schifrin's study of "blue grass" music came in especially handy when he was assigned to score *Cool Hand Luke,* a story of convicts in the South a few decades ago.

Lalo Schifrin at a party with singer Jan Daly and fellow film composer Ernest Gold.

Concerning his method and his manner of scoring films, Schifrin says, "I follow my instincts. When I try to rationalise, I cannot arrive at decisions. In general terms, I think that which is acoustical is a counterpoint to that which is visual—the *cantus firmus* concept: what is seen is tenor and what is heard is bass. My own taste runs to linear scoring, like a Japanese design, in which things are not told but suggested, implied. I admire the use of music in the Kabuki theatre in Japan, where the drama is punctuated by music. This is also similar to the traditional use of the chorus in Greek drama."

The Schifrin film scores are characterised by sparse, modernistic lines. In *The Fox* he used an orchestra of ten instruments of varying *timbres*, and managed to convey the bleak Canadian winter landscape and the odd relationship between the two women living together and the tension aroused by a young male interloper. In *Cool Hand Luke*, Schifrin wrote a guitar theme for Paul Newman, the existential hero, a silent man. Sparingly used, the theme had to mean something when it spoke for Newman— what it spoke of was his contempt for the prison, his rebellion and his strength. At those times, the music was foreground, not background. Dexterously used, a musical theme can sometimes become almost a character in the film.

Three of Schifrin's most interesting scores have been in films that met with little response from the public, *Che, The Brotherhood*, and *Hell in the Pacific*. Schifrin claims that the first script of the Che Guevara story was primarily an action vehicle and that it was later spoiled by attempts at political philosophising. The most vital part of the film, visually and musically, is the opening credit title sequence, in which split screen projection tells the story of the finding of Che's body and of bringing it by helicopter to an army base. "Che came from Argentina and he died in Bolivia. Coincidentally, the music of northern Argentina, Bolivia and Peru is from Inca sources. For the main title I used a dirge and scored it for drums and wooden flutes from the Andes, which have a piercing quality. I wanted these Bolivian scenes to have a primitive feeling, one of despair, in contrast to the Cuban scenes.

"In scoring *The Brotherhood*, I also considered it necessary to give a genuine ethnic feeling to the music because this was a story of an ancient Sicilian tradition, the Mafia. I went into research on Sicilian music and I think this helped convey the strange, medieval code of the main characters. The jew's harp came in useful in this score. With *Hell in the Pacific*, I didn't want to be ethnic. This was about two men marooned on a South Pacific island in the Second World War—a Japanese and an American, with neither of them able to speak the language of the other. You didn't need to comment on the fact that they were Japanese or American, only that they were afraid and suspicious and hostile. There was no dialogue, just snatches of monologue, so the music had to speak for them. The music doesn't have to be loud—what we see is the loneliness, the solitude, the sexual misery of these two men. Under these conditions, a flute can have the impact of an orchestra—an orchestra would be overpowering. I believe single instruments can be very communicative."

Lalo Schifrin was approached by the music department of the University of California, Los Angeles, to conduct a class in film composition. UCLA's rival, The University of Southern California, had long established an excellent course in film composition, first under Miklos Rozsa and then under David Raksin. Schifrin was puzzled by the request. "I told them I had had no experience in teaching and they said, 'It doesn't matter, just go ahead and do it.' I quickly devised a method. My first assignment to the students was: write a musical description of the colour orange, and do it with just one sound. They all came up with different solutions. Next class: write a description of a still photograph of a scene or a landscape. Afterwards came my requests for descriptions of an abstract painting; a photograph with human beings in it; and then a musical illustration of a comic strip. This seemed to me a functional way of teaching. Writing film music is a very personal form of composition. In addition to the understanding of drama, I want to encourage the students' sensitivity to audio-visual counterpoint."

Schifrin's own compositions are those that are likely to interest contemporary students, who tend to be impatient with the old-line film composers. Apart from his film scores, Schifrin has written a dramatic cantata based on his score for the TV film, *The Rise and Fall of the Third Reich*, an orchestral study called *The Ritual of Sound*, a trumpet concerto, a piano concerto, *A Jazz Suite on the Mass Texts*, and a piece for chamber orchestra —*Variants on a Madrigal by Gesualdo*. Some of these scores look like the blueprints of computing systems. It would seem that today's composer needs also to be a mathematical wizard with a head for electronics.

The assumption that Lalo Schifrin might take a disdainful view of the film music written by the previous Hollywood generation is false. "I am far from denying the past in any art. We owe to Max Steiner and Alfred Newman and the others all the things we do now—it is easier to improve upon something than it is to discover it. History is a continuity. Beethoven was a development of Mozart and Haydn, and Brahms was a development of Beethoven. *Avant-garde* music is not a negation of the musical past—it's an extension of it. When Schoenberg was young he wrote in the style of Mahler, and Mahler was a continuation of Wagner. And the Prelude of *Tristan and Isolde* was the beginning of contemporary music because it's so chromatic it's one step from atonality.

"Things are changing fast—the cycle of life is moving quickly. I belonged to a new generation but new people are coming into film and music all the time; and yet I think we are still at the beginning. A new art form has already started to shape: it's not impossible that the concert hall of the future will be a combination of music, movies, theatre, and choreography. Film-makers will get together with musicians to create abstract works of art with projections, paintings, still photographs and slides. It will be a conglomerate art, perhaps similar to the communes of the Middle Ages in which architects and various artists got together to build cathedrals. The arts of the future may well be collaborations, and film-making is already the first step in that direction."

# 8
# Film Music on Records

This chapter differs from the basic nature of this book in that it is not confined only to those composers mentioned in the previous chapters. My purpose here was to provide a listing of all the best examples of film composition, many of which did not originate in California. However, please bear in mind that the listing pertains to the North American market, and the labels and serial numbers may not be those issued in other parts of the world.

The listing is selective, and admittedly a shade arbitrary in that it is confined to scores that are original, and mostly orchestral, compositions for dramatic and comedy films. It does not include the scores of film musicals. Categories in this region tend to overlap each other but the category dealt with here is broadly that of incidental, background music. I like to think the selection represents much more than my own tastes in film music, although I have been personal in not listing those examples of scoring I truly believe to be downright inferior. By the same token, I am willing to concede that any and all omissions may be taken as lack of judgement on my part.

This listing is confined to Long Play (33⅓ rpm) recordings. It seemed to me to be futile to list 45 rpm and 78 rpm recordings: most serious film music which has appeared on 45 has also been available on LP. In the case of 78 rpm discs, the odds are against the collector locating the few worthwhile pieces of film music recorded at that speed and not later transferred to LP. Decca transferred their 78 rpm albums of Young's *For Whom the Bell Tolls*, and Newman's *The Song of Bernadette*, but RCA Victor did not, most regrettably, transfer to LP their 78 rpm sets of Raksin's *Forever Amber*, Rozsa's *The Jungle Book* (with Sabu as narrator) or the Boston Pops' eight sides of Tiomkin's *Duel in the Sun*. Lest it seem that these commercial considerations exist only in the United States, perhaps we should point out that no British record company deemed it viable to make LP transfers of the excellent 78 rpm recordings that were once available of Walton's *Spitfire* (Prelude and Fugue), John Ireland's suite from *The Overlanders*, or the Epilogue of Vaughan Williams's *49th Parallel*.

221

A word of caution: the term "soundtrack" has been badly abused. A genuine example of a soundtrack recording would be one directly from the film and including everything acoustical. Most albums are made up either of the pre-recorded music tracks or, very often, completely re-recorded selections from the score.

Additional points concerning this listing: in choosing between the monaural and stereo serial numbers of the discs, I have opted for the stereo, this method of recording having supplanted the other. On a more aesthetic level, I have omitted listing famous concert compositions that were derived from film scores, for example: Prokofiev's *Lt. Kije,* and *Alexander Nevsky,* or Richard Addinsell's *Warsaw Concerto.* It seemed to me that these pieces have become somewhat removed from the kind of film music recordings dealt with in this list, i.e., recordings of complete scores as they were heard in the film, or arrangements into suite form of selections from film scores with little change in concept or orchestral texture. The listing also does not include the many albums of film themes—single themes re-arranged into light orchestral pieces. Both Victor Young and Henry Mancini have produced many albums of this nature, containing themes from their own and other composers' scores. The Young and Mancini albums listed here are those each devoted to a single score.

Another sound reason for confining this listing to LP recordings is the fact of life that collecting recorded film music is a minority interest—the record companies are mainly concerned with the tastes of the majority—and the avid collector will have trouble enough locating LP's without needlessly frustrating himself in the search for other phonographic speeds. Such collectors are aware, as newcomers have possibly yet to learn, that film music recordings tend to be quickly deleted from the catalogues—some deserve to be, but, sadly, the tasty grains are oft discarded with the chaff.

**RICHARD ADDINSELL**
*Loss of Innocence (The Greengage Summer).*
Conducted by the composer.          Colpix CP 508

**JOHN ADDISON**
All recordings conducted by the composer:
| | |
|---|---|
| *Tom Jones.* | United Artists UAS 5113 |
| *The Amorous Adventures of Moll Flanders.* | RCA LOC 1113 |
| *Torn Curtain.* | Decca DL 9155 |
| *The Honeypot.* | United Artists UAS 5159 |
| *The Charge of the Light Brigade.* | United Artists UAS 5177 |

**WILLIAM ALWYN**
*Shake Hands with the Devil.* Conducted by
the composer.          United Artists UAS 5043

**DANIEL AMFITHEATROF**
All recordings conducted by the composer:
*The Mountain.*          Decca DL 8449

| | |
|---|---|
| *Spanish Affair.* | Dot DLP 3078 |
| *Major Dundee.* | Columbia OS 2780 |

**DAVID AMRAM**
All recordings conducted by the composer:

| | |
|---|---|
| *The Young Savages.* | Columbia CL 1672 |
| *The Arrangement.* | Warner Bros. 1824 |

**GEORGE ANTHEIL**

| | |
|---|---|
| *The Pride and the Passion.* Conducted by Ernest Gold. | Capitol W 873 |

**MALCOLM ARNOLD**
All recordings conducted by the composer:

| | |
|---|---|
| *Trapeze.* | Columbia CL 870 |
| *The Bridge on the River Kwai.* | Columbia CL 1100 |
| *The Inn of the Sixth Happiness.* | 20th Century-Fox 3011 |
| *The Key.* | Columbia CL 1185 |
| *Tunes of Glory.* | United Artists UAS 5086 |
| *The Roots of Heaven.* | 20th Century-Fox 3005 |
| *The Lion.* | London M 76001 |
| *Nine Hours to Rama.* | Decca LK 4527 |
| *The Heroes of Telemark.* | Mainstream 56064 |

**GEORGES AURIC**

| | |
|---|---|
| *Bonjour Tristesse.* Conducted by the composer. | RCA LOC 1040 |

**JOHN BARRY**
All recordings conducted by the composer:

| | |
|---|---|
| *Four in the Morning.* | Roulette OSS 805 |
| *The Ipcress File.* | Decca DL 9124 |
| *From Russia with Love.* | United Artists UAS 5114 |
| *Zulu.* | United Artists UAS 5116 |
| *Goldfinger.* | United Artists UAS 5117 |
| *The Knack.* | United Artists UAS 5129 |
| *Thunderball.* | United Artists UAS 5132 |
| *You Only Live Twice.* | United Artists UAS 5155 |
| *The Whisperers.* | United Artists UAS 5161 |
| *The Wrong Box.* | Mainstream 56088 |
| *The Chase.* | Columbia OS 2960 |
| *Born Free.* | MGM SE 4368 |
| *King Rat.* | Mainstream 56061 |
| *The Quiller Memorandum.* | Columbia OS 6660 |
| *Deadfall.* | 20th Century-Fox 4203 |
| *On Her Majesty's Secret Service.* | United Artists UAS 5204 |
| *Petulia.* | Warner Bros. 1755 |
| *The Lion in Winter.* | Columbia OS 3250 |
| *Midnight Cowboy.* | United Artists UAS 5198 |

**SIR ARNOLD BAX**

| | |
|---|---|
| *Oliver Twist (Suite).* Conducted by the composer. | Columbia ML 2092 |

**RICHARD RODNEY BENNETT**

| | |
|---|---|
| *Far From the Madding Crowd.* Conducted by the composer. | MGM SIE 11 ST |
| *Billion Dollar Brain.* Conducted by Marcus Dods. | United Artists UAS 5174 |

**ELMER BERNSTEIN**
All recordings conducted by the composer:
*Themes from: The Rat Race, Sudden Fear, Anna Lucasta, Sweet Smell of Success, The Man with the Golden Arm, and Walk on the Wild Side.*      Choreo A 11
*The Ten Commandments.* (Re-recorded version).      Dot DLP 25054 United Artists UAS 6495
*The Man with the Golden Arm.*      Decca DL 8527
*Drango.*      Liberty 3036
*God's Little Acre.*      United Artists UAL 40002
*Men in War.*      Imperial LP 9032
*Desire under the Elms.*      Dot DLP 3095
*The Buccaneer.*      Columbia CL 1278
*Sweet Smell of Success.*      Decca DL 8610
*Kings Go Forth.*      Capitol W 1063
*Some Came Running.*      Capitol W 1109
*Summer and Smoke.*      RCA LOC 1067
*The Carpetbaggers.*      MGM A 45
*The Great Escape.*      United Artists UAS 5107
*The Caretakers.*      Ava AS 31
*To Kill a Mocking Bird.*      Ava A 20
*The Hallelujah Trail.*      United Artists UAS 5127
*Cast a Giant Shadow.*      United Artists UAS 5138
*The Silencers.*      RCA LOC 1120
*The Sons of Katie Elder.*      Columbia OL 6420
*Baby, the Rain Must Fall.*      Ava A 53
*Hawaii.*      United Artists UAS 5143
*The Scalphunters.*      United Artists UAS 5176
*The Return of the Seven* (*The Magnificent Seven* score re-used).      United Artists UAS 5146
*True Grit.*      Capitol ST 263
*Where's Jack?*      Paramount PAS 5005

**LEONARD BERNSTEIN**
*On the Waterfront (Suite).* Conducted by the composer.      Columbia MS 6251

**SIR ARTHUR BLISS**
*Things to Come (Suite).* Conducted by the composer.      RCA LM 2257

**CHARLES CHAPLIN**
*The Chaplin Revue. Themes from: The Dog's Life, Shoulder Arms, and The Pilgrims.* Conducted by Eric Spears.      Decca DL 4040
*Modern Times.* Conducted by Alfred Newman.      United Artists UAL 4049
*The Countess from Hong Kong.* Conducted by Lambert Williamson.      Decca DL 71501

**AARON COPLAND**
*The Red Pony (Suite).* Conducted by Thomas Scherman.      Decca DL 9616
*Music for Movies Suite (Themes from Our Town, The City, and Of Mice and Men).* Conducted by Arthur Winograd.      MGM E 3334
*Our Town (Suite).* Conducted by the composer.      Columbia MS 7375
*Music for a Great City* (derived from the score of *Something Wild*). Conducted by the composer.      Columbia 32 11 0002

**FRANK CORDELL**
*Khartoum.* Conducted by the composer.          United Artists UAS 5140
*Cromwell.* Conducted by the composer.          Capitol SW 640

**GEORGES DELERUE**
All recordings conducted by the composer:
*King of Hearts.*                               United Artists UAS 5150
*Viva Maria.*                                   United Artists UAS 5135
*The 25th Hour.*                                MGM E 4464
*A Man for All Seasons.*                        RCA VDM 116
*Anne of the Thousand Days.*                    Decca DL 79174
*The Horsemen.*                                 Sunflower 5007

**ADOLPH DEUTSCH**
*The Apartment.* Conducted by Mitchell
Powell.                                         United Artists UAL 3105

**GEORGE DUNING**
*Salome.* Conducted by Morris Stoloff.          Decca DL 6026
*Picnic.* Conducted by Morris Stoloff.          Decca DL 8320
*From Here to Eternity.* Conducted by Morris
Stoloff.                                        Decca DL 8396
*Cowboy.* Conducted by Morris Stoloff.          Decca DL 8684
*Bell, Book and Candle.*                        Colpix 502
*The Devil at 4 O'Clock.*                       Colpix 509
*Me and the Colonel.*                           RCA LOC 1046
*The World of Suzie Wong.* Conducted by
Muir Mathieson.                                 RCA LSO 1059
*Any Wednesday.* Conducted by the com-
poser.                                          Warner Bros. 1669

**ROBERT FARNON**
*Shalako.* Conducted by Muir Mathieson.         Phillips 600-286

**JERRY FIELDING**
Both recordings conducted by the composer:
*Advise and Consent.*                           RCA LOC 1068
*The Wild Bunch.*                               Warner Bros. 1814

**BENJAMIN FRANKEL**
Both recordings conducted by the composer:
*The Night of the Iguana.*                      MGM E 4247
*The Battle of the Bulge.*                      Warner Bros. 1617

**HUGO FRIEDHOFER**
*Island in the Sky.* Conducted by Emil New-
man.                                            Decca DL 7029
*The Barbarian and the Geisha.* Conducted by
Kurt Graunke.                                   20th Century-Fox 3004
*Boy on a Dolphin.* Conducted by Lionel
Newman.                                         Decca DL 8580
*The Sun Also Rises.* Conducted by Lionel
Newman.                                         Kapp KDL 7001
*The Young Lions.* Conducted by Lionel
Newman.                                         Decca DL 8719
*This Earth Is Mine.* Conducted by Joseph
Gershenson.                                     Decca DL 8915
*One Eyed Jacks.*                               Liberty LOM 16001
*The Best Years of Our Lives (Main theme
only).* Conducted by Victor Young.              Decca DL 8364

**PAUL GLASS**
*Bunny Lake Is Missing.* Conducted by the
composer.                                       RCA LOC 1115

**ERNEST GOLD**
All recordings conducted by the composer, except where otherwise noted:
*Themes from: It's a Mad, Mad, Mad, Mad World, The Young Philadelphians, Judgment at Nuremberg, The Last Sunset, Inherit the Wind, Pressure Point, A Child Is Waiting, On the Beach, Saddle Pals, Exodus, and Too Much, Too Soon.*      London LL 3320
*Too Much, Too Soon.* Conducted by Ray Heindorf.      Mercury MG 20381
*On the Beach.*      Roulette 25098
*Judgment at Nuremberg.*      United Artists UAS 5095
*It's a Mad, Mad, Mad, Mad World.*      United Artists UAS 5110
*Exodus.*      RCA LSO 1058
*Ship of Fools*
*(Re-orchestrated score).* Conducted by Arthur Fiedler.      RCA LM 2817
*The Secret of Santa Vittoria.*      United Artists UAS 5200

**JERRY GOLDSMITH**
All recordings conducted by the composer, except where otherwise noted.
*Lilies of the Field.*      Epic LN 24094
*The Prize.*      MGM E 4192
*In Harm's Way.*      RCA LOC 1100
*Our Man Flint.*      20th Century-Fox 3179
*The Trouble with Angels.*      Mainstream 56073
*Stagecoach* (re-make).      Mainstream 56077
*A Patch of Blue.*      Mainstream 56068
*The Blue Max.*      Mainstream 56081
*The Sand Pebbles.* Conducted by Lionel Newman.      20th Century-Fox 4189
*In Like Flint.*      20th Century-Fox 4193
*The Hour of the Gun.*      United Artists UAS 5166
*Sebastian.*      Dot DLP 25845
*Planet of the Apes.*      Project S 5023
*Bandolero.* Conducted by Lionel Newman.      Project PR 5026
*Justine.*      Monument SLP 18123
*The Chairman.*      Tetragrammaton 5007
*Patton.*      20th Century-Fox 4208

**RON GOODWIN**
All recordings conducted by the composer:
*The Trap.*      Polydor 582004
*Those Magnificent Men in Their Flying Machines.*      20th Century-Fox 4174
*Where Eagles Dare.*      MGM SIE 16
*The Battle of Britain.* N.B. One segment written by Sir William Walton.      United Artists UAS 5201

**MORTON GOULD**
*Cinerama Holiday.* Conducted by Jack Shaindlin.      Mercury MG 20059
*Windjammer.* Conducted by Jack Shaindlin.      Columbia CL 1158
*World War One* (TV score). Conducted by the composer.      RCA LM 2791

**JOHN GREEN**
All recordings conducted by the composer:
*Raintree County.*      Complete version: RCA LOC 600
Highlights from above: RCA LOC 1038
Concert suite: Columbia CS 8913

| | |
|---|---|
| *Twilight of Honor.* | MGM E 4185 |
| *They Shoot Horses, Don't They?* | ABC OL 10 |

### DAVID GRUSIN
All recordings conducted by the composer:

| | |
|---|---|
| *Divorce, American Style.* | United Artists UAS 5163 |
| *The Heart Is a Lonely Hunter.* | Warner Bros. 1759 |
| *Winning.* | Decca DL 79169 |

### MANOS HADJIDAKIS
All recordings conducted by the composer:

| | |
|---|---|
| *Never on Sunday.* | United Artists UAS 5070 |
| *Topkapi.* | United Artists UAS 5118 |
| *America, America.* | Warner Bros. 1527 |
| *Blue.* | Dot DLP 25855 |

### BERNARD HERRMANN
All recordings conducted by the composer, except where otherwise noted:

| | |
|---|---|
| *Music from: Psycho, Marnie, North by Northwest, Vertigo, and The Trouble with Harry.* | London SP 44126 |
| *The Snows of Kilimanjaro (Memory Waltz only).* | Columbia CS 8913 |
| *Music from: Jane Eyre, The Snows of Kilimanjaro, Citizen Kane, and The Devil and Daniel Webster.* | London SP 44144 |
| *The Egyptian (part score).* Conducted by Alfred Newman | Decca DL 9014 |
| *Hangover Square (Piano concerto only).* Conducted by Werner Janssen, with Max Rabinowitsch, pianist. | RCA Camden CAL 205 |
| *The Three Worlds of Gulliver.* | Colpix 414 |
| *The Seventh Voyage of Sinbad.* | Colpix 504 |
| *Vertigo.* Conducted by Muir Mathieson. | Mercury MG 20384 |
| *Welles Raises Kane (Suite) and The Devil and Daniel Webster (Suite).* | Virtuoso 13010 |

N. B. Herrmann's opera, *Wuthering Heights*, contains a few themes derived from his film scores, and has been recorded in Britain: Pye CSCL 30173.

### KENYON HOPKINS
All recordings conducted by the composer, except where otherwise noted:

| | |
|---|---|
| *Baby Doll.* (Conducted by Ray Heindorf) | Columbia CL 958 |
| *The Strange One.* | Coral 57132 |
| *The Yellow Canary.* | Verve 8548 |
| *The Fugitive Kind.* | United Artists UAL 4065 |
| *The Hustler.* | Kapp KL 1264 |
| *This Property Is Condemned.* | Verve VG 8664 |
| *Mr. Buddwing.* | Verve V 8638 |

### MAURICE JARRE
All recordings conducted by the composer:

| | |
|---|---|
| *Lawrence of Arabia.* | Colpix 514 |
| *The Collector.* | Mainstream 56053 |
| *The Train.* | United Artists UAS 5122 |
| *Behold a Pale Horse.* | Colpix 519 |
| *Doctor Zhivago.* | MGM SIE 6 ST |
| *Is Paris Burning?* | Columbia OL 6630 |
| *The Professionals.* | RCA COMO 5001 |
| *Grand Prix.* | MGM IE 8 ST |
| *The Night of the Generals.* | RCA COMO 5002 |
| *The Damned.* | Warner Bros. 1829 |
| *Villa Rides!* | Dot DLP 25870 |
| *Ryan's Daughter.* | MGM 1SE—27 ST |

**BRONISLAU KAPER**

| | |
|---|---|
| *Lili.* Conducted by Hans Sommer. | MGM E 187 |
| *Themes from Lili, Invitation, The Glass Slipper, and The Power and the Prize.* Conducted by John Green. | MGM E 3694 |
| *The Swan.* Conducted by John Green. | MGM E 3399 |
| *Auntie Mame.* Conducted by Ray Heindorf. | Warner Bros. 1242 |
| *Mutiny on the Bounty.* Conducted by Robert Armbruster. | MGM IE4 |
| *Lord Jim.* Conducted by Muir Mathieson. | Colpix 521 |
| *The Way West.* Conducted by Andre Previn. | United Artists UAS 5149 |
| *A Flea in Her Ear.* Conducted by Lionel Newman. | 20th Century-Fox 4200 |

**SOL KAPLAN**

All recordings conducted by the composer:

| | |
|---|---|
| *The Victors.* | Colpix 516 |
| *The Spy Who Came in from the Cold.* | RCA LOC 1118 |
| *Judith.* | RCA LOC 1119 |

**CHRISTOPHER KOMEDA**

| | |
|---|---|
| *Rosemary's Baby.* Conducted by Dick Hazard. | Dot DLP 25875 |

**ERICH WOLFGANG KORNGOLD**

| | |
|---|---|
| *Selections from: Kings Row, Anthony Adverse, The Private Lives of Elizabeth and Essex, The Sea Hawk, The Prince and the Pauper, The Constant Nymph, and The Adventures of Robin Hood.* Conducted by Lionel Newman. | Warner Bros. 1438 |
| *Violin Concerto in D, Opus 35.* (The concerto is built on themes from: *Another Dawn, Anthony Adverse, Juarez,* and *The Prince and the Pauper).* Conducted by Alfred Wallenstein, with Jascha Heifetz, violin. | RCA LM 1782 |
| *The Constant Nymph (Suite).* Conducted by Charles Gerhardt. | Reader's Digest RD4-26 |
| *Kings Row (Suite) and title from Deception.* Conducted by Charles Gerhardt. | Reader's Digest RD3-39 |
| *Sea Hawk (Suite).* London Festival Orchestra conducted by Stanley Black. | London SP 44173 |

**ANGELO LAVAGNINO**

| | |
|---|---|
| *The Naked Maja.* Conducted by the composer. | United Artists UAL 4031 |

**MICHAEL LEWIS**

| | |
|---|---|
| *The Madwoman of Chaillot.* Conducted by the composer. | Warner Bros. 1805 |

**HENRY MANCINI**

All recordings conducted by the composer, with one exception:

| | |
|---|---|
| *Touch of Evil.* Conducted by Joseph Gershensen. | Challenge CHL 602 |
| *High Time.* | RCA LSP 2314 |
| *Breakfast at Tiffany's.* | RCA LSP 2362 |
| *Experiment in Terror.* | RCA LSP 2442 |
| *Hatari!* | RCA LSP 2559 |
| *Charade.* | RCA LSP 2755 |
| *The Pink Panther.* | RCA LSP 2795 |
| *The Great Race.* | RCA LSP 3402 |

| | |
|---|---|
| *Arabesque.* | RCA LSP 3623 |
| *What Did You do in the War, Daddy?* | RCA LSP 3648 |
| *Two for the Road.* | RCA LSP 3802 |
| *Gunn.* | RCA LSP 3840 |
| *The Party.* | RCA LSP 3997 |
| *Darling Lili.* | RCA LSPX 1000 |
| *Me, Natalie.* | Columbia OS 3350 |
| *Gaily, Gaily.* | United Artists UAS 5202 |
| *The Molly Maguires.* | Paramount PAS 6000 |
| *The Hawaiians.* | United Artists UAS 5210 |
| *Sunflower.* | Avco Embassy 11001 |
| *Sometimes a Great Notion.* | Decca 79185 |

**JOHNNY MANDEL**
All recordings conducted by the composer:

| | |
|---|---|
| *The Americanization of Emily.* | Reprise 6151 |
| *The Sandpiper.* | Mercury SR 61032 |
| *Harper.* | Mainstream 56078 |

**HUGO MONTENEGRO**

| | |
|---|---|
| *Hurry Sundown.* Conducted by the composer. | RCA LOC 1133 |

**JEROME MOROSS**

| | |
|---|---|
| *The Big Country.* Conducted by the composer. | United Artists UAS 5004 |
| *The Cardinal.* Conducted by the composer. | RCA LOC 1084 |
| *The War Lord.* Conducted by Joseph Gershensen. | Decca DL 9149 |

**STANLEY MYERS**

| | |
|---|---|
| *Ulysses.* Conducted by the composer. | RCA LOC 1138 |
| *No Way to Treat a Lady.* Conducted by the composer. | Dot DLP 25846 |

**MARIO NASCIMBENE**
All recordings conducted by Franco Ferrara:

| | |
|---|---|
| *Alexander the Great.* | Mercury 20148 |
| *Farewell to Arms.* | Capitol W 918 |
| *Francis of Assisi.* | 20th Century-Fox 3053 |
| *The Vikings.* | United Artists UAS 5003 |
| *Solomon and Sheba.* | United Artists UAS 5051 |
| *Barrabas.* | Colpix 510 |

**ALFRED NEWMAN**
All recordings conducted by the composer:

| | |
|---|---|
| *Themes from: A Man Called Peter, The President's Lady, The Seven Year Itch, David and Bathsheba, The Bluebird, The Hurricane, Desiree, Come to the Stable, Life Begins at 8.30, Wuthering Heights, The Snows of Kilimanjaro, and The Song of Bernadette.* | Decca DL 8123 |
| *Themes from: All about Eve, The Song of Bernadette, A Letter to Three Wives, The Razor's Edge, Pinky, and Wuthering Heights.* | Mercury MG 20037 |
| *Themes from: Anastasia, The Hurricane, and The Pleasure of His Company.* | Capitol T 1652 |
| *The Song of Bernadette.* | Decca DL 5358 |
| *Captain from Castille.* | Mercury MG 20005 |
| *The Robe.* | Decca DL 9012 |
| *The Egyptian* (part score). | Decca DL 9014 |

| | |
|---|---|
| *Themes from: The Robe, David and Bathsheba, Anastasia, Pinky, and Captain from Castille.* | Capitol P 8639 |
| *A Certain Smile.* | Columbia CL 1194 |
| *Anastasia.* | Decca DL 8460 |
| *The Diary of Anne Frank.* | 20th Century-Fox 3012 |
| *How the West Was Won.* | MGM ISE5 |
| *The Greatest Story Ever Told.* | United Artists UAS 5120 |
| *Nevada Smith.* | Dot DLP 3718 |
| *Airport.* | Decca DL 79173 |

**ALEX NORTH**

All recordings conducted by the composer, except where otherwise noted:

| | |
|---|---|
| *A Streetcar Named Desire (Suite).* Conducted by Ray Heindorf. | Capitol P 387 |
| *The Rose Tattoo.* | Columbia CL 727 |
| *The Bad Seed.* Conducted by Ray Heindorf. | RCA LPM 1395 |
| *The Wonderful Country.* | United Artists UAL 4050 |
| *Four Girls in Town.* | Decca DL 8424 |
| *The Rainmaker.* | RCA LPM 1434 |
| *Themes from: A Streetcar Named Desire, Wall Street Ballet, Hot Spell, American Road, Unchained, The Racers, The Rose Tattoo, and A Member of the Wedding.* | RCA LPM 1445 |
| *The Sound and the Fury.* Conducted by Lionel Newman. | Decca DL 8885 |
| *The Long Hot Summer.* Conducted by Lionel Newman. | Roulette 25026 |
| *South Seas Adventure.* | Audio Fidelity 1899 |
| *The Misfits.* | United Artists UAS 5087 |
| *Spartacus.* | Decca DL 9092 |
| *Cleopatra.* | 20th Century-Fox 5008 |
| *Who's Afraid of Virginia Woolf?* | Warner Bros. 1656 |
| *The Agony and the Ecstasy.* | Capitol MAS 2427 |
| *The Shoes of the Fisherman.* | MGM SIE 15 ST |
| *A Dream of Kings.* | National General 1000 |
| *Africa* (TV score). | MGM SE 4462 |

**VYACHESLAV OVCHINNIKOV**

| | |
|---|---|
| *War and Peace.* Conducted by the composer. | Capitol SWAO 2918 |

**GORDON PARKS**

| | |
|---|---|
| *The Learning Tree.* Conducted by Tom McIntosh. | Warner Bros. 1812 |

**ANDRE PREVIN**

All recordings conducted by the composer:

| | |
|---|---|
| *Invitation to the Dance (Ballet: Ring around the Rosy).* | MGM E 3207 |
| *Elmer Gantry.* | United Artists UAL 4069 |
| *The Subterraneans.* | MGM E 3812 |
| *The Four Horsemen of the Apocalypse.* | MGM S 3993 |
| *Two for the Seesaw.* | United Artists UAS 5103 |
| *Irma La Douce.* | United Artists UAS 5109 |
| *The Fortune Cookie.* | United Artists UAS 5145 |
| *Dead Ringer.* | Warner Bros. 1536 |
| *Inside Daisy Clover.* | Warner Bros. 1616 |

**JEAN PRODROMIDES**

| | |
|---|---|
| *Le Voyage en Ballon.* Conducted by Andre Girard. | Philips 200 029 |

**DAVID RAKSIN**
*Laura (Concert version of main theme).* Conducted by the composer. — Columbia CS 8913
*The Bad and the Beautiful (Concert version of main theme).* Conducted by Percy Faith. — Columbia CL 577
*The Unicorn in the Garden (Serenade).* — Classic Editions 1055
*Grounds for Marriage* (Toy Concertino only). Conducted by John Green. — MGM E 379
*Sylvia.* Conducted by the composer. — Mercury MG 21004
*Will Penny,* and five pieces from *Too Late Blues.* Conducted by the composer. — Dot DLP 25844

**NELSON RIDDLE**
All recordings conducted by the composer:
*El Dorado.* — Epic FLM 13114
*A Rage to Live.* — United Artists UAS 5130

**LEONARD ROSENMAN**
All recordings conducted by the composer:
*East of Eden (Suite)* and *Rebel Without a Cause (Suite).* Conducted by Ray Heindorf. — Columbia CL 940
*Edge of the City (Suite).* — MGM E 3501
*The Cobweb (Suite).* Conducted by John Green. — MGM E 3501
*The Chapman Report.* — Warner Bros. 1478
*Beneath the Planet of the Apes.* — Amos 8001
*A Man Called Horse.* — Columbia OS 3530

**LAURENCE ROSENTHAL**
*Becket.* Conducted by Muir Mathieson. — Decca DL 9117
*The Comedians.* Conducted by the composer. — MGM E 4494
*Hotel Paradiso.* Conducted by the composer. — MGM SE 4419

**NINO ROTA**
*War and Peace.* Conducted by Franco Ferrara. — Columbia CL 930
*La Dolce Vita.* — RCA FOL 1
*Rocco and His Brothers.* — RCA FOC 2
*8½* — RCA FOC 6
*The Leopard.* — 20th Century-Fox 5015
*Juliet of the Spirits.* Conducted by Carlo Savina. — Mainstream 56062
*The Taming of the Shrew.* — RCA VDM 117
*Romeo and Juliet.* — Capitol ST 400
*Fellini's Satyricon.* — United Artists UAS 5208
*Waterloo.* Conducted by Bruno Nicolai. — Paramount PAS 6003

**MIKLOS ROZSA**
All recordings conducted by the composer, except where otherwise noted:
*Suites from The Thief of Bagdad, and The Jungle Book.* Both suites narrated by Leo Genn. — RCA LM 2118
*The Lost Weekend (Main theme only).* Conducted by Al Goodman. — RCA LPT 1008
*Spellbound.* Conducted by Ray Heindorf. — Warner Bros. 1213
*Quo Vadis.* — MGM E 103
*Quo Vadis* (dramatic highlights). — MGM E 3524
*Quo Vadis Suite,* and *Spellbound Concerto* (conducted by Erich Kloss) and *Suite from The Red House* (conducted by the composer). — Capitol P 456
*Suites from Ivanhoe, Madame Bovary, and*

| | |
|---|---|
| *Plymouth Adventure.* | MGM E 3507 |
| *Julius Caesar.* | MGM E 3033 |
| *Lust for Life (Suite) and selections from: Brute Force, The Killers, and The Naked City.* | Decca DL 10015 |
| *A Time to Love and a Time to Die.* | Decca DL 8778 |
| *Ben-Hur.* | MGM S IEI |
| *Musical highlights from Ben-Hur.* Conducted by Erich Kloss. | MGM L 70123 |
| *More Music from Ben-Hur.* Conducted by Erich Kloss. | MGM E 3900 |
| *King of Kings.* | MGM SIE 2ST |
| *El Cid.* | MGM E 3977 |
| *Sodom and Gomorrah.* | RCA LOC 1076 |
| *The VIP's.* | MGM E 4152 |
| *Selections from Sodom and Gomorrah, Spellbound, Lydia, King of Kings, Quo Vadis, Ben-Hur, Madame Bovary, Diane, and El Cid.* The Rome Symphony Orchestra conducted by Carlos Savina and the composer. | MGM E 4112 |
| *Selections from Quo Vadis, Ben-Hur, King of Kings, and El Cid.* | Capitol ST 2837 |

N.B. Of the many recorded concert works of Miklos Rozsa, those that may most interest admirers of his film career are:
*Overture to a Symphony Concert, Opus 26; Three Hungarian Sketches; Theme, Variations and Finale, Opus 13; and Notturna Ungherese, Opus 28.*                    RCA LM 2802
The first three compositions in the previous listing are also available, in different performances, on Decca DL 9966.

**PHILLIP SAINTON**

| | |
|---|---|
| *Moby Dick.* Conducted by Louis Levy. | RCA LPM 1247 |

**LALO SCHIFRIN**

All recordings conducted by the composer:

| | |
|---|---|
| *The Cincinnati Kid.* | MGM E 4313 |
| *The Liquidator.* | MGM SE 4413 |
| *The Fox.* | Warner Bros. 1738 |
| *Cool Hand Luke.* | Dot DLP 25833 |
| *Murderers' Row.* | RCA COMO 5003 |
| *Sol Madrid.* | MGM SE 4541 |
| *Bullitt.* | Warner Bros. 1777 |
| *Mission Impossible* (TV score). | Dot DLP 3831 |
| *Che!* | Tetragammaton 5006 |
| *Mannix* (TV score). | Paramount PAS 5004 |
| *Kelly's Heroes.* | MGM ISE 23ST |
| *The Rise and Fall of the Third Reich* (Cantata based on a film score). Conducted by Lawrence Foster. | MGM SIE 12ST |

**WALTER SCHUMANN**

| | |
|---|---|
| *The Night of the Hunter.* Story and music from the score, narrated by Charles Laughton and conducted by the composer. | RCA LPM 1136 |

**BERNARDO SEGALL**

| | |
|---|---|
| *Custer of the West.* Conducted by the composer. | ABC OC5 |

**FRANK SKINNER**

All recordings conducted by Joseph Gershensen:

| | |
|---|---|
| *Magnificent Obsession.* | Decca DL 8078 |
| *Man of a Thousand Faces.* | Decca DL 8623 |
| *Imitation of Life.* | Decca DL 8879 |
| *Back Street.* | Decca DL 79097 |
| *Shenandoah.* | Decca DL 79125 |
| *Madame X.* | Decca DL 79152 |

**PAUL SMITH**
All recordings conducted by the composer:
| | |
|---|---|
| True Life Adventures: *Beaver Valley, Bear Country, Prowlers of the Everglades, Nature's Half Hour, and Olympic Elk.* | Disneyland 4011 |
| *Secrets of Life.* | Disneyland 4006 |
| *Westward Ho, the Wagons.* | Disneyland 4008 |
| *The Vanishing Prairie.* | Columbia CL 6332 |

**MISCHA SPOLIANSKY**
| | |
|---|---|
| Themes from *Idol of Paris, That Dangerous Age,* and *Wanted for Murder.* Conducted by Sidney Torch. | Columbia R 3029 |

**MAX STEINER**
All recordings conducted by the composer, except where otherwise noted:
| | |
|---|---|
| Suites from *Since You Went Away, Now Voyager,* and *The Informer.* | Capitol P 387 |
| Suites from *King Kong,* and *The Informer.* Conducted by Jack Shaindlin. | Decca DL 9079 |
| Themes from *Bird of Paradise, A Bill of Divorcement, Little Women, A Star Is Born, The Life of Emile Zola, Dark Victory, Saratoga Trunk, Adventures of Don Juan, Johnny Belinda, Helen of Troy, The McConnell Story,* and *The Last Command.* | RCA LPM 1170 |
| *Gone with the Wind* (Soundtrack). | MGM IE 10 ST |
| *Gone with the Wind* (Suite). Conducted by Muir Mathieson. | Warner Bros. 1322 |
| *Gone with the Wind (Suite),* and themes from *The Charge of the Light Brigade, The Searchers, The Fountainhead,* and *Four Wives (Symphonie Moderne).* | RCA LSP 3859 |
| *Gone with the Wind* (Suite arranged by Brian Fahey and conducted by Cyril Ornadel) N.B. This arrangement includes the Ballroom scene (reel and waltz) not available in other recordings. | MGM E 3954 |
| *Band of Angels.* | RCA LPM 1557 |
| *John Paul Jones.* | Warner Bros. 1293 |
| *Marjorie Morningstar.* | RCA LOC 1044 |
| *Parrish.* | Warner Bros. 1413 |
| *Rome Adventure.* | Warner Bros. 1458 |

**LEITH STEVENS**
| | |
|---|---|
| *Destination Moon.* Conducted by the composer. | Columbia CL 6151 |
| *The Wild One.* Conducted by the composer. | Decca DL 8349 |

**MIKIS THEODORAKIS**
All recordings conducted by the composer:
| | |
|---|---|
| *Phaedra.* | United Artists UAS 5102 |
| *Zorba the Greek.* | 20th Century-Fox 4167 |
| *Z.* | Columbia OS 3370 |

**VIRGIL THOMSON**

*Suite from Louisiana Story.* Conducted by
Eugene Ormandy.                               Columbia ML 2087
*Acadian Songs and Dances from Louisiana
Story.* Conducted by Thomas Scherman.        Decca DL 9616
*Suites from The River, and The Plow that
Broke the Plains.* Conducted by Leopold
Stokowski.                                   Vanguard VRS 1071

**DIMITRI TIOMKIN**

All recordings conducted by the composer:
*Themes from The High and the Mighty,
Champion, A Bullet Is Waiting, Strange Lady
in Town, Dial M for Murder, Return to Para-
dise, High Noon, Land of the Pharaohs, The
Adventures of Hajji Baba, Duel in the Sun,
I Confess, and Lost Horizon.*                 Coral CRL 57006
*Return to Paradise.*                         Decca DL 5489
*Giant.*                                      Capitol W 773
*Wild Is the Wind.*                           Columbia CL 1090
*Friendly Persuasion.*                        Unique (RKO) 110
*Search for Paradise.*                        RCA LOC 1034
*The Alamo.*                                  Columbia CS 8358
*The Unforgiven.*                             United Artists UAL 4068
*The Old Man and the Sea.*                    Columbia CS 8013
*The Guns of Navarone.*                       Columbia CS 8455
*55 Days at Peking.*                          Columbia CL 2028
*The Fall of the Roman Empire.*              Columbia OL 6060
*Circus World.*                               MGM E 4252
*36 Hours.*                                   Vee-Jay 1131

**RALPH VAUGHAN WILLIAMS**

*The Loves of Joanna Godden.* Conducted by
Ernest Irving.                               Columbia R 3029
*Symphony No. 7* (Based on the score of *Scott
of the Antarctic*). Conducted by Andre Previn.  RCA LSC 3066

**WILLIAM WALTON**

*Selections from Henry V,* conducted by the
composer, *and Hamlet,* conducted by Muir
Mathieson.                                   RCA LM 1924
*Richard the Third (soundtrack).*            RCA LM 6126
*Richard the Third (highlights).*            RCA LM 1940
*Suite from Richard the Third, Funeral March
from Hamlet, and Suite from Henry V.* Con-
ducted by the composer.                      Angel 36198

**FRANZ WAXMAN**

All recordings conducted by the composer:
*A Place in the Sun (Concert suite).*        Columbia CS 8913
*Crime in the Streets.*                      Decca DL 8376
*The Spirit of St. Louis.*                   RCA LPM 1472
*Sayonara.*                                  RCA LOC 1041
*Peyton Place.*                              RCA LOC 1042
*The Nun's Story.*                           Warner Bros. 1306
*My Geisha.*                                 RCA LOC 1070
*Hemingway's Adventures of a Young Man.*     RCA LOC 1074
*Taras Bulba.*                               United Artists UAS 5100
N.B. Also of possible interest to admirers of
Waxman's music:
*Sinfonietta for Strings and Timpani.* The Los
Angeles Festival Orchestra conducted by the
composer.                                    Decca DL 9889

**JOHN WILLIAMS**
All recordings conducted by the composer:

| | |
|---|---|
| *Diamond Head.* | Colpix 440 |
| *How to Steal a Million.* | 20th Century-Fox 4183 |
| *Penelope.* | MGM E 4426 |
| *Not with My Wife, You Don't.* | Warner Bros. 1668 |
| *Valley of the Dolls.* | 20th Century-Fox 4196 |
| *The Reivers.* | Columbia OS 3510 |
| *Jane Eyre.* | Capitol SW 749 |

**VICTOR YOUNG**
All recordings conducted by the composer:

| | |
|---|---|
| *Suites from For Whom the Bell Tolls, and Golden Earrings.* | Decca DL 8481 |
| *Suites from Samson and Delilah, and The Quiet Man.* | Decca DL 8566 |
| *For Whom the Bell Tolls (full score).* Conducted by Ray Heindorf. | Warner Bros. 1201 |
| *The Brave One.* | Decca DL 8344 |
| *Omar Khayyam.* | Decca DL 8449 |
| *Around the World in Eighty Days.* | Decca DL 79046 |
| *Run of the Arrow.* | Decca DL 8620 |

# 9
# The Score of the Scores

## By Clifford McCarty

A listing of the film scores of the twenty-four principal composers discussed in this book.

### GEORGE ANTHEIL

| | | |
|---|---|---|
| 1935 | Once in a Blue Moon | Paramount |
| | The Scoundrel | Paramount |
| 1937 | The Plainsman | Paramount |
| | Make Way for Tomorrow | Paramount |
| 1938 | The Buccaneer | Paramount |
| 1940 | Angels over Broadway | Columbia |
| 1946 | Specter of the Rose | Republic |
| | Plainsman and the Lady | Republic |
| | That Brennan Girl | Republic |
| 1947 | Repeat Performance | Eagle Lion |
| 1949 | Knock on any Door | Columbia |
| | We Were Strangers | Columbia |
| | The Fighting Kentuckian | Republic |
| | Tokyo Joe | Columbia |
| 1950 | House by the River | Republic |
| | In a Lonely Place | Columbia |
| 1951 | Sirocco | Columbia |
| 1952 | The Sniper | Columbia |
| | Actors and Sin | United Artists |
| 1953 | The Juggler | Columbia |
| | Dementia | Parker |
| 1954 | Hunters of the Deep (documentary) | DCA |
| 1955 | Not as a Stranger | United Artists |
| 1957 | The Young Don't Cry | Columbia |
| | The Pride and the Passion | United Artists |

### ELMER BERNSTEIN

| | | |
|---|---|---|
| 1951 | Saturday's Hero | Columbia |
| | Boots Malone | Columbia |
| 1952 | Sudden Fear | RKO |
| | Battles of Chief Pontiac | Realart |
| 1953 | Never Wave at a WAC | RKO |
| | Robot Monster | Astor |
| | Cat Women of the Moon | Astor |
| | Miss Robin Crusoe | 20th |
| 1954 | Make Haste to Live | Republic |
| | Silent Raiders | Lippert |
| 1955 | The Eternal Sea | Republic |
| | It's a Dog's Life | M-G-M |
| | The View from Pompey's Head | 20th |
| | The Man with the Golden Arm | United Artists |

| | | |
|---|---|---|
| | Storm Fear | United Artists |
| 1956 | The Naked Eye (documentary) | Stoumen |
| | The Ten Commandments | Paramount |
| 1957 | Drango | United Artists |
| | Men in War | United Artists |
| | Fear Strikes Out | Paramount |
| | Sweet Smell of Success | United Artists |
| | The Tin Star | Paramount |
| 1958 | Desire under the Elms | Paramount |
| | God's Little Acre | United Artists |
| | Kings Go Forth | United Artists |
| | Anna Lucasta | United Artists |
| | Some Came Running | M-G-M |
| | The Buccaneer | Paramount |
| 1959 | The Race for Space (documentary) | U. S. Government |
| | The Story on Page One | 20th |
| | The Miracle | Warners |
| 1960 | The Rat Race | Paramount |
| | From the Terrace | 20th |
| | Israel (documentary) | Warners |
| | The Magnificent Seven | United Artists |
| 1961 | By Love Possessed | United Artists |
| | The Young Doctors | United Artists |
| | The Comancheros | 20th |
| | Summer and Smoke | Paramount |
| 1962 | Walk on the Wild Side | Columbia |
| | Birdman of Alcatraz | United Artists |
| | A Girl Named Tamiko | Paramount |
| | Hud | Paramount |
| 1963 | To Kill a Mockingbird | Universal |
| | The Caretakers | United Artists |
| | The Great Escape | United Artists |
| | Rampage | Warners |
| | Kings of the Sun | United Artists |
| | Love with the Proper Stranger | Paramount |
| | The Carpetbaggers | Paramount |
| 1964 | The World of Henry Orient | United Artists |
| | Four Days in November (documentary) | United Artists |
| | Baby the Rain Must Fall | Columbia |
| 1965 | The Hallelujah Trail | United Artists |
| | The Sons of Katie Elder | Paramount |
| | The Reward | 20th |
| 1966 | The Silencers | Columbia |
| | Cast a Giant Shadow | United Artists |
| | Return of the Seven | United Artists |
| | Hawaii | United Artists |
| | Seven Women | M-G-M |
| 1967 | Thoroughly Modern Millie | Universal |
| 1968 | The Scalphunters | United Artists |
| | I Love You, Alice B. Toklas! | Warners |
| 1969 | True Grit | Paramount |
| | The Gypsy Moths | M-G-M |
| | Midas Run | Cinerama Releasing |
| | The Bridge at Remagen | United Artists |
| | Guns of the Magnificent Seven | United Artists |
| | Where's Jack? | Paramount |
| 1970 | The Liberation of L. B. Jones | Columbia |
| | A Walk in the Spring Rain | Columbia |
| | Cannon for Cordoba | United Artists |
| 1971 | Big Jake | National General |
| | See No Evil | Columbia |

## AARON COPLAND

| | | |
|---|---|---|
| 1939 | The City (documentary) | Civic Films |
| 1940 | Of Mice and Men | United Artists |
| | Our Town | United Artists |
| 1943 | The North Star | Goldwyn |
| 1945 | The Cummington Story (documentary) | U. S. Government |
| 1949 | The Red Pony | Republic |
| | The Heiress | Paramount |
| 1961 | Something Wild | United Artists |

## HUGO FRIEDHOFER

Friedhofer's contributions to film scoring have been too numerous and too varied to attempt a complete listing. Between 1930 and 1943 he composed portions of the scores of some sixty films, in addition to his many assignments as an arranger, adapter and orchestrator. His first screen credit for a complete original score was *The Adventures of Marco Polo* in 1938. This listing is limited to his work as a composer of complete scores:

| | | |
|---|---|---|
| 1943 | China Girl | 20th |
| | Chetniks! | 20th |
| | They Came to Blow Up America | 20th |
| | Paris after Dark | 20th |
| 1944 | The Lodger | 20th |
| | Lifeboat | 20th |
| | Roger Touhy, Gangster | 20th |
| | Home in Indiana | 20th |
| | Wing and a Prayer | 20th |
| 1945 | Brewster's Millions | United Artists |
| | Getting Gertie's Garter | United Artists |
| 1946 | The Bandit of Sherwood Forest | Columbia |
| | Gilda | Columbia |
| | So Dark the Night | Columbia |
| | The Best Years of Our Lives | Goldwyn |
| 1947 | Body and Soul | United Artists |
| | Wild Harvest | Paramount |
| | The Bishop's Wife | Goldwyn |
| | The Swordsman | Columbia |
| | A Song Is Born | Goldwyn |
| 1948 | Adventures of Casanova | Eagle Lion |
| | Black Bart | Universal |
| | Sealed Verdict | Paramount |
| | Joan of Arc | RKO |
| | Enchantment | Goldwyn |
| 1949 | Bride of Vengeance | Paramount |
| | Roseanna McCoy | Goldwyn |
| 1950 | Guilty of Treason | Eagle Lion |
| | Three Came Home | 20th |
| | Captain Carey, U.S.A. | Paramount |
| | No Man of Her Own | Paramount |
| | Broken Arrow | 20th |
| | Edge of Doom | Goldwyn |
| | Two Flags West | 20th |
| | The Sound of Fury | United Artists |
| 1951 | Queen for a Day | United Artists |
| | Ace in the Hole | Paramount |
| 1952 | Rancho Notorious | RKO |
| | The Marrying Kind | Columbia |
| | The Outcasts of Poker Flat | 20th |
| | Lydia Bailey | 20th |
| | Just for You | Paramount |
| | Above and Beyond | M-G-M |
| | Face to Face | RKO |
| 1953 | Thunder in the East | Paramount |

| | | |
|---|---|---|
| | Island in the Sky | Warners |
| | Hondo | Warners |
| 1954 | Vera Cruz | United Artists |
| 1955 | White Feather | 20th |
| | Violent Saturday | 20th |
| | Soldier of Fortune | 20th |
| | Seven Cities of Gold | 20th |
| | The Rains of Ranchipur | 20th |
| 1956 | The Harder They Fall | Columbia |
| | The Revolt of Mamie Stover | 20th |
| | Between Heaven and Hell | 20th |
| 1957 | Oh, Men! Oh, Women! | 20th |
| | Boy on a Dolphin | 20th |
| | An Affair to Remember | 20th |
| | The Sun Also Rises | 20th |
| 1958 | The Young Lions | 20th |
| | The Bravados | 20th |
| | The Barbarian and the Geisha | 20th |
| | In Love and War | 20th |
| 1959 | Woman Obsessed | 20th |
| | This Earth is Mine | Universal |
| | The Blue Angel | 20th |
| | Never So Few | M-G-M |
| 1960 | One-Eyed Jacks | Paramount |
| 1961 | Homicidal | Columbia |
| 1962 | Geronimo | United Artists |
| | Beauty and the Beast | United Artists |
| 1964 | The Secret Invasion | United Artists |
| 1971 | Richtofen and Brown | United Artists |

**ERNEST GOLD**

Between 1945 and 1957 Gold was employed on a large number of films as an orchestrator, arranger and collaborating composer. This listing is limited to his complete scores:

| | | |
|---|---|---|
| 1945 | The Girl of the Limberlost | Columbia |
| 1946 | The Falcon's Alibi | RKO |
| | Smooth as Silk | Universal |
| | G.I. War Brides | Republic |
| 1947 | Lighthouse | PRC |
| | Wyoming (with Nathan Scott) | Republic |
| | Exposed | Republic |
| 1948 | Old Los Angeles | Republic |
| 1951 | Unknown World | Lippert |
| 1953 | Jennifer | Allied Artists |
| | Man Crazy | 20th |
| 1954 | Karamoja (documentary) | Hallmark |
| | The Other Woman | 20th |
| 1955 | The Naked Street | United Artists |
| 1956 | Unidentified Flying Objects (documentary) | United Artists |
| | Edge of Hell | Universal |
| | Running Target | United Artists |
| 1957 | Affair in Havana | Allied Artists |
| | Man on the Prowl | United Artists |
| 1958 | Too Much, Too Soon | Warners |
| | Wink of an Eye | United Artists |
| | Tarzan's Fight for Life | M-G-M |
| | The Defiant Ones | United Artists |
| | The Screaming Skull | American International |
| 1959 | The Young Philadelphians | Warners |
| | Battle of the Coral Sea | Columbia |
| | On the Beach | United Artists |
| 1960 | Inherit the Wind | United Artists |

| | | |
|---|---|---|
| | Exodus | United Artists |
| 1961 | A Fever in the Blood | Warners |
| | The Last Sunset | Universal |
| | Judgment at Nuremberg | United Artists |
| 1962 | Pressure Point | United Artists |
| | A Child Is Waiting | United Artists |
| 1963 | It's a Mad, Mad, Mad, Mad World | United Artists |
| 1965 | Ship of Fools | Columbia |
| 1969 | The Secret of Santa Vittoria | United Artists |

**JERRY GOLDSMITH**

| | | |
|---|---|---|
| 1957 | Black Patch | Warners |
| 1959 | City of Fear | Columbia |
| | Face of a Fugitive | Columbia |
| 1960 | Studs Lonigan | United Artists |
| 1962 | Lonely Are the Brave | Universal |
| | The Spiral Road | Universal |
| | Freud | Universal |
| 1963 | The Stripper | 20th |
| | The List of Adrian Messenger | Universal |
| | A Gathering of Eagles | Universal |
| | Lilies of the Field | United Artists |
| | The Prize | M-G-M |
| | Take Her, She's Mine | 20th |
| 1964 | Seven Days in May | Paramount |
| | Shock Treatment | 20th |
| | Fate Is the Hunter | 20th |
| | Rio Conchos | 20th |
| 1965 | The Satan Bug | United Artists |
| | In Harm's Way | Paramount |
| | Von Ryan's Express | 20th |
| | Morituri | 20th |
| | A Patch of Blue | M-G-M |
| | Our Man Flint | 20th |
| 1966 | To Trap a Spy | M-G-M |
| | The Trouble with Angels | Columbia |
| | Stagecoach | 20th |
| | The Blue Max | 20th |
| | Seconds | Paramount |
| | The Sand Pebbles | 20th |
| | Warning Shot | Paramount |
| 1967 | In Like Flint | 20th |
| | The Flim-Flam Man | 20th |
| | Hour of the Gun | United Artists |
| | Sebastian | Paramount |
| 1968 | Planet of the Apes | 20th |
| | The Detective | 20th |
| | Bandolero! | 20th |
| 1969 | The Illustrated Man | Warners |
| | 100 Rifles | 20th |
| | The Chairman | 20th |
| | Justine | 20th |
| 1970 | The Ballad of Cable Hogue | Warners |
| | Patton | 20th |
| | Tora! Tora! Tora! | 20th |
| | Rio Lobo | National General |
| 1971 | The Mephisto Waltz | 20th |
| | Klute | Warners |

**JOHN GREEN**

Green's musical activities in films have been multi-varied, including much arranging, conducting, directing and supervision in addition to composition. His association with M-G-M began in 1944 and he was responsible for the music direction of many of that studio's successful musicals over the period of a dozen years. Many of these films contained underscoring which utilised original material by Green as well as arrangements of source material. The following listing is limited to scores composed or adapted by Green:

| | | |
|---|---|---|
| 1944 | Broadway Rhythm | M-G-M |
| | Bathing Beauty | M-G-M |
| 1945 | Week-End at the Waldorf | M-G-M |
| | The Sailor Takes a Wife | M-G-M |
| 1946 | Easy to Wed | M-G-M |
| 1947 | It Happened in Brooklyn | M-G-M |
| | Fiesta | M-G-M |
| | Something in the Wind | Universal |
| 1948 | Easter Parade | M-G-M |
| | Up in Central Park | Universal |
| 1949 | The Inspector General | Warners |
| 1950 | Summer Stock | M-G-M |
| 1951 | Royal Wedding | M-G-M |
| | The Great Caruso | M-G-M |
| | An American in Paris | M-G-M |
| 1952 | Because You're Mine | M-G-M |
| 1954 | Brigadoon | M-G-M |
| 1956 | High Society | M-G-M |
| 1957 | Raintree County | M-G-M |
| 1960 | Pepe | Columbia |
| 1963 | Twilight of Honor | M-G-M |
| 1966 | Alvarez Kelly | Columbia |
| 1968 | Oliver! | Columbia |
| 1969 | They Shoot Horses, Don't They? | Cinerama Releasing |

## BERNARD HERRMANN

| | | |
|---|---|---|
| 1941 | Citizen Kane | RKO |
| | All That Money Can Buy | RKO |
| 1942 | The Magnificent Ambersons | RKO |
| 1944 | Jane Eyre | 20th |
| 1945 | Hangover Square | 20th |
| 1946 | Anna and the King of Siam | 20th |
| 1947 | The Ghost and Mrs. Muir | 20th |
| 1951 | The Day the Earth Stood Still | 20th |
| | On Dangerous Ground | RKO |
| 1952 | Five Fingers | 20th |
| | The Snows of Kilimanjaro | 20th |
| 1953 | White Witch Doctor | 20th |
| | Beneath the 12-Mile Reef | 20th |
| | King of the Khyber Rifles | 20th |
| 1954 | Garden of Evil | 20th |
| | The Egyptian (with Alfred Newman) | 20th |
| 1955 | Prince of Players | 20th |
| | The Kentuckian | United Artists |
| | The Trouble with Harry | Paramount |
| 1956 | The Man in the Gray Flannel Suit | 20th |
| | The Man Who Knew Too Much | Paramount |
| 1957 | The Wrong Man | Warners |
| | A Hatful of Rain | 20th |
| | The Williamsburg Story (documentary) | Rockefeller |
| 1958 | Vertigo | Paramount |
| | The Naked and the Dead | Warners |
| | The 7th Voyage of Sinbad | Columbia |
| 1959 | North by Northwest | M-G-M |
| | Blue Denim | 20th |
| | Journey to the Center of the Earth | 20th |

| 1960 | Psycho | Paramount |
| | The 3 Worlds of Gulliver | Columbia |
| 1961 | Mysterious Island | Columbia |
| | Cape Fear | Universal |
| | Tender is the Night | 20th |
| 1963 | Jason and the Argonauts | Columbia |
| 1964 | Marnie | Universal |
| 1965 | Joy in the Morning | M-G-M |
| 1966 | Fahrenheit 451 | Universal |
| 1968 | The Bride Wore Black | Lopert |
| 1969 | Twisted Nerve | National General |
| | Obsessions | Scorpio |
| 1970 | The Battle of Neretva | National General |
| 1971 | The Night Digger | M-G-M |

**BRONISLAU KAPER**

| 1940 | I Take This Woman | M-G-M |
| | The Mortal Storm | M-G-M |
| | The Captain Is a Lady | M-G-M |
| | We Who Are Young | M-G-M |
| | Dulcy | M-G-M |
| | Comrade X | M-G-M |
| 1941 | Blonde Inspiration | M-G-M |
| | Rage in Heaven | M-G-M |
| | A Woman's Face | M-G-M |
| | I'll Wait for You | M-G-M |
| | Barnacle Bill | M-G-M |
| | Whistling in the Dark | M-G-M |
| | Dr. Kildare's Wedding Day | M-G-M |
| | When Ladies Meet | M-G-M |
| | The Chocolate Soldier | M-G-M |
| | H. M. Pulham, Esquire | M-G-M |
| | Johnny Eager | M-G-M |
| 1942 | Two-Faced Woman | M-G-M |
| | We Were Dancing | M-G-M |
| | Fingers at the Window | M-G-M |
| | Crossroads | M-G-M |
| | The Affairs of Martha | M-G-M |
| | Somewhere I'll Find You | M-G-M |
| | A Yank at Eton | M-G-M |
| | White Cargo | M-G-M |
| | Keeper of the Flame | M-G-M |
| 1943 | Slightly Dangerous | M-G-M |
| | Above Suspicion | M-G-M |
| | Bataan | M-G-M |
| | The Cross of Lorraine | M-G-M |
| 1944 | The Heavenly Body | M-G-M |
| | Gaslight | M-G-M |
| | Marriage Is a Private Affair | M-G-M |
| | Mrs. Parkington | M-G-M |
| 1945 | Without Love | M-G-M |
| | Bewitched | M-G-M |
| | Our Vines Have Tender Grapes | M-G-M |
| 1946 | Three Wise Fools | M-G-M |
| | The Stranger | RKO-International |
| | Courage of Lassie | M-G-M |
| | The Secret Heart | M-G-M |
| 1947 | Cynthia | M-G-M |
| | Song of Love | M-G-M |
| | Green Dolphin Street | M-G-M |
| 1948 | High Wall | M-G-M |

|  |  |  |
|---|---|---|
|  | B. F.'s Daughter | M-G-M |
|  | Homecoming | M-G-M |
|  | The Secret Land (documentary) | M-G-M |
|  | Act of Violence | M-G-M |
| 1949 | The Secret Garden | M-G-M |
|  | The Great Sinner | M-G-M |
|  | That Forsyte Woman | M-G-M |
|  | Malaya | M-G-M |
| 1950 | Key to the City | M-G-M |
|  | The Skipper Surprised His Wife | M-G-M |
|  | A Life of Her Own | M-G-M |
|  | To Please a Lady | M-G-M |
|  | Grounds for Marriage | M-G-M |
| 1951 | Three Guys Named Mike | M-G-M |
|  | Mr. Imperium | M-G-M |
|  | The Red Badge of Courage | M-G-M |
|  | Too Young to Kiss | M-G-M |
|  | It's a Big Country | M-G-M |
|  | Shadow in the Sky | M-G-M |
| 1952 | Invitation | M-G-M |
|  | The Wild North | M-G-M |
| 1953 | The Naked Spur | M-G-M |
|  | Lili | M-G-M |
|  | Ride, Vaquero! | M-G-M |
|  | The Actress | M-G-M |
|  | Saadia | M-G-M |
| 1954 | Them! | Warners |
|  | Her Twelve Men | M-G-M |
| 1955 | The Glass Slipper | M-G-M |
|  | The Prodigal | M-G-M |
|  | Quentin Durward | M-G-M |
|  | Forever, Darling | M-G-M |
| 1956 | The Swan | M-G-M |
|  | The Power and the Prize | M-G-M |
|  | Somebody Up There Likes Me | M-G-M |
| 1957 | The Barretts of Wimpole Street | M-G-M |
|  | Jet Pilot | RKO |
|  | Don't Go Near the Water | M-G-M |
|  | The Brothers Karamazov | M-G-M |
| 1958 | Auntie Mame | Warners |
|  | The Scapegoat | M-G-M |
| 1959 | Green Mansions | M-G-M |
|  | Home from the Hill | M-G-M |
| 1960 | The Angel Wore Red | M-G-M |
|  | Butterfield 8 | M-G-M |
| 1961 | Two Loves | M-G-M |
|  | Ada | M-G-M |
| 1962 | Mutiny on the Bounty | M-G-M |
| 1964 | Kisses for My President | Warners |
| 1965 | Lord Jim | Columbia |
| 1967 | Tobruk | Universal |
|  | The Way West | United Artists |
| 1968 | Counterpoint | Universal |
|  | A Flea in Her Ear | 20th |

### ERICH WOLFGANG KORNGOLD

|  |  |  |
|---|---|---|
| 1935 | A Midsummer Night's Dream | Warners |
|  | Captain Blood | Warners |
| 1936 | Give Us This Night | Paramount |
|  | The Green Pastures | Warners |
|  | Anthony Adverse | Warners |

| 1937 | The Prince and the Pauper | Warners |
| | Another Dawn | Warners |
| 1938 | The Adventures of Robin Hood | Warners |
| 1939 | Juarez | Warners |
| | The Private Lives of Elizabeth and Essex | Warners |
| 1940 | The Sea Hawk | Warners |
| 1941 | The Sea Wolf | Warners |
| 1942 | King's Row | Warners |
| 1943 | The Constant Nymph | Warners |
| 1944 | Between Two Worlds | Warners |
| 1946 | Devotion | Warners |
| | Of Human Bondage | Warners |
| | Deception | Warners |
| 1947 | Escape Me Never | Warners |
| 1955 | Magic Fire | Republic |

## HENRY MANCINI

Mancini was under contract to Universal from 1952 to 1958, during which time he worked on dozens of routine films as an arranger, orchestrator and collaborating composer. His most important films of this period were *The Glenn Miller Story* (1953), *The Benny Goodman Story* (1955) and *Touch of Evil* (1958).

| 1960 | High Time | 20th |
| | The Great Imposter | Universal |
| 1961 | Breakfast at Tiffany's | Paramount |
| | Bachelor in Paradise | M-G-M |
| | Hatari | Paramount |
| 1962 | Experiment in Terror | Columbia |
| | Mr. Hobbs Takes a Vacation | 20th |
| | Days of Wine and Roses | Warners |
| 1963 | Man's Favorite Sport? | Universal |
| | Charade | Universal |
| | Soldier in the Rain | Allied Artists |
| 1964 | The Pink Panther | United Artists |
| | A Shot in the Dark | United Artists |
| 1965 | Dear Heart | Warners |
| | The Great Race | Warners |
| 1966 | Moment to Moment | Universal |
| | What Did You Do in the War, Daddy? | United Artists |
| | Arabesque | Universal |
| | Two for the Road | 20th |
| 1967 | Gunn | Paramount |
| | Wait Until Dark | Warners |
| 1968 | The Party | United Artists |
| 1969 | Me, Natalie | National General |
| | Gaily, Gaily | United Artists |
| 1970 | The Molly Maguires | Paramount |
| | Darling Lili | Paramount |
| | The Hawaiians | United Artists |
| | Sunflower | Avco Embassy |
| 1971 | Salem Come to Supper | UMC |

## ALFRED NEWMAN

The exact amount of composition contributed by Newman to the more than two hundred films on which he worked during his forty years in Hollywood is difficult to determine. He conducted every score but the actual music was often provided by his staff under his supervision. This listing is limited to films on which Newman was the principal composer as well as the music director:

| 1931 | The Devil to Pay | Goldwyn |
| | Reaching for the Moon | United Artists |
| | Kiki | United Artists |
| | Indiscreet | United Artists |

| | | |
|---|---|---|
| | Street Scene | Goldwyn |
| | The Unholy Garden | Goldwyn |
| | The Age for Love | United Artists |
| | Corsair | United Artists |
| | Around the World in Eighty Minutes | United Artists |
| | Tonight or Never | Goldwyn |
| 1932 | Arrowsmith | Goldwyn |
| | Cock of the Air | United Artists |
| | The Greeks Had a Word for Them | Goldwyn |
| | Sky Devils | United Artists |
| | Mr. Robinson Crusoe | United Artists |
| | Rain | United Artists |
| | Cynara | Goldwyn |
| 1933 | Secrets | United Artists |
| | I Cover the Waterfront | United Artists |
| | The Masquerader | Goldwyn |
| | The Bowery | United Artists |
| | Blood Money | United Artists |
| | Advice to the Lovelorn | United Artists |
| 1934 | Gallant Lady | United Artists |
| | Looking for Trouble | United Artists |
| | Nana | Goldwyn |
| | The House of Rothschild | United Artists |
| | Born to be Bad | United Artists |
| | The Affairs of Cellini | United Artists |
| | The Last Gentleman | United Artists |
| | Bulldog Drummond Strikes Back | United Artists |
| | The Cat's Paw | Fox |
| | Our Daily Bread | United Artists |
| | We Live Again | Goldwyn |
| | The Count of Monte Cristo | United Artists |
| 1935 | The Mighty Barnum | United Artists |
| | Clive of India | United Artists |
| | The Wedding Night | Goldwyn |
| | Les Miserables | United Artists |
| | Cardinal Richelieu | United Artists |
| | The Call of the Wild | United Artists |
| | The Dark Angel | Goldwyn |
| | Barbary Coast | Goldwyn |
| | The Melody Lingers On | United Artists |
| | Splendor | Goldwyn |
| 1936 | These Three | Goldwyn |
| | Ramona | 20th |
| | Dodsworth | Goldwyn |
| | Come and Get It | Goldwyn |
| 1937 | Beloved Enemy | Goldwyn |
| | You Only Live Once | United Artists |
| | History Is Made at Night | United Artists |
| | Woman Chases Man | Goldwyn |
| | Slave Ship | 20th |
| | Wee Willie Winkle | 20th |
| | Stella Dallas | Goldwyn |
| | Dead End | Goldwyn |
| | The Prisoner of Zenda | United Artists |
| 1938 | The Hurricane | Goldwyn |
| | The Cowboy and the Lady | Goldwyn |
| | Trade Winds | United Artists |
| 1939 | Gunga Din | RKO |
| | Wuthering Heights | Goldwyn |
| | Young Mr. Lincoln | 20th |
| | Beau Geste | Paramount |

|      |                                    |               |
| ---- | ---------------------------------- | ------------- |
|      | The Rains Came                     | 20th          |
|      | The Real Glory                     | Goldwyn       |
|      | Drums Along the Mohawk             | 20th          |
|      | The Hunchback of Notre Dame        | RKO           |
| 1940 | The Blue Bird                      | 20th          |
|      | The Grapes of Wrath                | 20th          |
|      | Vigil in the Night                 | RKO           |
|      | Little Old New York                | 20th          |
|      | Earthbound                         | 20th          |
|      | Foreign Correspondent              | United Artists |
|      | Brigham Young                      | 20th          |
|      | They Knew What They Wanted         | RKO           |
|      | The Mark of Zorro                  | 20th          |
|      | Hudson's Bay                       | 20th          |
| 1941 | That Night in Rio                  | 20th          |
|      | Blood and Sand                     | 20th          |
|      | A Yank in the R.A.F.               | 20th          |
|      | Ball of Fire                       | Goldwyn       |
|      | Son of Fury                        | 20th          |
|      | How Green Was My Valley            | 20th          |
| 1942 | Roxie Hart                         | 20th          |
|      | To the Shores of Tripoli           | 20th          |
|      | This Above All                     | 20th          |
|      | The Pied Piper                     | 20th          |
|      | Girl Trouble                       | 20th          |
|      | The Black Swan                     | 20th          |
|      | Life Begins at Eight-Thirty        | 20th          |
| 1943 | The Moon Is Down                   | 20th          |
|      | My Friend Flicka                   | 20th          |
|      | Heaven Can Wait                    | 20th          |
|      | Claudia                            | 20th          |
|      | The Song of Bernadette             | 20th          |
| 1944 | The Purple Heart                   | 20th          |
|      | Wilson                             | 20th          |
|      | Sunday Dinner for a Soldier        | 20th          |
|      | The Keys of the Kingdom            | 20th          |
| 1945 | A Tree Grows in Brooklyn           | 20th          |
|      | A Royal Scandal                    | 20th          |
|      | A Bell for Adano                   | 20th          |
| 1946 | Leave Her to Heaven                | 20th          |
|      | Dragonwyck                         | 20th          |
|      | Centennial Summer                  | 20th          |
|      | Margie                             | 20th          |
|      | The Razor's Edge                   | 20th          |
| 1947 | Gentleman's Agreement              | 20th          |
|      | Captain from Castille              | 20th          |
| 1948 | Call Northside 777                 | 20th          |
|      | Sitting Pretty                     | 20th          |
|      | The Walls of Jericho               | 20th          |
|      | Cry of the City                    | 20th          |
|      | The Snake Pit                      | 20th          |
|      | Yellow Sky                         | 20th          |
| 1949 | Chicken Every Sunday               | 20th          |
|      | A Letter to Three Wives            | 20th          |
|      | Down to the Sea in Ships           | 20th          |
|      | Mother Is a Freshman               | 20th          |
|      | Mr. Belvedere Goes to College      | 20th          |
|      | You're My Everything               | 20th          |
|      | Pinky                              | 20th          |
|      | Prince of Foxes                    | 20th          |
|      | Twelve O'Clock High                | 20th          |

| | | |
|---|---|---|
| 1950 | When Willie Comes Marching Home | 20th |
| | The Big Lift | 20th |
| | The Gunfighter | 20th |
| | Panic in the Streets | 20th |
| | No Way Out | 20th |
| | All about Eve | 20th |
| | For Heaven's Sake | 20th |
| 1951 | Fourteen Hours | 20th |
| | Take Care of My Little Girl | 20th |
| | David and Bathsheba | 20th |
| 1952 | With a Song in My Heart | 20th |
| | Wait Till the Sun Shines, Nellie | 20th |
| | What Price Glory? | 20th |
| | O. Henry's Full House | 20th |
| | Stars and Stripes Forever | 20th |
| 1953 | Tonight We Sing | 20th |
| | Call Me Madam | 20th |
| | The President's Lady | 20th |
| | The Robe | 20th |
| 1954 | Hell and High Water | 20th |
| | The Egyptian (with Herrmann) | 20th |
| 1955 | A Man Called Peter | 20th |
| | The Seven Year Itch | 20th |
| | Love Is a Many-Splendored Thing | 20th |
| 1956 | Anastasia | 20th |
| 1958 | A Certain Smile | 20th |
| 1959 | The Diary of Anne Frank | 20th |
| | The Best of Everything | 20th |
| 1961 | The Pleasure of His Company | Paramount |
| | The Counterfeit Traitor | Paramount |
| 1962 | How the West Was Won | M-G-M |
| 1965 | The Greatest Story Ever Told | United Artists |
| | Nevada Smith | Paramount |
| 1967 | Firecreek | Warners |
| 1970 | Airport | Universal |

**ALEX NORTH**

| | | |
|---|---|---|
| 1951 | A Streetcar Named Desire | Warners |
| | The 13th Letter | 20th |
| | Death of a Salesman | Columbia |
| 1952 | Viva Zapata! | 20th |
| | Les Miserables | 20th |
| | Pony Soldier | 20th |
| 1953 | The Member of the Wedding | Columbia |
| 1954 | Go, Man, Go! | United Artists |
| | Desiree | 20th |
| 1955 | The Racers | 20th |
| | Unchained | Warners |
| | Man With the Gun | United Artists |
| | The Rose Tattoo | Paramount |
| 1956 | I'll Cry Tomorrow | M-G-M |
| | The Bad Seed | Warners |
| | The Rainmaker | Paramount |
| | Four Girls in Town | Universal |
| | The King and Four Queens | United Artists |
| 1957 | The Bachelor Party | United Artists |
| 1958 | The Long, Hot Summer | 20th |
| | Stage Struck | RKO |
| | Hot Spell | Paramount |
| | South Seas Adventure | Cinerama |
| 1959 | The Sound and the Fury | 20th |

|  |  |  |
|---|---|---|
|  | The Wonderful Country | United Artists |
| 1960 | Spartacus | Universal |
| 1961 | The Children's Hour | United Artists |
|  | Sanctuary | 20th |
|  | The Misfits | United Artists |
| 1962 | All Fall Down | M-G-M |
| 1963 | Cleopatra | 20th |
| 1964 | The Outrage | M-G-M |
| 1965 | Cheyenne Autumn | Warners |
|  | The Agony and the Ecstasy | 20th |
| 1966 | Who's Afraid of Virginia Woolf? | Warners |
| 1967 | Africa (documentary) | ABC |
| 1968 | The Devil's Brigade | United Artists |
|  | The Shoes of the Fisherman | M-G-M |
| 1969 | A Dream of Kings | National General |
|  | Hard Contract | 20th |
| 1971 | Willard | Crosby |

## ANDRE PREVIN

|  |  |  |
|---|---|---|
| 1948 | The Sun Comes Up | M-G-M |
| 1949 | Scene of the Crime | M-G-M |
|  | Border Incident | M-G-M |
|  | Challenge to Lassie | M-G-M |
|  | Tension | M-G-M |
|  | Shadow on the Wall | M-G-M |
| 1950 | The Outriders | M-G-M |
|  | Three Little Words | M-G-M |
|  | Dial 1119 | M-G-M |
|  | Kim | M-G-M |
| 1951 | Cause for Alarm | M-G-M |
| 1953 | Small Town Girl | M-G-M |
|  | The Girl Who Had Everything | M-G-M |
|  | Kiss Me Kate | M-G-M |
|  | Give a Girl a Break | M-G-M |
| 1954 | Bad Day at Black Rock | M-G-M |
| 1955 | It's Always Fair Weather | M-G-M |
|  | Kismet | M-G-M |
| 1956 | The Catered Affair | M-G-M |
|  | The Fastest Gun Alive | M-G-M |
| 1957 | Hot Summer Night | M-G-M |
|  | Designing Woman | M-G-M |
|  | Silk Stockings | M-G-M |
|  | House of Numbers | M-G-M |
| 1958 | Gigi | M-G-M |
| 1959 | Porgy and Bess | Columbia |
| 1960 | Who Was That Lady? | Columbia |
|  | The Subterraneans | M-G-M |
|  | Bells Are Ringing | M-G-M |
|  | Elmer Gantry | United Artists |
| 1961 | All in a Night's Work | Paramount |
|  | One, Two, Three | United Artists |
|  | The Four Horsemen of the Apocalypse | M-G-M |
| 1962 | Long Day's Journey into Night | Embassy |
|  | Two for the Seesaw | United Artists |
| 1963 | Irma La Douce | United Artists |
| 1964 | Dead Ringer | Warners |
|  | My Fair Lady | Warners |
|  | Goodbye Charlie | 20th |
|  | Kiss Me, Stupid | Lopert |
| 1965 | Inside Daisy Clover | Warners |
| 1966 | The Fortune Cookie | United Artists |

## DAVID RAKSIN

Raksin has been one of the most prolific and versatile of Hollywood's composers. Between 1936 and 1943 he was employed as an arranger, adapter and collaborating composer on a large number of features, shorts, cartoons and documentaries.

| | | |
|---|---|---|
| 1944 | Tampico | 20th |
| | Laura | 20th |
| 1945 | Attack in the Pacific (documentary) | U.S. Navy |
| | Where Do We Go from Here? | 20th |
| | Don Juan Quilligan | 20th |
| | Fallen Angel | 20th |
| 1946 | Smoky | 20th |
| | The Shocking Miss Pilgrim | 20th |
| 1947 | The Homestretch | 20th |
| | The Secret Life of Walter Mitty | Goldwyn |
| | Forever Amber | 20th |
| | Daisy Kenyon | 20th |
| 1948 | Fury at Furnace Creek | 20th |
| | Apartment for Peggy | 20th |
| 1949 | Force of Evil | M-G-M |
| 1950 | Whirlpool | 20th |
| | The Reformer and the Redhead | M-G-M |
| | A Lady without Passport | M-G-M |
| | Giddyap (cartoon) | UPA |
| | Right Cross | M-G-M |
| | The Next Voice You Hear | M-G-M |
| | The Magnificent Yankee | M-G-M |
| 1951 | Kind Lady | M-G-M |
| | Across the Wide Missouri | M-G-M |
| | The Man with a Cloak | M-G-M |
| 1952 | Sloppy Jalopy (cartoon) | UPA |
| | The Girl in White | M-G-M |
| | Pat and Mike | M-G-M |
| | Carrie | Paramount |
| | Madeline (cartoon) | UPA |
| | The Bad and the Beautiful | M-G-M |
| 1953 | The Unicorn in the Garden (cartoon) | UPA |
| 1954 | Apache | United Artists |
| | Suddenly | United Artists |
| 1955 | The Big Combo | Allied Artists |
| 1956 | Jubal | Columbia |
| | Seven Wonders of the World | Cinerama |
| | Hilda Crane | 20th |
| | Bigger Than Life | 20th |
| 1957 | The Vintage | M-G-M |
| | Man on Fire | M-G-M |
| | Until They Sail | M-G-M |
| | Gunsight Ridge | United Artists |
| 1958 | Twilight for the Gods | Universal |
| | Separate Tables | United Artists |
| 1959 | Al Capone | Allied Artists |
| 1960 | Pay or Die | Allied Artists |
| 1961 | Night Tide | Harrington |
| | Too Late Blues | Paramount |
| 1962 | Two Weeks in Another Town | M-G-M |
| 1964 | The Patsy | Paramount |
| | Invitation to a Gunfighter | United Artists |
| | Sylvia | Paramount |
| 1965 | Love Has Many Faces | Columbia |
| 1966 | A Big Hand for the Little Lady | Warners |
| | The Redeemer | Empire |
| 1968 | Will Penny | Paramount |

| | | |
|---|---|---|
| 1970 | Glass Houses | Columbia |
| 1971 | What's the Matter with Helen? | American-International |

**LEONARD ROSENMAN**

| | | |
|---|---|---|
| 1955 | East of Eden | Warners |
| | The Cobweb | M-G-M |
| | Rebel without a Cause | Warners |
| 1956 | Edge of the City | M-G-M |
| 1957 | The Young Stranger | RKO |
| | Bombers B-52 | Warners |
| 1958 | Lafayette Escadrille | Warners |
| | The Hidden World (documentary) | Small World |
| 1959 | Pork Chop Hill | United Artists |
| | The Savage Eye | Trans-Lux |
| 1960 | The Rise and Fall of Legs Diamond | Warners |
| | The Bramble Bush | Warners |
| | The Crowded Sky | Warners |
| | The Plunderers | Allied Artists |
| 1961 | The Outsider | Universal |
| | Hell Is for Heroes | Paramount |
| 1962 | Convicts 4 | Allied Artists |
| | The Chapman Report | Warners |
| 1966 | Fantastic Voyage | 20th |
| 1967 | A Covenant with Death | Warners |
| 1968 | Countdown | Warners |
| | Hellfighters | Universal |
| 1970 | A Man Called Horse | National General |
| | Beneath the Planet of the Apes | 20th |
| 1971 | Skipper | National General |

**LAURENCE ROSENTHAL**

| | | |
|---|---|---|
| 1955 | Yellowneck | Republic |
| 1957 | Naked in the Sun | Allied Artists |
| 1961 | A Raisin in the Sun | Columbia |
| | Dark Odyssey | Era |
| 1962 | The Miracle Worker | United Artists |
| | Requiem for a Heavyweight | Columbia |
| 1964 | Becket | Paramount |
| 1966 | Hotel Paradiso | M-G-M |
| 1967 | The Comedians | M-G-M |
| 1969 | Three | United Artists |
| 1971 | A Gunfight | Paramount |

**MIKLOS ROZSA**

| | | |
|---|---|---|
| 1937 | Thunder in the City | Columbia |
| | Knight without Armor | Korda |
| | The Squeaker | Korda |
| 1938 | The Divorce of Lady X | Korda |
| 1939 | The Four Feathers | Korda |
| | The Spy in Black | Columbia |
| | Ten Days in Paris | Columbia |
| 1940 | The Green Cockatoo | New World |
| | On the Night of the Fire | Universal |
| | The Thief of Bagdad | Korda |
| 1941 | That Hamilton Woman | Korda |
| | Lydia | Korda |
| | Sundown | United Artists |
| 1942 | The Jungle Book | Korda |
| | Jacare | United Artists |
| 1943 | Five Graves to Cairo | Paramount |
| | So Proudly We Hail! | Paramount |

| Year | Title | Studio |
|---|---|---|
| | **Sahara** | Columbia |
| | The Woman of the Town | United Artists |
| 1944 | The Hour Before the Dawn | Paramount |
| | Double Indemnity | Paramount |
| | Dark Waters | United Artists |
| | The Man in Half Moon Street | Paramount |
| 1945 | Blood on the Sun | United Artists |
| | The Lost Weekend | Paramount |
| | Lady on a Train | Universal |
| | Spellbound | United Artists |
| 1946 | Because of Him | Universal |
| | The Strange Love of Martha Ivers | Paramount |
| | The Killers | Universal |
| 1947 | The Red House | United Artists |
| | The Macomber Affair | United Artists |
| | Time Out of Mind | Universal |
| | Desert Fury | Paramount |
| | Brute Force | Universal |
| | The Other Love | United Artists |
| 1948 | Secret Beyond the Door | Universal |
| | A Woman's Vengeance | Universal |
| | A Double Life | Universal |
| | The Naked City | Universal |
| | Kiss the Blood Off My Hands | Universal |
| | Criss Cross | Universal |
| 1949 | Command Decision | M-G-M |
| | The Bribe | M-G-M |
| | Madame Bovary | M-G-M |
| | The Red Danube | M-G-M |
| | Adam's Rib | M-G-M |
| | East Side, West Side | M-G-M |
| 1950 | The Asphalt Jungle | M-G-M |
| | Crisis | M-G-M |
| 1951 | The Light Touch | M-G-M |
| | Quo Vadis | M-G-M |
| 1952 | Ivanhoe | M-G-M |
| | Plymouth Adventure | M-G-M |
| 1953 | Julius Caesar | M-G-M |
| | The Story of Three Loves | M-G-M |
| | Young Bess | M-G-M |
| | All the Brothers Were Valiant | M-G-M |
| | Knights of the Round Table | M-G-M |
| 1954 | Men of the Fighting Lady | M-G-M |
| | Valley of the Kings | M-G-M |
| | Crest of the Wave | M-G-M |
| | Green Fire | M-G-M |
| 1955 | Moonfleet | M-G-M |
| | The King's Thief | M-G-M |
| | Diane | M-G-M |
| 1956 | Tribute to a Bad Man | M-G-M |
| | Bhowani Junction | M-G-M |
| | Lust for Life | M-G-M |
| 1957 | Something of Value | M-G-M |
| | The Seventh Sin | M-G-M |
| | Tip on a Dead Jockey | M-G-M |
| 1958 | A Time to Love and a Time to Die | Universal |
| | The World, the Flesh and the Devil | M-G-M |
| 1959 | Ben-Hur | M-G-M |
| 1961 | King of Kings | M-G-M |
| | El Cid | Allied Artists |
| 1962 | Sodom and Gomorrah | 20th |

| 1963 | The V.I.P.s | M-G-M |
| 1968 | The Power | M-G-M |
| | The Green Berets | Warners |
| 1970 | The Private Life of Sherlock Holmes | United Artists |

### LALO SCHIFRIN

| 1963 | Rhino! | M-G-M |
| 1964 | Joy House | M-G-M |
| | Once a Thief | M-G-M |
| 1965 | The Cincinnati Kid | M-G-M |
| | The Liquidator | M-G-M |
| 1966 | I Deal in Danger | 20th |
| | Blindfold | Universal |
| | Way . . . Way Out! | 20th |
| | Murderers' Row | Columbia |
| 1967 | The Venetian Affair | M-G-M |
| | Sullivan's Empire | Universal |
| | Who's Minding the Mint? | Columbia |
| | Cool Hand Luke | Warners |
| | The President's Analyst | Paramount |
| | The Fox | Warners |
| | Where Angels Go . . . Trouble Follows! | Columbia |
| 1968 | Sol Madrid | M-G-M |
| | The Brotherhood | Paramount |
| | Bullitt | Warners |
| | Coogan's Bluff | Universal |
| | Hell in the Pacific | CR |
| 1969 | Che! | 20th |
| | Eye of the Cat | Universal |
| 1970 | Kelly's Heroes | M-G-M |
| | Pussycat, Pussycat, I Love You | United Artists |
| | Imago | Emerson |
| | WUSA | Paramount |
| | I Love My Wife | Universal |
| 1971 | THX 1138 | Warners |

### MAX STEINER

Steiner began a six-year association with RKO Radio Pictures in late 1929. A completely accurate listing of his credits for that period seems impossible due to Steiner's himself having kept no record of his activities. For much of the period he was in charge of the studio's music department and responsible for the scoring of all RKO films. However, in almost all cases the actual amount of scoring was minimal, consisting of a brief main and closing title. Perhaps only a dozen of Steiner's RKO films received extensive scoring, whereas most of his films for Warner Brothers were given considerable musical treatment.

Herewith the Steiner RKO credits:

| 1929 | Rio Rita |
| 1930 | Dixiana |
| | Half Shot at Sunrise |
| | Check and Double Check |
| | Cimarron |
| | Beau Ideal |
| 1931 | Kept Husbands |
| | Cracked Nuts |
| | Young Donovan's Kid |
| | Transgression |
| | The Public Defender |
| | Traveling Husbands |
| | The Runaround |
| | The Gay Diplomat |
| | Fanny Foley Herself |
| | Consolation Marriage |

Way Back Home
Are These Our Children?
Secret Service
1932 Men of Chance
Girl of the Rio
Ladies of the Jury
The Lost Squadron
Young Bride
Symphony of Six Million
State's Attorney
Westward Passage
Is My Face Red?
What Price Hollywood
Roar of the Dragon
Bird of Paradise
The Most Dangerous Game
A Bill of Divorcement
Thirteen Women
The Phantom of Crestwood
Little Orphan Annie
Renegades of the West
Secrets of the French Police
The Conquerors
The Sport Parade
Rockabye
The Half Naked Truth
Penguin Pool Murder
The Animal Kingdom
The Monkey's Paw
1933 No Other Woman
The Cheyenne Kid
Lucky Devils
The Great Jasper
Topaze
Our Betters
King Kong
Christopher Strong
Sweepings
Diplomaniacs
The Silver Cord
Son of the Border
Emergency Call
Professional Sweetheart
Flying Devils
Melody Cruise
Bed of Roses
Double Harness
Headline Shooter
Before Dawn
No Marriage Ties
Morning Glory
Blind Adventure
One Man's Journey
Rafter Romance
Midshipman Jack
Ann Vickers
Ace of Aces
Chance at Heaven
After Tonight
Little Women
The Right to Romance

Aggie Appleby
If I Were Free
The Son of Kong
Flying Down to Rio
1934  Man of Two Worlds
The Meanest Gal in Town
Long Lost Father
Two Alone
The Lost Patrol
Keep 'Em Rolling
Spitfire
Success at Any Price
This Man Is Mine
Sing and Like It
The Crime Doctor
Finishing School
Strictly Dynamite
Where Sinners Meet
Stingaree
Murder on the Blackboard
The Life of Vergie Winters
Let's Try Again
Of Human Bondage
We're Rich Again
His Greatest Gamble
Hat, Coat and Glove
Bachelor Bait
Their Big Moment
Down to Their Last Yacht
The Fountain
The Age of Innocence
The Richest Girl in the World
The Gay Divorcee
Dangerous Corner
Gridiron Flash
Wednesday's Child
Kentucky Kernels
By Your Leave
Anne of Green Gables
The Little Minister
1935  Romance in Manhattan
Enchanted April
Roberta
Laddie
Star of Midnight
The Informer
Break of Hearts
Becky Sharp
She
Alice Adams
Top Hat
The Three Musketeers
I Dream Too Much
1936  Follow the Fleet
Two in Revolt
M'liss

Steiner left RKO in 1936 and began an association with Warner Brothers. All the films in the remainder of this listing are Warners, except where otherwise noted:

1936  Little Lord Fauntleroy (Selznick)
The Charge of the Light Brigade
The Garden of Allah (Selznick)

God's Country and the Woman
1937 Green Light
Slim
Kid Galahad
A Star Is Born (Selznick)
The Life of Emile Zola
That Certain Woman
First Lady
Submarine D-I
Tovarich
1938 Gold Is Where You Find It
Jezebel
The Adventures of Tom Sawyer (Selznick)
Crime School
White Banners
The Amazing Dr. Clitterhouse
Four Daughters
The Sisters
Angels with Dirty Faces
The Dawn Patrol
1939 They Made Me a Criminal
The Oklahoma Kid
Dodge City
Dark Victory
Confessions of a Nazi Spy
Daughters Courageous
Each Dawn I Die
The Old Maid
Dust Be My Destiny
Intermezzo (Selznick)
We Are Not Alone
Gone with the Wind (Selznick-M-G-M)
1940 Four Wives
Dr. Ehrlich's Magic Bullet
Virginia City
All This and Heaven Too
City for Conquest
A Dispatch from Reuter's
The Letter
Santa Fe Trail
1941 The Great Lie
Shining Victory
The Bride Came C.O.D.
Dive Bomber
Sergeant York
One Foot in Heaven
1942 They Died with Their Boots On
Captains of the Clouds
In This Our Life
The Gay Sisters
Desperate Journey
Now, Voyager
1943 Casablanca
Mission to Moscow
Watch on the Rhine
This Is the Army
1944 Passage to Marseille
The Adventures of Mark Twain
Since You Went Away (Selznick)
Arsenic and Old Lace
The Conspirators

1945    Roughly Speaking
        The Corn Is Green
        Rhapsody in Blue
        Mildred Pierce
        Tomorrow Is Forever (RKO)
1946    San Antonio
        My Reputation
        Saratoga Trunk
        One More Tomorrow
        A Stolen Life
        The Big Sleep
        Cloak and Dagger
1947    The Man I Love
        The Beast with Five Fingers
        Pursued
        Love and Learn
        Cheyenne
        The Unfaithful
        Deep Valley
        Life with Father
        The Voice of the Turtle
1948    The Treasure of the Sierra Madre
        My Girl Tisa
        Winter Meeting
        The Woman in White
        Silver River
        Key Largo
        Johnny Belinda
        Fighter Squadron
        The Decision of Christopher Blake
        A Kiss in the Dark
1949    Adventures of Don Juan
        South of St. Louis
        Flamingo Road
        The Fountainhead
        Without Honor (United Artists)
        Beyond the Forest
        White Heat
        Mrs. Mike (United Artists)
        The Lady Takes a Sailor
1950    Caged
        The Flame and the Arrow
        The Glass Menagerie
        Rocky Mountain
        Sugarfoot
        Dallas
1951    Operation Pacific
        Lightning Strikes Twice
        Raton Pass
        I Was a Communist for the F.B.I.
        On Moonlight Bay
        Jim Thorpe—All-American
        Force of Arms
        Close to My Heart
        Distant Drums
1952    Room for One More
        The Lion and the Horse
        Mara Maru
        The Miracle of Our Lady of Fatima
        Springfield Rifle
        The Iron Mistress

1953   The Jazz Singer
       This Is Cinerama (Cinerama)
       Trouble along the Way
       By the Light of the Silvery Moon
       The Desert Song
       The Charge at Feather River
       So This Is Love
       So Big
1954   The Boy from Oklahoma
       The Caine Mutiny (Columbia)
       King Richard and the Crusaders
       The Violent Men (Columbia)
1955   Battle Cry
       The Last Command (Republic)
       The McConnell Story
       Illegal
       Come Next Spring (Republic)
1956   Hell on Frisco Bay
       Helen of Troy
       The Searchers
       Bandido (United Artists)
       Death of a Scoundrel (RKO)
1957   China Gate (theme by Victor Young—20th)
       Band of Angels
       Escapade in Japan (RKO)
       All Mine to Give (RKO)
1958   Fort Dobbs
       Darby's Rangers
       Marjorie Morningstar
1959   The Hanging Tree
       John Paul Jones
       The FBI Story
       A Summer Place
1960   Cash McCall
       Ice Palace
       The Dark at the Top of the Stairs
1961   The Sins of Rachel Cade
       Portrait of a Mobster
       Parrish
       Susan Slade
       A Majority of One
1962   Rome Adventure
1963   Spencer's Mountain
1964   A Distant Trumpet
       FBI Code 98
       Youngblood Hawke
1965   Those Calloways (Disney)
       Two on a Guillotine

## VIRGIL THOMSON

| | | |
|---|---|---|
| 1936 | The Plow That Broke the Plains (documentary) | U.S. Government |
| 1937 | The Spanish Earth (documentary) | Contemporary Historians |
| | The River (documentary) | U.S. Government |
| 1945 | Tuesday in November (documentary) | U.S. Government |
| 1948 | Louisiana Story | Robert Flaherty |
| 1958 | The Goddess | Columbia |
| 1959 | Power among Men (documentary) | United Nations |
| 1964 | Voyage to America (documentary) | N.Y. World's Fair |

## DIMITRI TIOMKIN

Tiomkin's first film assignments were writing ballet sequences in four M-G-M films in 1930: *Devil May Care, Lord Byron of Broadway, The Rogue Song,* and *Our Blushing Brides.*

| 1931 | Resurrection | Universal |
| 1933 | Broadway to Hollywood (ballet) | M-G-M |
| | Alice in Wonderland | Paramount |
| 1935 | Naughty Marietta (ballet sequence) | M-G-M |
| | The Casino Murder Case | M-G-M |
| | Mad Love | M-G-M |
| | I Live My Life | M-G-M |
| 1937 | Lost Horizon | Columbia |
| | The Road Back | Universal |
| 1938 | Spawn of the North | Paramount |
| | You Can't Take It with You | Columbia |
| | The Great Waltz | M-G-M |
| 1939 | Only Angels Have Wings | Columbia |
| | Mr. Smith Goes to Washington | Columbia |
| 1940 | Lucky Partners | RKO |
| | The Westerner | United Artists |
| 1941 | Meet John Doe | Warners |
| | Forced Landing | Paramount |
| | Scattergood Meets Broadway | RKO |
| | Flying Blind | Paramount |
| | The Corsican Brothers | United Artists |
| 1942 | A Gentleman After Dark | United Artists |
| | Twin Beds | United Artists |
| | The Moon and Sixpence | United Artists |
| | Shadow of a Doubt | Universal |
| 1943 | Unknown Guest | Monogram |
| 1944 | The Imposter | Universal |
| | The Bridge of San Luis Rey | United Artists |
| | Ladies Courageous | Universal |
| | When Strangers Marry | Monogram |
| | Forever Yours | Monogram |
| 1945 | Dillinger | Monogram |
| | China's Little Devils | Monogram |
| | Pardon My Past | Columbia |
| 1946 | Whistle Stop | United Artists |
| | Black Beauty | 20th |
| | Angel on My Shoulder | United Artists |
| | The Dark Mirror | Universal |
| | Duel in the Sun | Selznick |
| 1947 | It's a Wonderful Life | RKO |
| | The Long Night | RKO |
| 1948 | Tarzan and the Mermaids | RKO |
| | The Dude Goes West | Allied Artists |
| | So This Is New York | United Artists |
| | Red River | United Artists |
| 1949 | Canadian Pacific | 20th |
| | Champion | United Artists |
| | Portrait of Jennie | Selznick |
| | Home of the Brave | United Artists |
| | Red Light | United Artists |
| 1950 | Dakota Lil | 20th |
| | Guilty Bystander | Film Classics |
| | Champagne for Caesar | United Artists |
| | D.O.A. | United Artists |
| | The Men | United Artists |
| | Cyrano de Bergerac | United Artists |
| | Mr. Universe | United Artists |
| 1951 | The Thing | RKO |
| | Strangers on a Train | Warners |
| | Peking Express | Paramount |

| | | |
|---|---|---|
| | The Well | United Artists |
| | Drums in the Deep South | RKO |
| | Bugles in the Afternoon | Warners |
| 1952 | Mutiny | United Artists |
| | My Six Convicts | Columbia |
| | Lady in the Iron Mask | 20th |
| | The Happy Time | Columbia |
| | The Big Sky | RKO |
| | High Noon | United Artists |
| | The Four Poster | Columbia |
| | The Steel Trap | 20th |
| | Angel Face | RKO |
| 1953 | Jeopardy | M-G-M |
| | I Confess | Warners |
| | Return to Paradise | United Artists |
| | Blowing Wild | Warners |
| | Take the High Ground! | M-G-M |
| | Cease Fire! | Paramount |
| 1954 | His Majesty O'Keefe | Warners |
| | The Command | Warners |
| | Dial M for Murder | Warners |
| | The High and the Mighty | Warners |
| | A Bullet Is Waiting | Columbia |
| | The Adventures of Hajji Baba | 20th |
| 1955 | Strange Lady in Town | Warners |
| | Land of the Pharaohs | Warners |
| | The Court-Martial of Billy Mitchell | Warners |
| 1956 | Friendly Persuasion | Allied Artists |
| | Tension at Table Rock | RKO |
| | Giant | Warners |
| 1957 | Gunfight at the O.K. Corral | Paramount |
| | Night Passage | Universal |
| | Search for Paradise | Cinerama |
| | The Young Land | Columbia |
| 1958 | Wild Is the Wind | Paramount |
| | The Old Man and the Sea | Warners |
| 1959 | Rio Bravo | Warners |
| | Last Train from Gun Hill | Paramount |
| 1960 | The Unforgiven | United Artists |
| | The Alamo | United Artists |
| | The Sundowners | Warners |
| 1961 | The Guns of Navarone | Columbia |
| | Town without Pity | United Artists |
| 1962 | Without Each Other | Allen Klein |
| 1963 | 55 Days at Peking | Allied Artists |
| 1964 | The Fall of the Roman Empire | Paramount |
| | Circus World | Paramount |
| 1965 | 36 Hours | M-G-M |
| 1967 | The War Wagon | Universal |
| 1968 | Great Catherine | Warners |

### FRANZ WAXMAN

| | | |
|---|---|---|
| 1935 | Bride of Frankenstein | Universal |
| | Diamond Jim | Universal |
| | The Affair of Susan | Universal |
| | His Night Out | Universal |
| | Three Kids and a Queen | Universal |
| | Remember Last Night? | Universal |
| | East of Java | Universal |
| | The Great Impersonation | Universal |
| | Magnificent Obsession | Universal |

| | | |
|---|---|---|
| 1936 | The Invisible Ray | Universal |
| | Next Time We Love | Universal |
| | Don't Get Personal | Universal |
| | Love before Breakfast | Universal |
| | Sutter's Gold | Universal |
| | Absolute Quiet | M-G-M |
| | Trouble for Two | M-G-M |
| | Fury | M-G-M |
| | The Devil-Doll | M-G-M |
| | His Brother's Wife | M-G-M |
| | Love on the Run | M-G-M |
| 1937 | Personal Property | M-G-M |
| | Captains Courageous | M-G-M |
| | The Emperor's Candlesticks | M-G-M |
| | The Bride Wore Red | M-G-M |
| | Man-Proof | M-G-M |
| 1938 | Arsene Lupin Returns | M-G-M |
| | Test Pilot | M-G-M |
| | Port of Seven Seas | M-G-M |
| | Three Comrades | M-G-M |
| | Too Hot to Handle | M-G-M |
| | The Shining Hour | M-G-M |
| | The Young in Heart | Selznick |
| | Dramatic School | M-G-M |
| | A Christmas Carol | M-G-M |
| 1939 | Honolulu | M-G-M |
| | The Adventures of Huckleberry Finn | M-G-M |
| | On Borrowed Time | M-G-M |
| | Lady of the Tropics | M-G-M |
| 1940 | Strange Cargo | M-G-M |
| | Florian | M-G-M |
| | Rebecca | Selznick |
| | Sporting Blood | M-G-M |
| | Boom Town | M-G-M |
| | I Love You Again | M-G-M |
| | Escape | M-G-M |
| | The Philadelphia Story | M-G-M |
| | Flight Command | M-G-M |
| 1941 | The Bad Man | M-G-M |
| | Dr. Jekyll and Mr. Hyde | M-G-M |
| | Unfinished Business | Universal |
| | The Feminine Touch | M-G-M |
| | Honky Tonk | M-G-M |
| | Kathleen | M-G-M |
| | Suspicion | RKO |
| | Design for Scandal | M-G-M |
| 1942 | Woman of the Year | M-G-M |
| | Tortilla Flat | M-G-M |
| | Her Cardboard Lover | M-G-M |
| | Seven Sweethearts | M-G-M |
| | Journey for Margaret | M-G-M |
| | Reunion in France | M-G-M |
| 1943 | Air Force | Warners |
| | Edge of Darkness | Warners |
| | Old Acquaintance | Warners |
| 1944 | Destination Tokyo | Warners |
| | In Our Time | Warners |
| | Mr. Skeffington | Warners |
| | The Very Thought of You | Warners |
| 1945 | To Have and Have Not | Warners |
| | Objective, Burma! | Warners |

| Year | Title | Studio |
|---|---|---|
| | Hotel Berlin | Warners |
| | God Is My Co-Pilot | Warners |
| | The Horn Blows at Midnight | Warners |
| | Pride of the Marines | Warners |
| | Confidential Agent | Warners |
| 1946 | Her Kind of Man | Warners |
| 1947 | Humoresque | Warners |
| | Nora Prentiss | Warners |
| | The Two Mrs. Carrolls | Warners |
| | Possessed | Warners |
| | Cry Wolf | Warners |
| | Dark Passage | Warners |
| | The Unsuspected | Warners |
| | That Hagen Girl | Warners |
| | The Paradine Case | Selznick |
| 1948 | Sorry, Wrong Number | Paramount |
| | No Minor Vices | M-G-M |
| 1949 | Whiplash | Warners |
| | Alias Nick Beal | Paramount |
| | Rope of Sand | Paramount |
| | Night unto Night | Warners |
| | Task Force | Warners |
| 1950 | Johnny Holiday | United Artists |
| | Night and the City | 20th |
| | The Furies | Paramount |
| | Sunset Boulevard | Paramount |
| | Dark City | Paramount |
| 1951 | Only the Valiant | Warners |
| | He Ran All the Way | United Artists |
| | A Place in the Sun | Paramount |
| | Anne of the Indies | 20th |
| | The Blue Veil | RKO |
| | Red Mountain | Paramount |
| | Decision Before Dawn | 20th |
| 1952 | Phone Call from a Stranger | 20th |
| | Lure of the Wilderness | 20th |
| | My Cousin Rachel | 20th |
| 1953 | Come Back, Little Sheba | Paramount |
| | Man on a Tightrope | 20th |
| | Stalag 17 | Paramount |
| | I, the Jury | United Artists |
| | A Lion Is in the Streets | Warners |
| | Botany Bay | Paramount |
| 1954 | Prince Valiant | 20th |
| | Elephant Walk | Paramount |
| | Demetrius and the Gladiators | 20th |
| | Rear Window | Paramount |
| | This Is My Love | RKO |
| 1955 | The Silver Chalice | Warners |
| | Untamed | 20th |
| | Mister Roberts | Warners |
| | The Virgin Queen | 20th |
| | The Indian Fighter | United Artists |
| 1956 | Miracle in the Rain | Warners |
| | Crime in the Streets | Allied Artists |
| | Back From Eternity | RKO |
| 1957 | The Spirit of St. Louis | Warners |
| | Love in the Afternoon | Allied Artists |
| | Peyton Place | 20th |
| | Sayonara | Warners |
| 1958 | Run Silent, Run Deep | United Artists |

|      | Home Before Dark | Warners |
|------|------------------|---------|
| 1959 | Count Your Blessings | M-G-M |
|      | The Nun's Story | Warners |
|      | Career | Paramount |
|      | Beloved Infidel | 20th |
| 1960 | The Story of Ruth | 20th |
|      | Sunrise at Campobello | Warners |
|      | Cimarron | M-G-M |
| 1961 | Return to Peyton Place | 20th |
|      | King of the Roaring '20's | Allied Artists |
|      | My Geisha | Paramount |
| 1962 | Hemingway's Adventures of a Young Man | 20th |
|      | Taras Bulba | United Artists |
| 1966 | Lost Command | Columbia |

## VICTOR YOUNG

Young was another musician whose musical activities were so numerous and varied that a listing of his film compositions is difficult. He worked on more than 350 films in the various capacities of conductor, arranger, music director, composer and song writer. This list focuses on his work as a composer of film scores:

| | | |
|------|------------------|---------|
| 1937 | Champagne Waltz | Paramount |
|      | Maid of Salem | Paramount |
|      | Swing High, Swing Low | Paramount |
|      | Vogues of 1938 | United Artists |
|      | Ebb Tide | Paramount |
|      | Wells Fargo | Paramount |
| 1938 | Army Girl | Republic |
|      | Breaking the Ice | RKO |
|      | Peck's Bad Boy with the Circus | RKO |
|      | Flirting with Fate | M-G-M |
| 1939 | Fisherman's Wharf | RKO |
|      | Man of Conquest | Republic |
|      | Heritage of the Desert | Paramount |
|      | Way Down South | RKO |
|      | Golden Boy | Columbia |
|      | Range War | Paramount |
|      | Our Neighbors—the Carters | Paramount |
|      | The Night of Nights | Paramount |
|      | The Llano Kid | Paramount |
|      | Gulliver's Travels | Paramount |
| 1940 | Raffles | United Artists |
|      | The Light That Failed | Paramount |
|      | Dark Command | Republic |
|      | Buck Benny Rides Again | Paramount |
|      | The Way of All Flesh | Paramount |
|      | Three Faces West | Republic |
|      | Untamed | Paramount |
|      | I Want a Divorce | Paramount |
|      | Moon over Burma | Paramount |
|      | Arise My Love | Paramount |
|      | Three Men from Texas | Paramount |
|      | North West Mounted Police | Paramount |
|      | Arizona | Columbia |
|      | The Mad Doctor | Paramount |
| 1941 | Virginia | Paramount |
|      | The Outlaw | United Artists |
|      | Reaching for the Sun | Paramount |
|      | Caught in the Draft | Paramount |
|      | I Wanted Wings | Paramount |
|      | Aloma of the South Seas | Paramount |
|      | Hold Back the Dawn | Paramount |

| | | |
|---|---|---|
| | Skylark | Paramount |
| 1942 | The Remarkable Andrew | Paramount |
| | Reap the Wild Wind | Paramount |
| | The Great Man's Lady | Paramount |
| | Beyond the Blue Horizon | Paramount |
| | Take a Letter, Darling | Paramount |
| | The Forest Rangers | Paramount |
| | Mrs. Wiggs of the Cabbage Patch | Paramount |
| | Flying Tigers | Republic |
| | Young and Willing | United Artists |
| | The Glass Key | Paramount |
| | The Palm Beach Story | Paramount |
| | The Crystal Ball | United Artists |
| | Silver Queen | United Artists |
| 1943 | Buckskin Frontier | United Artists |
| | China | Paramount |
| | For Whom the Bell Tolls | Paramount |
| | Hostages | Paramount |
| | True to Life | Paramount |
| | No Time for Love | Paramount |
| 1944 | The Uninvited | Paramount |
| | The Story of Dr. Wassell | Paramount |
| | The Great Moment | Paramount |
| | Frenchman's Creek | Paramount |
| | Ministry of Fear | Paramount |
| | Practically Yours | Paramount |
| | And Now Tomorrow | Paramount |
| 1945 | A Medal for Benny | Paramount |
| | The Great John L | United Artists |
| | You Came Along | Paramount |
| | Kitty | Paramount |
| | Love Letters | Paramount |
| | Masquerade in Mexico | Paramount |
| | Hold That Blonde! | Paramount |
| 1946 | The Blue Dahlia | Paramount |
| | The Searching Wind | Paramount |
| | Our Hearts Were Growing Up | Paramount |
| | To Each His Own | Paramount |
| | Two Years Before the Mast | Paramount |
| 1947 | Suddenly It's Spring | Paramount |
| | California | Paramount |
| | The Imperfect Lady | Paramount |
| | Calcutta | Paramount |
| | The Trouble with Women | Paramount |
| | I Walk Alone | Paramount |
| | Unconquered | Paramount |
| | Golden Earrings | Paramount |
| 1948 | State of the Union | M-G-M |
| | The Big Clock | Paramount |
| | The Emperor Waltz | Paramount |
| | Dream Girl | Paramount |
| | So Evil My Love | Paramount |
| | Beyond Glory | Paramount |
| | The Night Has a Thousand Eyes | Paramount |
| | Miss Tatlock's Millions | Paramount |
| | The Paleface | Paramount |
| 1949 | The Accused | Paramount |
| | A Connecticut Yankee in King Arthur's Court | Paramount |
| | Streets of Laredo | Paramount |
| | Thelma Jordan | Paramount |
| | Samson and Delilah | Paramount |

|      |                              |               |
|------|------------------------------|---------------|
|      | Song of Surrender            | Paramount     |
|      | Chicago Deadline             | Paramount     |
|      | Sands of Iwo Jima            | Republic      |
|      | Deadly Is the Female         | United Artists|
|      | My Foolish Heart             | Goldwyn       |
|      | Our Very Own                 | Goldwyn       |
| 1950 | Paid in Full                 | Paramount     |
|      | Bright Leaf                  | Warners       |
|      | The Fireball                 | 20th          |
|      | Rio Grande                   | Republic      |
| 1951 | September Affair             | Paramount     |
|      | Belle Le Grand               | Republic      |
|      | Payment on Demand            | RKO           |
|      | Bullfighter and the Lady     | Republic      |
|      | The Lemon Drop Kid           | Paramount     |
|      | Appointment with Danger      | Paramount     |
|      | Honeychile                   | Republic      |
|      | A Millionaire for Christy    | 20th          |
|      | The Wild Blue Yonder         | Republic      |
|      | My Favorite Spy              | Paramount     |
| 1952 | The Quiet Man                | Republic      |
|      | Anything Can Happen          | Paramount     |
|      | Something to Live For        | Paramount     |
|      | The Greatest Show on Earth   | Paramount     |
|      | Scaramouche                  | M-G-M         |
|      | The Story of Will Rogers     | Warners       |
|      | One Minute to Zero           | RKO           |
|      | Thunderbirds                 | Republic      |
|      | Blackbeard the Pirate        | RKO           |
|      | The Star                     | 20th          |
| 1953 | Fair Wind to Java            | Republic      |
|      | A Perilous Journey           | Republic      |
|      | The Sun Shines Bright        | Republic      |
|      | Shane                        | Paramount     |
|      | Flight Nurse                 | Republic      |
|      | Little Boy Lost              | Paramount     |
|      | Forever Female               | Paramount     |
| 1954 | Jubilee Trail                | Republic      |
|      | Johnny Guitar                | Republic      |
|      | Three Coins in the Fountain  | 20th          |
|      | Trouble in the Glen          | Republic      |
|      | About Mrs. Leslie            | Paramount     |
|      | Drum Beat                    | Warners       |
|      | The Country Girl             | Paramount     |
|      | Timberjack                   | Republic      |
| 1955 | Strategic Air Command        | Paramount     |
|      | Son of Sinbad                | RKO           |
|      | A Man Alone                  | Republic      |
|      | The Left Hand of God         | 20th          |
|      | The Tall Merr                | 20th          |
|      | The Conqueror                | RKO           |
| 1956 | The Maverick Queen           | Republic      |
|      | The Vagabond King            | Paramount     |
|      | The Proud and Profane        | Paramount     |
|      | Around the World in 80 Days  | United Artists|
|      | The Brave One                | RKO           |
| 1957 | The Buster Keaton Story      | Paramount     |
|      | Run of the Arrow             | RKO           |
|      | Omar Khayyam                 | Paramount     |

# Index

*Italicized* numbers refer to photographs, **boldface** numbers to score and record lists.

265

Caron, Leslie, *85*, 88
Cash, Johnny, *32*
Cassavetes, John, 166
Castelnuovo-Tedesco, Mario, 42, 199
Chandler, Raymond, 120
Chaplin, Charles, 161, *162*, **224**
Chavez, Carlos, 157, 182
Chevalier, Maurice, 49
Chopin, Frederic, 40, 138
Clift, Montgomery, 79
Cocteau, Jean, 170
Colman, Ronald, 67, 96
Cook, Page, 9, 23–24, 145, 148, 213
Cooper, Gary, 18, 157, 170
Cooper, Merian C., 115
Copland, Aaron, 19, *20*, 113, 144, 174–79, *175*, 181, 187, **224, 238**
Cordell, Frank, **225**
Cortez, Ricardo, 113
Corwin, Norman, 103, 187
Courage, Alexander, 155
Crane, Stephen, 89
Crawford, Joan, 188
Cregar, Laird, 144
Cummings, Robert, 136
Curtis Institute of Music, 179
Custer, George Armstrong, 119

Dallapiccola, Luigi, 203
Daly, Jan, *217*
Darby, Ken, 60–62, *63*
Darwin, Bobby, 166
Daves, Delmer, 153
Davis, Bette, 116, 120, 137, *138*
Davis, Miles, 87
Day, Doris, 145
Dean, James, 203
Debussy, Claude, 64, 103–4
Delerue, Georges, **225**
Delius, Frederick, 153
De Havilland, Olivia, 119, 130, 134
DeMille, Cecil B., 170
De Packh, Maurice, 117, 150
Des Prez, Josquin, 103
De Sylva, Buddy, 95
Deutsch, Adolph, 18, 51, 117, **225**
Diaghilev, Serge, 66
Dieterle, William, 129, 139
Dietrich, Angelika, 111
Dietrich, Marlene, 76, 77, 93
Dods, Marcus, 223
Dolin, Anton, 92
Donat, Robert, 93
Douglas, Kirk, 103, 155, 210
Dowding, Air Marshal, 16
Dreiser, Theodore, 79
Duke, Vernon, 23
Du Maurier, Daphne, 78
Duning, George, **225**

Dunne, Irene, 113
Durbin, Deanna, 50

Eastman School of Music, 30
Eddy, Nelson, 87
Edens, Roger, 51
Edison, Thomas, 107
Edwards, Blake, 199
Edwards, George, 112
Edwards, Gus, 55
Ellington, Duke, 181
Elman, Mischa, 128
Esterhazy, Count, 158

Fahey, Brian, 233
Fain, Sammy, 49, 168
Faith, Percy, 231
Fairbanks, Douglas, Sr., 38
Fall, Leo, 129
Farnon, Robert, **225**
Federal Theater Project, 181, 182
Ferrara, Franco, 229, 231
Feyder, Jacques, 93
Fiedler, Arthur, 226
Fielding, Jerry, **225**
*Films In Review*, 9, 23, 61–62, 135, 145, 213
Fine, Robert, *172*
Fischer, Carl, 37
Flaherty, Robert, *172*, *173*, 257
Flynn, Errol, 2, 11, 17, 78–79, 114, 116, 120, 131, 132, 134, 136, 137
Fonda, Henry, 187
Fontaine, Joan, 18, 78
Forbstein, 109, *110*, 118, 133–34, 151–52
Ford, John, 115, 184
Foster, Lawrence, 232
Frankel, Benjamin, **225**
Frankenheimer, John, 205, 211
Freed, Arthur, 50
Friedhofer, Hugo, 18, 23, 62, 117, 125, 131, 133, 140, 141, 148–59, *149*, *156*, **225, 238–39**
Fuchs, Robert, 111, 126

Gabrieli, Giovani, 184
Gardner, Ava, 88
Garfein, Jack, 178
Garland, Judy, 50
Garner, Errol, 208
Genn, Leo, 94, 231
Gerhardt, Charles, 228
Gershenson, Joseph, 198, 229, 232
Gershwin, George, 66, 112, 161, 168
Getz, Stan, 216
Gillespie, Dizzy, 215, 216
Gimpel, Jakob, 208
Girard, Andre, 230

Glass, Paul, **225**
Glazounov, Alexander, 64
Gold, Ernest, 9, 24–30, *26, 217,* 223, **226, 239**
Goldsmith, Jerry, 203, 208–14, *209, 212,* **226, 240**
Goldwyn, Samuel, 30, 38, 42–43, 55, 64, 152, 153, 154, 176
Goodman, Al, 161
Goodman, Benny, 161, 182
Goodwin, Ron, 16, **226**
Gould, Morton, 150, **226**
Grabner, Herman, 92
Graham, Martha, 181
Grant, Cary, 154
Grauman, Sid, 45
Graunke, Kurt, 225
Green, John, 43, 48–53, *51, 52,* 72, 84–85, 96, 188, **226–27,** 228, 231, **240–41**
Grieg, Edvard, 38
Grusin, David, **227**
Guevara, Che, 218
Guinness, Sir Alec, 88

Hadjidakis, Manos, **227**
Hadley, Henry, 109
Hagen, Earle, 150
Hale, Alan, 119
Hammerstein, Oscar, 2nd, 77, 131
Handel, George Frederic, 62
Hanslick, Eduard, 126, 208
Harris, Roy, 80
Hart, Henry, 9
Hart, William S., 38
Haydn, Franz Josef, 19, 21, 138, 158, 189
Hayton, Lennie, 51
Hayworth, Rita, 165
Hecht, Ben, 42–43
Heifetz, Jascha, 96, 128, 139, 228
Heindorf, Ray, 150, 226, 227, 228, 230, 231, 235
Hellinger, Mark, 96
Hemingway, Ernest, 145, 155
Henreid, Paul, 137, *138*
Hepburn, Audrey, 196
Hepburn, Katharine, 113
Herbert, Victor, 112
Herrmann, Bernard, 18, 59, 141–48, *141, 146,* 188, **227, 241**
Heston, Charlton, 166
Heuberger, Richard, 24
Heyman, Edward, 49
Hindemith, Paul, 47, 75, 80
Hitchcock, Alfred, 15, 78, 145, *146,* 147
Hitler, Adolf, 64, 134
Hollaender, Friedrich, 76
Hopkins, Kenyon, **227**
Horowitz, Vladimir, 65
Honegger, Arthur, 82, 94
Hope, Bob, 117

Houseman, John, 103, 205
Howard, Leslie, 113
Howe, James Wong, 202
Hurst, Fannie, 113
Huston, John, 89, 210
Huston, Walter, 113

Ibert, Jacques, 94
Ingram, Rex, 132
Ireland, John, 221
Irving, Ernest, 234

Jannssen, Werner, 227
Jarre, Maurice, 18, **227**
Jeritza, Maria, 128
Jones, Jennifer, 18, 70, 71, 121
Jourdan, Louis, 88
Juilliard School of Music, 142, 179, 187, 198, 205

Kaper, Bronislau, 51, 64, *83,* 84–91, *85,* 202, 216, **228, 242–43**
Kaplin, Sol, **228**
Kariton, Michael, 65–66
Kaun, Bernard, 117
Kaye, Danny, 50
Kazan, Elia, 181–82, 183, 203
Kelly, Grace, 88
Kennedy, Margaret, 136
Kerker, Gustave, 111
Kern, Jerome, 77, 112, 150, 168
Kiepura, Jan, 86, 131
King, Henry, 58
Kloss, Erich, 231–32
Kodaly, Zoltan, 96
Komeda, Christopher, **228**
Korda, Sir Alexander, 93
Korngold, Erich Wolfgang, 11, 17, 19, 22, 58, 70, 107, 108, 109, 123–40, *123, 135, 138,* 150, 151, 152, 188, **228, 243–44**
Korngold, Ernst, *135*
Korngold, Josephine Witrofsky, 125
Korngold, Dr. Julius, 125, 126, 128, *135,* 138
Korngold, Luzi, *135,* 140
Koussevitsky, Serge, 203
Kramer, Stanley, 25, *26,* 170
Krasner, Milton, 155
Kreisler, Fritz, 128
Krenek, Ernst, 42, 199
Krumgold, Sigmund, 133

Lamour, Dorothy, 95
Lancaster, Burt, 157, 165
Lang, Fritz, 77
Lassus, Orlando, 103
Laughton, Charles, 232